THE   STORIES   THAT   SHAPE   US

THE STORIES THAT

CONTEMPORARY WOMEN WRITE ABOUT THE WEST

SHAPE US

An Anthology Edited by

TERESA JORDAN AND
JAMES R. HEPWORTH

W. W. NORTON & COMPANY

NEW YORK   LONDON

Copyright ©1995 by Theresa Jordan and James R. Hepworth

Since this page cannot accommodate all of the copyright notices,
pages 395 and 396 constitute an extension of the copyright page.

The text of this book is composed in Monotype Bell
with the display set in Oblong
Composition and manufacturing by the Haddon Craftsmen, Inc.
Book design by Beth Tondreau Design

LIBRARY OF CONGRESS CATALOGING-IN-PUBLICATION DATA
The stories that shape us : contemporary women write about the West :
an anthology / edited by Teresa Jordan and James R. Hepworth.
p. cm.
1. Women authors, American—West (U.S.)—Biography.   2. West
(U.S.)—Social life and customs—20th century.   3. Women authors,
American—20th century—Biography.   4. Women—West (U.S.)—
Biography.   5. West (U.S.)—Biography.   6. Authorship.   I. Jordan,
Teresa.   II. Hepworth, James, 1948– .
PS271.S76   1995
814'.540803278—dc20   94-20846
ISBN 0-393-31451-0

W. W. Norton & Company, Inc., 500 Fifth Avenue, New York, N.Y. 10110
W. W. Norton & Company Ltd., 10 Coptic Street, London WC1A 1PU

1   2   3   4   5   6   7   8   9   0

For the daughters
and most especially for

Anneliese Cannon,
Cheyenne Quintana Hepworth
and Mariah Layne Hepworth

Contents

THE STORIES THAT SHAPE US

Introduction

Teresa Jordan

No story has shaped American culture more than the Winning of the West. It is a story of promise and conquest, of risk and achievement, of men alone in a world of unlimited resources. It is our national myth but it tells only part of the story. If someone won, others had to lose. Still, as long as conquest was our only story, it had its appeal. We could believe we didn't have to measure our actions by their consequences. We could use up people and places and move on.

Today, a hundred years after Frederick Jackson Turner declared the end of the frontier, we have dammed and polluted our rivers, killed off our native salmon runs, overfished our oceans, and cut our old-growth forests. We have developed an energy policy based on exploitation rather than conservation. We have paved over much of our richest agricultural land, and we farm the rest with oil-hungry machines and polluting chemicals that produce amazing but unsustainable yields. We are pumping our deep water aquifers dry, salinating vast tracts of land, and losing more topsoil than we did during the Dust Bowl. We have pushed 13 million people off the land in the last forty years and we are well on our way to gutting our inner cities. As we approach the end of the twentieth century and the beginning of the third millennium, one thing is clear: we need new stories to live by.

Over the past several years, a chorus of women's voices has emerged from the West. These women tell stories of family and community, of race and gender, of commitment and displacement, of grief and repair, of spirituality and connection to the earth. Their stories are not new, but until recently we seemed unable to hear them. They have been shaped by their particular regions and cultures, but they speak to the nation. We listen to them now because we need them in order to survive. These are the voices in *The Stories that Shape Us*.

SEVERAL YEARS AGO, when I was looking at the role storytelling played in different cultures, I read an article (by anthropologist Sally Snyder) about storytelling within the Skagit tribe. "Even acculturated Skagits were compulsive about telling stories 'right,'" Snyder wrote. "If a story was imperfectly recalled, it was wrong to 'guess,' meaning to pad, improvise, or omit. It was better not to tell it at all for it is dangerous to omit scenes or to shorten myths. Nubile women in the audience might give birth to deformed children, incomplete or malformed like the abbreviated or truncated story. And shortening of myths would shorten the lives of all listeners . . ." (*Anthropologica*, 1968).

The idea that our well-being depended on the truth of the stories we heard fascinated me, but the article was written with academic distance. No voices of actual Skagit storytellers were recorded; information, paraphrased rather than quoted, came from "informants" rather than individuals with names and personalities; the stories were described rather than told. It all seemed distant from real people and real lives, most especially my own.

But that was before I understood how much stories shape all of our lives. My epiphany came when I started to write about the ranching culture in which I was raised. I wanted to address the rugged individualism that has so shaped the way white rural Westerners see themselves, and I had in mind a historical overview, drawing on a variety of primary sources: journals of the first explorers, Thomas Jefferson's letters, women's diaries of the overland trail, cattlemen's memoirs. I had not intended to write a personal essay but I thought I would introduce it with a personal story, a short sketch of my grandfather.

Sunny Jordan, my father's father, lived with us all the time I was growing up. He was a ranchman of the old school, gruff and not given to small talk. Too many bad horses and too much bad weather had crippled him some; later, he had a series of strokes. By the time I was old enough to remember, he no longer worked outside. Still, he dressed for work, in starched khaki shirts and blue denim Levis pressed to a knife-edge crease.

He made no secret of the fact that children annoyed him. He frightened me, as he did all children, and I knew he didn't like me. Yet, he was my best friend. I wouldn't have called him that at the time, but I spent more time with him than anyone else. Every afternoon I joined him in his apartment on the second floor of our house and we played cards. I learned to count playing blackjack on his red leather ottoman; I learned fractions mixing him martinis. Sometimes something outside would distract him and he would look out his picture window at the big corrals where the men were working cattle; other times he'd gaze off in the distance, at the brakes he had ridden all his life. But he never lost track of his cards.

Sunny died when I was in college and I came home for his funeral. Strokes had gradually stripped him of both consciousness and continence and he lived his final years in a rest home recognizing no one, his memory a tangle of incoherent events. His death came as a relief. But at his grave site I couldn't stop crying and it took me years to figure out why. His funeral was the first time I realized I had loved him. It was the first time I realized that he had loved me.

I wanted to start my essay with Sunny's story because it captured for me some of the ways "strength" can make us weak and keep us from each other. I thought I could sketch him in a few hard lines and leave him. But stories don't always release us when we think we're through with them. I found myself thinking about other stories, stories Sunny had passed on to me. Foremost among them was our family creation myth, the story of Sunny's father coming to Wyoming.

My great-grandfather J. L. Jordan grew up in Maryland. He had wanted to join his brothers fighting the Civil War but he was only fourteen. When his parents refused him permission to go, he ran away, but before he could reach the front, Lee surrendered. Since he had disobeyed his parents, he couldn't return home so he headed out West. He worked his way across the country, building bridges in Illinois and railroads in Nebraska. He ended up in Wyoming and found a job on a ranch. A few years later his employer died, owing J. L. several years' wages, and he received title to what would become the core of the Jordan ranch. Through the years he bought more cattle and more land, and he never wrote home until he had made himself into a success.

That, at any rate, was the family gospel. But when I sat down to write about Sunny, I remembered a packet of letters that a distant relative back East had sent to my great-aunt Marie (Sunny's sister and J. L.'s daughter) a few years earlier, letters J. L. had written his father back in Maryland. When Marie died, the letters came to me. I had glanced through them enough to recognize familiar details—in one, J. L. mentioned the bridge gang; in another, the railroad crew—but I hadn't really read them. Now I put the letters in chronological order, and the dates leapt out at me. The earliest were written in 1886, over twenty years after Lee surrendered. I consulted the family Bible. J. L. had been born in 1861. He would have been four years old when the Civil War came to an end.

I started to read the correspondence in earnest. J. L. hadn't run away from home; he left at the age of twenty-five with his family's blessing. He hadn't cut himself off; rather, he chronicled his trip across the country in letters to his father, and he was often homesick. He found his work in Wyoming particularly dismal, with its wind and cold and loneliness. But his boss offered him the chance to buy cattle and his father lent him money to make it possible. Later, when his brothers' sawmill burned down back in Maryland, J. L. lent them money to start up again.

The letters told a story, but not the one I had heard at Sunny's knee. His tale was of a fourteen-year-old orphan who had come West and done it all alone. The real story was of a family that had sent out one of its members when he was ready, and helped him get a start. Once he established himself, he helped the family back home in return.

I cannot describe the revelation that these two stories, laid side by side, provided for me. It was the first time I fully understood how much our stories shape us, how much we are the stories we tell about ourselves. My grandfather had died without making the arrangements that would have allowed the ranch to pass to my father. Like many Western families—like many American families—mine had a history of fathers fighting sons. And as I thought about the generations of tension that had distanced Sunny from J. L., my father from Sunny, and my brother from the men who preceded him, I thought: How could it have been any different? They had all measured themselves and each other against someone who had never existed.

I'm certain Sunny never consciously changed his father's story. Rather, he absorbed it from the culture at large. Owen Wister's Virginian, the hero of the most popular Western ever written, was a fourteen-year-old orphan, as were many of the heroes of the Horatio Alger stories. These orphans turn up in so many popular novels and have been absorbed into so many family stories that one would think the trails West were blazed by armies of homeless fourteen-year-olds. And as the Skagit know, an incomplete or improper story can cause harm. My family told one story about ourselves. It severed the bonds between us and put us off the land. Things might have been different if we had told a story somewhat closer to the truth.

I AM A WESTERNER. As I look at the many terms that describe me—woman, writer, wife, feminist, environmentalist, rural advocate—"Westerner" comes close to the top of the list if not at its pinnacle. When I first meet people, I always want to know where they are from. I don't mean to be nosy; I'm not passing judgment. It just seems that home should matter to them because it matters so deeply to me.

As someone born into the mythic West, a Wyoming rancher's daughter, the fourth generation in the same house on the same piece of land, I grew up with certain confidences and assumptions: that I belonged to a place; that I was competent in nature, which is to say with large spaces, large animals, and large weather; that, as a descendant of pioneers who had stuck it out, I played a role in the American Dream. I grew up with certain insecurities as well which, paradoxically, derived from many of the same things that gave me confidence. If I had the pride of place, I also had the shame of place that many rural people share, the fear of being backward in the eyes of the larger, more sophisticated world. Still, however this mixture of pride and shame balanced out, I was confident that I was a "real" Westerner.

If my family story departed from the facts, it was still a story of the "real" West, full of cowboys and open country. And if, as a child, I thought that "my" West was the only one that mattered, I knew by the time I graduated from college that there were many Wests. I had come to understand that the pioneer story, the story of the American frontier as viewed through the eyes of the Anglos who came to it, is a lens that filters out other stories. It is an important story, but it is not the only one.

When I first began to look at my roots, I started to look at the stories of women and family. Until the last fifteen or twenty years, ranching—and the larger, pioneer story of which it is a part—had been told as the story of men. A change in emphasis changed the narrative radically. Stories that had been invisible before suddenly burst into view. And when I stepped back further to view the West in its many manifestations, the various lenses of class, gender, and ethnicity revealed a hundred Wests I had been blind to before.

Early photocopy machines had a lens that didn't read blue. An editor could scribble all over a manuscript with blue pencil and then make a copy that wouldn't show the marks at all. It is as if these other stories of the West were written in blue pencil. They have been there all along, but too often we didn't have a lens through which we could read them. Some of them were told within their own cultures, if only from woman to woman. Others couldn't be voiced at all.

It takes courage to tell stories where there has been silence before, and many of the essays in this collection address that fear. When the poet Judith Barrington ventured from her home in Portland, Oregon, to teach in rural and small-town schools in eastern Oregon, a part of the state she loved, she consciously hid her sexuality. She feared that if her students and their families knew she was a lesbian, her job—and even her life—would be in danger. Then a young man in one of her classes read a poem in which he dreamed of killing all the gays in the world, and Judith had to decide whether or not to speak out. Judith Freeman faced a different sort of wrath, that of her father, when she drew from her Mormon background to write her first novel. Dorothy Allred Solomon risked losing those close to her when she wrote about the polygamous household in which she was raised. Mary Clearman Blew braved one of the gravest taboos of American motherhood when she wrote about not wanting a child. And Evelyn C. White watched white students and colleagues enjoying the wilderness during a writing workshop in a remote part of the Northwest while she quaked in her cabin in fear—wilderness was where her African-American ancestors had always been hunted.

Race factors in many of these essays. Kathleen Tyau stepped from being a member of the majority, an Asian in Hawaii, to being one of a minority when she went to the mainland for college. Mary Crow Dog was ripped from her home and placed in the cruel St. Francis mission school, a kidnapping her mother and grandmother had also experienced. Janet Campbell Hale writes of the less publicized urban Indian experience. Maxine Scates remembers her Hispanic grandmother, shamed into silence and even into insanity by her Irish grandfather. Mary Helen Ponce recalls her childhood in a barrio near Los Angeles where the loving embrace of her extended, Mexican-American family brought with it confusions of language and custom. Judy Blunt remembers her fascination with the Native American boy who entered her one-room school in rural Montana, and her parents' warnings against him.

Sometimes the stories of one culture can heal the wounds inflicted by another, as folklorist Joanne Mulcahy discovered when her work with native midwives in Alaska helped her repair from the trauma of her own girlhood. Other times, stories translate in less benevolent ways and they can travel a long way. Laurie Gunst traces the ways that legends of desperados from America's Wild West have influenced members of Jamaica's violent "posses."

Some of these stories tell secrets that have to do with the natural world. Brenda Peterson writes of the mixture of reverence and horror, hunger and awe that she feels when she eats wild game. And Page Lambert guides her children through the complicated responsibilities involved when her family must shoot a porcupine.

As Jim Hepworth and I started to collect these stories, we wanted them in all their variety. Still, we retained a tint of blue in our glasses. We are both white and middle class; our very definition of what is "Western" has been shaped by our own experience in the

region. Constantly, as we poured over manuscripts and published
works, we found ourselves saying, "This is wonderful, but is it
Western?" By that we meant, did it make reference to the vastness
of the West, the landscape, the dreams of possibility? These questions led us, sometimes, to favor one piece rather than another. For
instance, we first chose Maxine Hong Kingston's story about her
uncle Kau Goong because it seemed to fit within certain Western
parameters—he had worked in the gold fields of California. We
wanted something tied more directly to Kingston's own experience,
but her autobiography, *The Woman Warrior*, wasn't "Western"
enough. And then we realized: Kingston's experience as a young
girl shamed into silence by her fear of speaking English *is* a story of
the "real" West, for, in the history of this region, Chinatown is as
Western as sagebrush.

AS WE APPROACH the dawn of a new millennium, the chal-
lenges that greet us seem almost overwhelming. Our population
keeps increasing, even as we deplete the earth that supports us. We
must live together in new ways if we are to live at all, shaped by
stories of nurture and interdependence rather than conquest. When
shifting paradigms, the historian Patricia Nelson Limerick has
quipped, it is important to remember to put in the clutch. Stories
ease our passage from one way of seeing ourselves to another. We
have included some of those stories here. Only some. This is just a
beginning. Have a good trip.

Introduction

James R. Hepworth

ecause I grew up without sisters, and, after the age of ten without a mother, I always felt deprived of knowledge about the opposite sex. Furthermore, I have to admit that my reading of women writers in general has been haphazard. Surely all men compelled to reflect upon the subject of women must at some time have felt the same dread of their own ignorance as I do.

Women, Faulkner writes somewhere, and, as if he had just expressed the sum of everything he knew, he lets the word stand alone as its own paragraph. Yet few American novelists have created more unforgettable women characters than his Dilsey or Lena Grove or Mrs. Armstid or Nancy or Caddy or Eula or Temple Drake. . . . Eudora Welty said that being a writer in Mississippi after Faulkner was like living next door to a mountain. Until I read that, I didn't know Mississippi had any mountains.

But where in the West is our mountain?

The only male Western writer I know who has come even close to creating women equal in depth to Faulkner's is Wallace Stegner, who peoples his fiction with strong female characters. Nearly all of them are Western women but of no single type, for there is no single type of Western woman, or even a set of types: like her experiences, each woman is unique.

But the real question I want to raise here is whether a recognizably "Western" culture even exists. And if it does, where, and at what, shall we look to find it? In other words, as Westerners do we have an immanent, vital society that is uniquely ours? Or do we actually live in exile and fool ourselves with the regional success story that has purportedly shaped us: the hardships already endured, the violences remembered, the troubles of a romanticized frontier behind us? In that story, it goes without saying, the only recognizably feminine story is that of the life devoted primarily to male destiny.

That the frontier still exists I am quite sure. True, it is not the same frontier that Frederick Jackson Turner declared officially dead in 1890, that point in history when American life began to turn urban and industrial and our literature at the same time turned from hopefulness to disillusionment. The frontier I speak of is the power of renewal that I and thousands of Americans find every year in the deserts and mountains of the West. Recently, I spent a few days at a ranch I used to work near Howe, Idaho. The nearest telephone was still twenty miles away, along with the nearest neighbor, and at night the only lights on all the dark rounding earth were the pickup headlights of a woman rancher who twice drove up for a visit.

If a recognizably Western society does exist, one way to characterize it might be to see how much of its literature takes place outdoors, for open space is still one of the West's most salient geographic features. Trying to define America in a sentence, Gertrude Stein once wrote, "Conceive a space filled with motion." As she knew, having been born in Oakland, space enforces mobility, and no culture in the United States is more mobile than the West's. What happens, then, when we look at the essays in this volume exclusively in terms of space and mobility?

From the forced mobility that created internment boomtowns like the one Jeanne Wakatsuki Houston writes about in *Farewell to Manzanar* to Sharmon Apt Russell's portraits of peripatetic "Illegal

Aliens" and Kathleen Norris's farmers kneeling before an open grave in "Getting to Hope," the essays in this volume are in this sense recognizably "Western." Much, perhaps even a preponderance, of the action in these essays takes place outdoors. Even the mental action. When Terry Tempest Williams of Salt Lake, for instance, writes about her uncle Alan in "The Village Watchman," she is not sitting at home in front of a computer screen but outside in the deep woods of Sitka, Alaska, in front of a totem pole. When Shannon Applegate decides to write about her dream and the family ancestral home in "Dear Uncle Vince," she is miles away in a tent on the Oregon coast. The plentiful rising and falling action in Teresa Jordan's essay, "Bones," all takes place in the open air on or near the family's Iron Mountain ranch in Wyoming. In "Waist-high in the West," Nancy Mairs does not let multiple sclerosis keep her from visiting remote places like Chaco Canyon. Of course not. Judging by these essays, we can say that Western space, often big and impressive, sometimes empty, and always fragile, is still a crucial shaping influence. And the people in the essays, even the wheelchair-bound ones, are highly mobile. But these pieces also contain other noteworthy characteristics—self-reliance and rugged individualism, stoicism and grit, optimism and hope, tenacity and courage, the ability to bear pain and hardship, and even some of the true piety and adventurous but cooperative spirit that I believe are emblematic of Western people, women and men alike.

I'm tempted to say, though, that the men in these essays come off less favorably than the women. I'm thinking, for instance, of those yahoos urinating in the ditch as Linda Hasselstrom pulls up her drive on her way to the mailbox in "Why One Peaceful Woman Carries a Pistol." Or the lecherous and abusive priests in Mary Crow Dog's "Civilize Them with a Stick." Or the high school student and aspiring queer-killer in Judith Barrington's piece. Nevertheless, plenty of strong men also surface in these essays. Often, they make only a quick, walk-on appearance like Derek, who counterpoints the abusive husband in Janet Campbell Hale's "Transitions." Sometimes, however, as in the case of Williams's exceptional uncle, they become the primary focus of the discussion.

Of course, until very recently, literary critics (male and female alike) regarded the writing of most American women, especially Western American women, as little more than "local color." As with so much nonfiction writing, if scholars regarded women's personal biographies at all, they considered them subliterary. In fact, as William Zinsser notes in *On Writing Well*, critics and scholars have almost exclusively defined "literature" by genre, limiting it to forms that were "certified as 'literary' in the nineteenth century: novels, short stories, and poems." And yet the "great preponderance of what writers now write and sell, what book and magazine publishers publish, and what readers demand is nonfiction."

Obviously, poetry and fiction are entirely legitimate and enduring literary forms. From time to time I suppose we have all heard it said that one or the other was a threatened species. But they are only threatened until some writer like Toni Morrison or Leslie Marmon Silko or Mary Oliver comes along to astonish us. It also used to be said (and still is) that the novelists alone could take us into those hidden places where other writers could not go: deep into the texture of our interior lives and emotions. But every once in a while literature, like science, comes to a place where it encounters a man or woman who overturns it and sets it going forever in a different direction. That is exactly what has happened, I believe, in the case of Maxine Hong Kingston, for the sources and substance of her two autobiographies, *The Woman Warrior* (1976) and *China Men* (1980), are dreams, memories, ancient myths, and desires. Both books are wildly imaginative kaleidoscopic visions that investigate the interior soul in exile from its roots, books that set new standards for autobiography and opened up new possibilities for nonfiction.

So much, indeed, has changed in the last fifty years that

younger writers in the West now have difficulty believing that their elders could ever have had serious problems getting a hearing. But the narrow literary consciousness that made a stepsister out of non-fiction in the royal house of literature also plagued Western writers of both genders well into the 1970s. For many years, serious writers in the West were practically voiceless, a situation with which many women can still easily identify. As evidence, though, of recent changes in attitude on the part of Eastern publishers, one has only to look at the number of books by Western writers being published in New York every year to know that something has radically altered.

As a publisher, of course, I'd like to believe that the dispersal of book and magazine publishing beyond New York and Boston into places as culturally isolated as Lewiston, Idaho, has spurred along the increasing ascendancy of Western writers, particularly women. For instance, whereas sixty years ago literary magazines in the West were practically nonexistent, today we have hundreds of them that devote thousands of pages to writing by Western women. In *Calyx*, published in Corvallis, Oregon, we have in fact an exquisitely produced award-winning magazine exclusively devoted to writing by women. As for books, I know from experience that it is possible, even from out here in the sticks, to publish volumes that escape the regional label to reach a national audience. One of my favorite writers in this anthology, Linda Hasselstrom, has yet to bring out a book with a publisher outside the West. Others, like Kathleen Norris, Nancy Mairs, Judy Blunt, and Mary Clearman Blew, all published their first or second books with university or small Western presses. I even published a couple of them myself.

Another thing has also changed: we have better and stronger educational support structures for writers in the West than we ever had before. Beginning with Iowa and Stanford back in the 1930s and '40s, Western colleges and universities, institutions that used to look upon all writers with profound suspicion, finally began providing many of them with jobs. Even the gender and ethnic imbalances have now begun to shift. Nearly all of the women with essays in this volume have taught at a college or university, if only on a part-time basis. And the same revolution that placed writers into colleges and universities also produced a new reading and lecture circuit.

Independent bookstores, too, now flourish in the West. One thinks immediately of the big stores: Elliott Bay in Seattle, Powell's in Portland, Black Oak Books in Berkeley, The Tattered Cover in Denver. Of course, many of those who own or manage the independent stores are Western women, like Jean Wilson of The Bookshop in Boise or Chris O'Harra of Auntie's Bookstore in Spokane. But even the smallest of the great independent stores—Bookpeople in Moscow, Idaho, or The Country Bookshelf in Bozeman, Montana— offer Western women writers and their books a significant forum. What's more, as New York publishers are slowly beginning to learn, the crowd that turns out for the reading and the book signing in a town the size of Missoula may be larger than the one in Salt Lake or L.A., if only because rural people in the West are still culturally starved. Along with the colleges and the bookstores, private, state, and federal agencies now also offer their services to writers, including residencies and fellowships.

In fact, grants and fellowships, whether from the National Endowment or the state arts commissions, have often provided Western women with the very things they have most needed: not only money for a room of one's own but time to write.

Regardless, I don't think it could be said that the women writers in this volume are homogeneous enough to be labeled a "movement" or "school." While several are close friends, many don't know each other and still others are only casual acquaintances. They live spread out all the way from the Dakotas to California. What's more, even for women we might presume to share the same cultural values, differences are likely to count more than similarities. Dorothy Allred Solomon's experiences with Mormonism and the Principle of Plural Marriage, for instance, are at some remove from the Mormonism of Judith Freeman or Terry Tempest Williams.

The country is too big and various and the time still too short for Western women to have developed a collective native voice. Mary Crow Dog, a Lakota born in a one-room cabin on the reservation, is a very different woman even from Janet Campbell Hale, a Coeur d'Alene woman raised in northern Idaho and continually uprooted throughout her childhood and adolescence, and even more different from Sharmon Apt Russell or Jeanne Wakatsuki Houston.

Reading the essay of any one writer in this volume, we may not be much reminded of the others. Yet each is as Western, which I take to mean as prototypically American, as the others, and all are attempts by women to uncover and to know their traditions and their inheritances. Rather than a melting pot, the contemporary West is much closer to what the Canadians claim as their cultural metaphor: a mosaic, an anthology.

Shannon Applegate

hannon Applegate is an editor, fiction writer, and historian. She co-edited her most recent book, Talking on Paper: The Letters and Diaries of Oregon *(1994)*, *with Terence O'Donnell. The title word of her own tour de force in the genre,* Skookum *(1988), comes from Chinook jargon, an early trade language of the Pacific Northwest rooted firmly in several indigenous languages as well as in English (*oleman *= "old man") and French (*slwash *= "savage"). The word* skookum *means "power or spirit." For native Westerners, of course, particularly those in Oregon, the word* Applegate *also resounds with cultural authority and complexity, for it can refer not only to a trail, a town, a river, and even a mountain peak but also to any one of many, many individuals in a legendary and populous pioneer family. Born in 1944 to a riot control expert in the Office of Strategic Services (OSS), Colonel Rex Applegate, and Edith LaCaille, Applegate early determined to become a painter and printmaker. She attended the Maryland Institute of Art and took her academic classes at Johns Hopkins. In Calgary, however, she began showing some of her early writing to a woman named Peggy (Margaret Atwood), who encouraged Applegate to continue writing. A 1967 visit with her Applegate elders in Yoncalla Valley prompted her to change the course of her creative life. Soon after, she moved into the old Applegate house, her ancestral home, Oregon's* *oldest house, and the book's principal setting. Once there, she began to sift through literally thousands of family documents, including 6,000 letters, as well as recollections, journals, manuscripts, sketchbooks, and photographs. These she used to create* Skookum, *a continuous narrative that employs many of the same literary forms, particularly the two forms we associate most closely with Western women and the Westering experience in general: the letter and the journal. In all, Shannon Applegate spent seventeen years researching and writing her family's history and lore. The book spans nearly a century and a half (1843–1988). She now lives on 110 acres in her great-grandfather Buck's house with her husband, Dan Robertson, in Roseburg, Oregon. It is the same house in which her father was born.*

"Dear Uncle Vince"

from *Skookum*

1981
Oregon Coast

Dear Uncle Vince,

Why am I writing to you?—you whom the minister eulogized ten years ago and more; you, lying there alone on an island of dark ribboned flowers; you, whom I loved, however imperfectly, whom I could not bear to look upon as I filed past. I saw only the big hand resting over your heart, the sleeve of your one good suit, a glimpse of your old bald head—the unmistakable peak of an Applegate nose looming over the unseen face.

Uncle Vince, for weeks now I have been pulling and pushing, yet my mind seems closed—the door shut tight or not there at all. A wall. No, the memories of you and me and those days we shared in the old house have not come easily. Even on good days, they seem no more than summer westerlies—like the little gusts I remember that rustle through the orchard every now and then.

The truth is that on most days I have felt as if I were standing on the kitchen porch, calling and calling again, waiting for some wayward child or half-deaf hound who will not come. Yet I feel different this morning: Relieved. Released. Last night I had a dream. The dream:

Darkness had fallen but the sky was a vibrant blue. There was no moon; yet in the distance, the Old Place emanated such a bright white light, it was like the moon, or so I thought to myself as I walked along.

I was following a long, winding brick pathway, which resembled the one you said your father made when you were a boy. After walking for what seemed a long time indeed, I turned to see the landscape from whence I'd come. The ocean was utterly silver. I was not surprised to see it in the least. I knew I'd started there and had climbed over huge rocks to find the path.

I was pleased with myself, feeling calm, not hurrying when I resumed my journey.

But as I came closer and closer to the house, some apprehension began to stir in me. I knew that something or someone was waiting for me up ahead.

Mists hovered over the fields on either side of me. I wanted to turn back after a while, for now there was no view at all, but I knew I couldn't. I walked very slowly, concentrating upon the bricks, which were laid unevenly—the moss seeming to eat around their edges even as I watched.

I was still some distance from the glow of the house when I heard the sound. I puzzled over it for some moments. It was resonant but brief, almost bell-like. Suddenly I recognized it. A hoe was striking the earth again and again. I was listening so intently, I lost my sense of self. The pitch was like that of a temple or meditation bell. The sound was all. I was still walking, but it was more like floating, as though caught in some stream or current that was not my own. Yet when I passed beneath the locust trees in the front yard, I heard the black leaves whispering. It was as if they were saying, "Call back your alertness." And I did, feeling incredibly alive again.

The pathway did not lead to the front doors as it does in reality, nor did it pass beneath the lattice of the pergola and on to the kitchen door. Instead, the path bordered an immense flowerbed, and Uncle Vince, I have never seen such dahlias.

All were pearl-white, their long stems wavering slightly with each chime of the hoe. Some had heavy heads, larger than dinner plates, and their fringed petals were almost translucent. Others were daintier and wonderfully iridescent. I left the pathway and found myself amidst the maze of flowers.

Did I hear the sound any longer? I can't remember. Before me I see flowers so tall, they are as a swaying wall of lace. But I seem to be looking down now. I see the blade of the hoe. No. That's not right. What I see first are the shoes, dusty and brown. Now there is the blade. The hoe handle. The hand. The man. I knew who it was, Uncle Vince, from the moment I saw those old shoes. His frayed suspenders clipped to baggy pants, the collarless shirt. How many times have I stared at that face caught in those yellowed photographs? Yes. It was your father. It was Buck. Great-grandfather was tending his night garden. And when I was finally able to return his gaze, his eyes told me that he had known me all my life.

How is such a thing possible? He died—what?—twenty-five years before I was born. I knew that: even as I was dreaming. Yet this morning I still feel it. He knows me, Uncle Vince, or some aspect of me. He knows me and sees me and accepts me, in ways that you never did, and I know him.

He said the most amazing things to me, Uncle Vince. No, not in words. He just kept looking at me, oh so deeply.

But I was afraid of him, those first moments. All manner of things were racing through my mind. After all, I have not always been flattering—in terms of Buck, I mean—and as I stood there, the voices of all those men and women I've interviewed over the years were somehow spliced together, whirring round and round. Buck Applegate: "He may have been brilliant, no doubt about that: inventions and those inlaid violins he made for the twins, and apple trees, too; grafting them and watching over them as if they were babies . . . that acre of wheat Buck grew one time as an experiment, the yield so high and each stock so long it extended clear acrosst the bumper of a Model A, and the people at the agricultural college came down. Yes, it was that good. . . . Why, he could do anything— built hisself a record player and made his own recording, too . . . had the first carbide gas setup in the whole danged valley, so he didn't have to bother with kerosene anymore. . . . Drew pictures, played the fiddle . . . but did Buck Applegate ever bother to turn his clever hands at anything that might make his family a little money? . . . Flora, his wife, she did the work over there. . . . She worried, he whittled and fiddled, holed up in that big front room, and when his poor wife couldn't make ends meet anymore and he realized how hard up they were, what did Buck Applegate do? Why, he sold a little more of the land, got rid of it bit by bit. . . ."

How can a person gloss over such things? And Uncle Vince, you yourself told me that your pappa had failings. How could I not at least allude to all that? And I was standing there, feeling embarrassed and even guilty, arguing with myself, and fearful, yes.

My God, he was looking at me—through me almost—and it came to me suddenly he was reading my thoughts and that nothing whatever had missed him, and I began trembling, fully expecting his anger to fall upon me like a blow.

He put down his hoe. His look was quizzical, then amused in some way, his big white moustache lifting a little as he came toward me. He put his hand upon my shoulder.

How I wish I could remember exactly what passed from his mind to mine.

"On the contrary," . . . I remember those words. . . . "I'm very interested in what you and others think of me. How can I know if no one tells me?"

And there was something else, too. This is as close as I'm able to come, because this was more like a feeling, a feeling given expression. In some way he let me know that I was doing exactly what I ought to be doing. Yes. Somehow, in some way what I was doing might *help him.*

Help him? I was quite literally stunned. What did he mean? But we were off then—his old gnarled hand still on my shoulder. He was leading me toward the back porch. And a woman opened the kitchen door. Her hair was incredibly thick and auburn in color. She was very animated: "Why, Shannon," she said aloud, "don't you know me? I'm Irene, of course."

And Uncle Vince, others were there, waiting for me: family women all. But this part is the most remarkable:

The women were not in the west room, making quilts or sewing. No, there they were, sitting around the big table in the east room. They had sheafs of paper in their hands, things I'd written or they had written, old letters and documents. Buck took me there and sat back, enjoying all our talk.

Do you understand? It is your father who has led me to the men's side. Buck: my doorway to you.

"What in the Sam Hill is she going on and on about all this dream business?" I can almost hear you saying. "What's she getting at?"

She. Her. "She's in the kitchen." "She's Rex's girl." "She's trying to write herself a book." "She don't know anything; she's been
back east mostly." "Now, what's got into *her?*"

Uncle Vince, I can't remember a single time when you used my
given name.

As for the "dream business," I'll have you know that talking
about dreaming is an honorable tradition in this family. No, not
"just the women," either. I could tell you of a half-dozen dreams
that have been passed down in one way or another. The dreamers—
all family men: Charley and Jesse, your uncle John and uncle Al and
Buck. My own father. Three generations, skipping yours and
Grandpa's.

If I'd had my wits back then when you and I lived together, I
would have asked you about your dreams. I know you had them. I
used to watch you sleeping in your favorite chair. Every so often,
you'd mutter something and then you'd tremble a little and jerk
your head like some old dog reliving the chase.

Do you know what I'd think when I saw you drifting off, or
shoveling hash browns into your mouth, or slouching toward the
bathroom in your dingy long johns? "Oh, how the mighty have
fallen."

You reminded me of some secondary Faulkner character or one
of Hardy's listless Derbyvilles. And who was I, pray? A quiet short
lady on a very high horse indeed.

In those days, I was straining to fit you into the group portrait
I was painting in my mind—"The Three Brothers," I called them.
Lindsay, Jesse, and Charles were front and center. Larger than life.

They had led notable lives. *They* had rubbed shoulders with famous men: the doyens of the British and American fur trade, Indian
chiefs, missionaries, explorers, and politicians. Why, as a boy,
Great-great-great-uncle Lindsay hunted coon with Abraham Lincoln, and Jesse corresponded with governors, senators, and vice-
presidents who sought his advice.

Those men were "movers and shakers," trailblazers and lawmakers. Even Great-great-grandfather made his mark, in my mind, however faint. Charley, at least, had the gumption to be well-to-do.

Yet you, Charley's grandson, Buck's beloved baby boy, carried nary a trace of either gumption or genius, as far as I could see. You decided to become a dairy inspector, pleased with yourself because they gave you a county car to drive on your rounds. And before that—someone told me you'd run some little grocery store in a town almost as small as Yoncalla. Oh, you could shoot the breeze amicably enough with the customers, but you had trouble keeping up on your inventory. Those bins of sugar, flour, beans, and macaroni apparently had not inspired you. And who were your friends? Why, their lives had been as prosaic as your own. Retired farmers, ranchers, loggers, and maybe one or two who ventured into the world of commerce: a feed and seed salesman who once had been on the road; a gas-station owner.

I was a snob, Uncle Vince. The countryside, rural folk, it was all new to me. "She" had been back east mostly.

Those elderly cronies of yours who sometimes congregated on the back porch on summer afternoons. "Dee-vorced?" I'd hear them whisper raspily to you, then they'd look me over when they thought I couldn't see them, as though they were gauging some heifer being auctioned.

How could I feel comfortable? I see that now. Yet I see other things, too. When those old men came to visit, "just-a-sitting" or playing cribbage and talking, why didn't I have the sense to sit quietly and eavesdrop until they got used to having me around? But I always felt the need to interject something or ask something. Right then. No, I couldn't wait. I was a backseat driver trying to steer the conversation toward some subject of more interest to me. Such as what crops had their grandfathers grown in the old days, or when had sheep arrived in the valley? Were they more lucrative than cattle? And they'd stop their own talk then and give me a funny look, those old male relatives of ours with spots on their baggy pants, their belts cinched tight, their shirts drizzled with "snooze" or bacon grease, their knotty, tobacco-stained fingers moving the little matchstick pegs or silently reshuffling the plastic playing cards. You could hear a pin drop. I knew how to stop talk dead in its tracks, all right. Even so, those old men were objects of interest to me—antiques, not unlike the Seth Thomas on the men's side that chimed according to a time all its own, and those rusty, ancient pieces of farm equipment lying along the banks of the old creekbed whose names and uses I did not know.

Yet I felt "right at home" when I visited the wives and sisters of those old men. I could follow a woman around in her kitchen and think nothing of it: shucking corn or coring apples, watching her put up green beans while I washed Mason jars. I didn't expect their undivided attention.

And talk? Yes, talk. The air hummed with it. It positively percolated, mixing with the hiss of the canning kettle or trailing along beside us like smoke as we passed in and out of the kitchen to the vegetable garden and back again:

"Great-aunt Susie was a one . . . people came from miles around to try out her sour biscuits. . . . Jane Applegate painted pictures of wild flowers and sewed up a storm. . . . Irene Applegate? Why, my mother told me that old doctor got out his knives and operated on her cancers right there in an upstairs bedroom. Just imagine. No one would go through that today."

They took to me right away, Uncle Vince, asking me questions: How old were the children? did I get lonely over there? how did it happen I had a pretty name like Shannon?—so uncommon . . .

And when the talker finally landed on an overstuffed chair, the talk slowed down somewhat, more or less keeping time with the clickety-click of the knitting needles or crochet hooks. Anything I wanted to know that they knew, it was gladly told, Uncle Vince, and when it was time to go, I left feeling I was a part of something. All these years have passed, yet I have never known more industrious women. Neither age nor infirmity seemed to keep them from their appointed rounds. But those old men you introduced me to never seemed to be around when I called upon their wives, now that I think about it. And when I saw them in town or at our place, they were always either sitting or standing. As though waiting for something. I had that feeling about you too, Uncle Vince, especially toward the last.

Last week I got out all the old pictures I'd brought from Yoncalla. I was looking for you, I guess. There you were, decked out for World War I. And in one picture, you had curls to your shoulders and a cunning little suit on. But the best one showed you—oh, you must have been as old as Colin is now—riding on a bull in the front yard. Grandpa was behind you, smiling. And I was smiling too by then, until I found that newspaper clipping at the bottom of the box. The obituary notice.

Uncle Vince, you were born in 1894—though I don't suppose I need to tell you that. Why didn't I ask you about the influenza epidemic; were you at home then or off soldiering? Did you go to Europe? Did Buck ever own a motorcar? Did *you* ever play the violin?

And the story you told me one afternoon—I must not have been listening carefully: the Yoncalla ball team that licked all comers—were all the players named Applegate except for one Indian, or was it the other way around?

Oh, Uncle Vince, I wish I could go to the kitchen now and get the Jim Beam down from the cupboard for you, or fry you an egg or make you a blackberry cobbler. Then, by God, we'd talk; or rather, you'd talk and I'd listen.

But there was one evening close to the end—remember?—when the licorice darkness lapped outside the window, and you and I sat by ourselves inside, sipping our ration of bourbon. And you had shown me how to trim the wicks of those kerosene lamps suspended on the walls of the dining room. "Well, go ahead if you want to," you said, "fire 'em up." We turned off the electric lights and sat there in that still pool of glowing yellow: the room itself and you and I, muted and mellow.

But I was afraid you'd fall asleep on me, and I poked at you a little, trying to stir the talk before it died out altogether.

I think I was asking you about Charley: why he, Jesse, and Lindsay had left their homesteads in the Willamette Valley and headed south to Yoncalla instead.

"Aw, honey," you said, "that's history." You drained your cup and told me how you didn't need to tell me about all that history "stuff" because it was already written up. I should go up to Portland to that historical society, or to the library in Eugene at the college. And you yawned, giving in to the hour and the soft light, and muttering something about how you wished your grandpappy's barrel of whiskey was still out on the back porch.

And this is why I remember. It was at the last. Maybe a week before it happened. You sighed and said, "Well, I guess I don't have to worry what will happen to the Old Place anymore now that you and the kids are here." And there it was again, like a cold current or a chill wind slipping unexpectedly beneath a door. I was so lonely suddenly. The night train whistled as it rumbled past the Yoncalla siding and you shut your eyes, asleep in your rocking chair.

Good-bye, Uncle Vince. It's all said. It's all right.

"She" loves you.

Judith Barrington

J udith Barrington was born in England in 1944 and, after the death of her parents in an accident at sea, lived in Spain for three years in her early twenties. She came to Oregon in 1976 to spend a summer at Portland State University as part of a writing project, and never left. "I probably had to leave my home in order to become a serious writer," Barrington says, echoing the sentiments of expatriate writers all over the world. "It took going away to see what I was truly close to."

The American West gave Barrington a sense of both space and permission. Her imagination responded to the landscape, and in the Portland community she found freedom and support for both her writing and her desire to live openly as a lesbian.

Barrington is the author of two collections of poetry, Trying to Be an Honest Woman (1985) and History and Geography (1989); Lifesaving: A Spanish Memoir (forthcoming in 1996); and is the editor of An Intimate Wilderness: Lesbian Writers on Sexuality (1991). Central to her work is the power of place, the experience of loss and grief, the importance of living a physical life, and, as so compellingly revealed in this essay, the challenge of telling the truth.

Poetry and Prejudice

IF ONLY I HAD KNOWN WHAT HE WAS GOING TO say when he stood up, I would have stopped him. But how? *Don't read your poem out loud, Brad—you have no idea of the effect it will have on me?* Or, as I had said every other morning: *Please hand your papers up to me and I'll read a few of them aloud?* That had worked fine for the first four class meetings. I had been able to screen out the worst of the blood and gore. I had read the hunting poems, with their slitting of throats, removal of scalps, antlers, ears, and eyes, and their dragging out of guts. But I hadn't read the poems in which the throats being slit were human. As a criterion for selection I have some doubts about this now, but I had to think on my feet those mornings, leafing through a sheaf of unappetizing poems.

I was the poet-in-residence at Enterprise High School, in the shadow of Oregon's Wallowa Mountains near the Idaho border. This first-period class consisted of twelve seniors—and I didn't like them. Unlike all the classes I had worked with the previous week, this one had not responded to any of my attempts to interest them in poetry. With only one more day, I had begun to think it wasn't going to happen. This frustrated me. Always before I had managed to make a good connection with my students.

Earlier that morning, I had driven, as I did every day before school, down the road from my borrowed cabin on Wallowa Lake towards Joseph, where I had worked several times as a visiting poet. I loved this part of the state. In fact, it had become one of those rare, special places where I could relax into the beauty of the landscape and work on my own writing in the quiet hours after school—one of those places that imprints its colors and its contours on my mind forever. Each time I had completed a residency here, I'd angled for return invitations, which, so far, had always been forthcoming.

As I approached the Indian burial ground, I turned for a last look at snow-covered Chief Joseph Mountain, paying deliberate attention to the shadows playing across the surface of the lake, on which patches of ice still floated in the shady spots. I didn't want to grow too accustomed to this breathtakingly beautiful place; I wanted to be amazed, every day, that this was my drive to work. Along the side of the lake, deer lifted their heads from the grass, which was pale and limp where it had just emerged from the snow, and turned their huge, dished ears my way, while I wondered how to connect with this unusually difficult group of students—wondered how to like them better.

They didn't like me either. It wasn't hard to tell. The ten boys overflowed from chairs and desks, long legs in skin-tight blue jeans sprawled forward with the pointed toes of their cowboy boots sticking up defiantly, as if giving me the finger. The two girls giggled together and never finished writing anything, but screwed up their papers and threw them away in loud disgust, as if to reassure the boys over and over that they had appropriately low expectations of themselves. At first, seeing how outnumbered they were, I had felt sorry for them, but by now I was exasperated. Of course, I had encountered all these common teenage behaviors in other classes at other schools, but I had usually managed to bypass the careful indifference of the kids and find something that excited them, however reluctant they were to show it.

Brad, for instance, seemed like other teenagers I had known: intent on looking cool at all costs, but underneath perhaps more interested in the poems than he let on. He was the tall one who always sat in the back left corner of the room. His jeans were so tight they must have impeded both movement and circulation, but he tried, not very successfully, to imitate the relaxed style of someone who was both comfortable and self-confident. Underneath the studied pose, he seemed intense; often he stared out of the windows behind me, his expression so passionate that sometimes I turned to

look outside too: the line of snow-covered peaks stood out like cardboard cutouts against the brilliant blue sky. It was stunning. But
what did Brad see, I wondered. Was he thinking about being out
there on the slopes? About hunting? His poems this week had described the thrill of early-morning stalking; a twig snapping underfoot; a doe's eye in the sights of his gun.

If only I had known what he was going to say when he stood
up, I would have planned my response the way I carefully, obses-
sively, planned it later—after the event, when it was too late. "Bigotry," I would have written in large letters on the blackboard, and I
would have started with racism, which surely these students already knew was frowned upon, at least in some circles. What they
heard at home, of course, might be another matter. Most of them, I
imagined, were not exposed to progressive views. In fact, I had just
heard about a lawsuit filed against Wallowa Lodge, the old hotel up
on the lake, which had refused accommodation to a woman with a
multi-racial child. Later I heard that she won her case and got some
damages, but still the incident told me something about how imper-
vious many people up here were to the moral standards that had
finally been written into law—how free they felt, not only to hold
on to their prejudice, but also to act on it in a public and visible way.

It was an isolated community, rife with tensions between the
long-term inhabitants, most of whom were loggers and ranchers,
and the new, many of whom were artists, writers, and reclusive intellectuals, enjoying the beauty and peace of what had come to be
called the "little Switzerland" of Oregon. The isolation was, in fact,
beginning to break down, whether the old-timers liked it or not, as
hikers came in to climb the mountains, llama trekking became fash-
ionable, and—most controversial of all—the old sewer system that
had polluted Wallowa Lake was replaced by a new one, which
would allow for the development of more summer homes. It's not
hard to imagine how what must have seemed like an invasion to
some, got translated into various prejudices in the privacy of my

students' homes—variations on the "Jews, commies, and queers" theme. But I had never thought about any of this until Brad read his poem that morning.

The teacher, Dan, was sitting at the back of the room. I had talked to him a couple of times about this unresponsive group, and he had been concerned. Dan hadn't given up like so many of the teachers I had met in my frequent visits to schools around the state: he communicated his excitement about literature; he wrote poems for my classroom assignments, which he shared with the group; and he coached the students in reading dramatically, which some of them enjoyed. But nothing had made much of a dent with this class.

That morning, I started by handing out a William Stafford poem, which we read aloud. In "Serving with Gideon," Stafford describes a moment of decision he faced when he had to throw in his lot with the "good old white boys" of his town or take a stand against them, in Kansas during the segregated thirties. In the poem, the young Stafford symbolically carries his Coke from the drugstore and goes to stand with the black elevator man, who is not allowed to drink at the counter—a small act, perhaps, but a very large decision. As we talked about the poem, I was aware that this group probably had little ability to empathize with the black man—and perhaps not even with the young white man troubled by racism, but I figured that, a few weeks away from graduation, they might know what it felt like to face important choices.

"Write a poem about an important decision in *your* life," I suggested.

For the next ten minutes there was a lot of squirming, writing, balling up of paper, and giggling. I tried to write too, as I always do, using my own assignments to generate lines or images that I might use later. But I found it hard to concentrate in the atmosphere, which was anything but peaceful. The two girls, who were sitting in front, whispered to each other until I stared at them, when they pouted and looked at their paper, but made it clear they were just waiting till I looked away so they could resume their conversation.

A couple of boys were reading paperbacks, which I decided to let go, since they were at least being quiet. Brad was staring out at the mountains again and I found myself speculating about his thoughts. In one of his hunting poems, he had come close to lyricism as he described the aromatic smell of the pines and the breeze humming and sighing at that moment before he fired. Was this dreamy smile caused by his recollection of the deer looking up at him as he softly squeezed the trigger?

I checked my watch. Another five minutes was all they would manage.

I knew Brad's father had taught him to hunt—he had written about that yesterday, though he refused to read the poem aloud. Learning to hunt was part of learning to be a man up here—I understood that, just as I understood that reading a poem aloud was a definite challenge to that tenuous manhood. Yet many of these kids would get out of Wallowa County as fast as they could. The smart ones would be off to college or to jobs in the city, where some of the others would find only unemployment and trouble. Few wanted to farm or cut trees like their fathers, and hunting deer would be no passport to manhood in their new lives. For all I knew, Brad was dreaming about high life in the city. Staring out at the spectacular scenery, which he had seen his whole life, maybe he saw, instead, the skyscrapers of New York and himself—all decked out in his suede jacket with the fringes swaying to the rhythm of his stride, swaggering into some dive where everyone looked up through smoke and saxophone vibes to admire his entrance.

I checked my watch again, and asked, "Anyone want to read a poem?"

Brad leapt to his feet, once again a six-foot-two-inch cowboy, his face reverting to its habitual smirk. His poem, he announced, was called "On a Mission." Gesturing melodramatically with his arm, he declaimed:

Once on the mountaintop
I heard a voice say
"You can be a Hero
if you choose, and this is how.
Go out and find all the gays
and kill them. You will be
a Hero, praised by the whole world."
I had to decide.
I don't want to remain
obscure.
So I made my decision:
I got my gun and began my task.

As he finished, bowing low from the waist, the room erupted into wild guffaws and applause. Sitting on a high stool up front, I watched as the laughter seemed to take over, sweeping wildly around the room, seizing them all, even the girls, until they were in the grip of some emotion that had nothing to do with humor. For once utterly satisfied to be who they were, they laughed until tears glistened on their flushed faces.

I was sitting very still on my stool. It took a while for it to dawn on them that I was not laughing—that my cheeks were, in fact, bright red, although I have no idea what expression my face registered as I struggled to keep control of myself. Inside, my body registered hot fury. It was *me* Brad wanted to kill—but I was afraid to say so, and while the laughter whirled around the room like a tornado, I sat at its center, my heart drumming in my ears, my mind turning over and over like an engine that won't fire.

The first thought that came into my head was that if I told them I was a lesbian I would not be physically safe in the cabin. There was no phone there and I was one of only a handful of inhabitants up at the lake this early in the season. I could already see the pickup truck full of rowdy boys with a couple of guns in the rack,

hurtling down the track in the dark; I imagined the headlights pene-
trating the living room windows as it swung onto the grass in front
of the cabin; I knew how their big, competent hands would hold the
knives and guns they had been writing about all week. Then it
flashed through my mind that there would be other repercussions:
in this contract work, which I relied on for a significant part of my
income, it would be easy to phase me out—I wouldn't have to be
fired; I just wouldn't get invited back to any of the schools up here
when word got around.

It certainly wasn't my first confrontation with homophobia,
yet it entered my body in a way that was different from anything I
had encountered before. As the laughter tore around me, it was as if
the outrage I had politely suppressed throughout my life was suddenly unlocked. It heated up my body from inside. Indignation, a
sense of injustice, and the kind of frustration that makes you want
to be a baby, yelling and waving your fists, all pulsed through my
bloodstream. I felt hot enough to explode.

If only I had known what he was going to say when he stood
up, I would have gathered my courage inside me, as I have done so
often when preparing to take that leap off the cliff, but probably,
even then, I wouldn't have said the words, "I am a lesbian." It's true
that I wasn't physically safe up there alone in that cabin, and it's
true that I would probably have lost all or part of my school work,
but it's also true that I was just plain afraid of revealing myself in
that room. I had no sense of being able to bridge the huge chasm
between me and those twelve kids—no belief that my simple, true
statement would reach them through the bubble of camaraderie inside which they floated.

Perhaps if we had already established a good relationship, I
could have done it, could have gambled that whatever tenuous lik-
ing for me they had would withstand the shock of the revelation—
that they would somehow incorporate my being a lesbian into an
already established picture of me as a real person. But it wasn't like

that. I had no rapport in the bank, no goodwill savings to draw on at this moment. Suddenly I remembered an occasion some twenty-six years earlier when, at the age of twenty, I had been sitting at an outdoor cafe table in Spain with a group of Spanish boys, all of them my friends. They were talking about a soldier, whose body had been found on the road to the army camp outside the town where we lived. The body, they said, had been left to rot, picked at by crows and other scavengers. I remembered the wave of guilt I felt as the boys muttered the word *maricon* ("faggot"), almost unable to say it aloud. I remembered the profound silence of the cafe as I sat there blushing. And the sultry heat of that evening touched my skin again now, the smell of car exhaust rolling back over the years in great, noxious waves, as I remembered, most clearly of all, how much I wanted to cry out, but how I did not know what words would leap from my mouth if I did.

I sat quite still in the classroom until the laughter had died away and the students were uncomfortable with my silence. As it grew quiet, little eruptions of congratulation broke out again, as one or other of them tried to prolong their shared pleasure.

"Hey, man, great poem!" said one, and a ripple of agreement ran round the room, like an aftershock.

"Right on Brad!" said another, accompanied by murmurs of "Yeah, yeah!"

But they couldn't keep it up as they glanced sideways at me, bewildered by my red face.

At the back of the room Dan was poring over some papers with his head down. I could tell he was scared by what was happening and it didn't seem as if he intended to help me out. I struggled to make a plan, but my body was buzzing, almost as if I were touching a low-voltage electric fence, and my mind refused to follow a normal sequence of thought. It would formulate the first few words of a declaration intended to change the lives of these students, but then it would jump sideways, derailed by an incongruous memory, or by the words I should have said on some other occasion. I was talking in my mind to family, friends, strangers on buses, politicians. I was sitting in my brother's oak-paneled dining room as his wife described the women at her tennis club as a bunch of dykes. I was watching myself smile complicitly as my family sneered at the woman only I knew was my lover. I was on a stone terrace overlooking the Mediterranean, my heart tearing inside my ribs as the man with the gold tooth smoothly flirted with the woman I loved, and she responded to this stranger as if she were available so that no one would suspect us.

"I want to tell you something," I said finally, my voice shaking and higher pitched than usual. I grasped the sides of the stool with both my sweaty hands, willing myself to look casual, but terrified I might burst into tears. As I affected what felt like an unconvincingly nonchalant pose, it flashed through my mind that I was doing with my body exactly what Brad did with his: I was trying to convince the class I was invulnerable, unshaken and unshakeable. I was trying to be cool.

"It is a known fact," I said, "statistically proven, that about ten percent of every population, no matter where it is, is gay."*

There was a lot of shifting around. Someone muttered "dirty queers."

"So what?" said someone else, defiantly.

I paid no attention but waited until the uncomfortable silence returned. "There are twelve of you here in this room," I continued. "Statistics would indicate that at least one of you will turn out to be gay."

* The figure of 10 percent for the gay and lesbian segment of the population in the United States has recently been challenged as too high. At the time of this incident, however, it was accepted and quoted widely. No matter what the figure actually might be, my response would be the same: some percentage of any student body is gay and therefore likely to be in particular need of exposure to positive role models and protection from bigotry.

I paused as another, much louder wave of discomfort ran round the room and I heard the words "No way, man!" surface from the scared babble. For a moment, it seemed as if the room might not contain the emotion that was packing the air. But still I took my time.

"A great many teenage gays commit suicide," I said, "because of attitudes like yours. I hope that won't happen to anyone here." I paused and looked at them deliberately. "If it does, you will bear a terrible responsibility."

It was impersonal, stern, and just the kind of lecturing I had always ignored from old people when I was seventeen. But it was the best I could manage, and I was grateful to change the subject without losing all my equilibrium. I turned decisively to the side of the room furthest from Brad's seat and asked, "Anyone else want to read a poem?"

I MOVED TO PORTLAND, OREGON, from London almost twenty years ago. Although Portland is a fairly cosmopolitan city, my first few years in the West were marked by an enormous sense of culture gap. It took a long time to stop feeling foreign, even though I picked up the vocabulary and the accent much too fast for the comfort of my family back in England. I explored the area, taking long hikes in the Cascades, visiting the high desert, the Malheur wildlife refuge, and other beautiful and remote areas unlike anywhere I had seen before. On these trips, I would pass through little one-store towns that looked to me more like movie sets than places people actually lived. Joseph was like that, though a bit bigger, with its wide main street heading up from the valley, mountains off to the right and the left, and the red, wooden hotel with its swinging doors, its boardwalk, and its hitching posts, looking for all the world as if the Lone Ranger or Wyatt Earp might come swaggering out under the "Saloon" sign at any minute.

Who knows how long it would have taken me to put down real

roots here if I had continued taking hikes and car trips, stopping at cafes that made home-baked pies, and chatting with the owners of small-town stores, many of whom eyed me with suspicion? It was the Arts in Education program that allowed me to go out and live in my adopted state, instead of cruising through it, a perpetual tourist.

I started with a six-week stint up the Columbia River in Hermiston, where I learned a lot about potatoes, irrigation, and the amazing number and diversity of churches that could thrive in a small community. Then in Toledo, a mill-town near the coast, where I lived with the science teacher for a couple of weeks, I watched what happens to kids when the mill closes, families are out of work, and tensions at home skyrocket. It was the only school where I've ever seen a teacher's room with a combination lock on the door to protect the teachers' lunches in the refrigerator. Later, in Yamhill, set among rolling hills and vineyards, I witnessed the warmth and hospitality of the small town, as well as the determination of parents in an impoverished school district to get what they want for their children. This was the school where I was greeted with a message of welcome on the signboard outside the school, and then invited to buy a candy bar from a huge bin in the front hall, to help pay for my residency!

Over the years, I became an Oregonian. I met enough people who were more recent transplants than me to start feeling like an old-timer. In Portland, I made friends, became part of various arts groups, taught classes at a number of colleges, and slowly, over time, came to feel at home. I learned to love this city that grew more sophisticated each year, yet retained its endearing ability to imitate a village from time to time. What other city's population would turn out the way Portlanders did when the magnificent statue of Portlandia, created for the new city office building, floated up the Columbia on her stately barge? Where else would a tightrope walker dance across a wire to open the new Performing Arts Center, the streets below packed solid with well-wishers? And while I let Portland work its magic on me, gradually I found acceptance and support for my work as a teacher and writer, as well as for my life as a lesbian in a committed partnership.

But, as I visited schools in central and eastern Oregon or at the coast, schools in small rural communities up mountains, in forests, or lost in vast tracts of high desert, I found myself prevaricating when a teacher asked about my poetry books.

"I'm sure your bookstore will be able to order them," I would say, knowing that the books could not arrive until after I left. And, although I always carry a few copies of my books when I travel around giving readings, I never offered them to the schools I visited.

There were, however, almost always a few parents and teachers like Dan, who had bothered to read my work ahead of time and were comfortable with the fact that my lesbian identity was present in some of my poems. I latched on to these friendly souls with gratitude, never, until the incident in Enterprise, fully aware of how nervous I was in their communities, whose friendliness was conditional on my silence. I rarely contradicted the widespread assumption that I was heterosexual.

My greatest ambivalence about this deception came up around the kids, not the adults. In question-and-answer sessions, the students asked me all kinds of things about being a poet and, inevitably, sooner or later one of them would ask, "Are you married?"

"No," I would say. "But I used to be."

This was true but misleading. I could tell they saw me as a woman alone. No children. No husband. A direct descendent of the reclusive and equally misrepresented Emily Dickinson. It was hardly an accurate picture of my life in which my partner and I had been together for more than a decade. I hated this lie—hated that it deprived the students of seeing the true diversity among us—hated that it withheld a model from some kid who would one day need it.

RIGHT AFTER BRAD READ HIS POEM that day, I had a free period, during which I fled down the street and sat in the little cafe behind the bookstore with a cup of tea, my hands still shaking. I told the bookstore owner, Mary, what had happened. She listened, murmuring sympathetically, and then gave me one of her home-made muffins. She didn't seem quite able to understand the extremity of my distress, which is not surprising since I didn't understand it myself. I walked back to school and got through the rest of the day with little enthusiasm for the poems, but warmed by the genuine thanks of the students I was working with for the last time.

Before I left school that afternoon, Dan came to find me and steered me into his classroom.

"I talked with Brad about what had happened in class," he said awkwardly.

"Oh yes?" I said.

"Brad was confused. He saw how angry you were, but he didn't understand why."

Dan shifted uncomfortably as he told me this, and I sensed he wanted to apologize for his silence in the classroom but I didn't want his apology. I knew he couldn't afford to risk his job, which, unlike mine, was permanent.

"So what did you tell him?" I asked.

"I suggested that he talk to you about it. And I told him that bigotry was unacceptable, no matter what he heard other people say. He seemed startled when I said 'bigotry' and then he said he couldn't talk to you because he was leaving for a golf tournament and wouldn't be back till Monday."

"Oh," I said. And then, rather ungraciously, "Thanks."

I was still pretty angry at Brad as I drove back up the valley to Joseph and then on past the lake. I parked my car at my cabin and went for a walk through the silent resort, past the pack station and a couple of closed motels. The late afternoon sun lit up the top of the mountains but left me in the shade, where patches of icy snow still huddled under the pines. Groups of deer, their ribs standing out after the hard winter, looked up fearlessly as I walked by, then returned to munching on the hay someone had put out for them. As the sun dipped behind the mountaintop, I turned back towards the cabin, thinking about Brad's confusion. How could he *not* know why I was angry? Had he never heard anyone question his attitude— could he really believe it would be an act of heroism to kill all the gays in the world? Had no one ever shown him that there was another point of view?

Later, as I sat by the embers of my fire, the night a deep well outside the windows, my head nodded and my book fell from my hand. The occasional crackles from the fire faded as I fell asleep and immediately found myself inside a dream. I was high up on Chief Joseph Mountain, crouched under a clump of salal. Far below, the lake glinted in late afternoon sun, but I barely noticed it, so intently was I listening. I felt my scalp tighten as I slowly turned my head, trying to scoop the sounds out of the air into the hollows of my ears. As my face revolved, I noted the direction of the breeze by its cool touch on my cheek. I knew instinctively that I was hearing much more from the south, where the wind was blowing from, so I turned away and faced north, straining to hear the minute sounds which the breeze carried away and flung out into the valley.

In the dream, I did not know who I was. For a while it was the soldiers who were after me, my brothers having followed Chief Joseph down the canyon towards Imnaha, while I lurked up at the timberline, separated from them and vulnerable. Down the Imnaha gorge were many small arroyos in which they would be able to hide: the soldiers, though many, were stupid when it came to rocks. They saw nothing. Then I became a deer. I felt my ears stand up on my head, clarifying and magnifying the chitter of a chipmunk under a heap of stones far off to my left. I felt my nostrils flare. I felt my heart beat. And then somehow I was human again, my clumsy feet unsure on the shale, my ears failing to identify the one sound that mattered—the crack of the twig under Brad's boot. When I heard the metallic click of the gun, I knew it was too late.

I woke sweating in spite of the freezing temperature in the cabin. My breath condensed in a cloud as I stumbled into the bedroom, rubbing my eyes and switching on lights to dispel the power of the dream. I remembered what Dan had said about Brad's confusion and I saw that the problem was not Brad, but the absence of information available to him. Then I saw that I had participated in withholding that information from him.

Sitting up in bed, wrapped in a sleeping bag, I reflected on my role here in Wallowa County. I was, after all, however temporarily, a member of this farming and logging community. The teachers and parents had welcomed me, lent me a cabin, and invited me to their homes for dinner. Furthermore, I had come here with a certain amount of respect already granted me, at least by those who made my visit happen. They had chosen me from a catalog full of artists; they admired my work and wanted my skills. No matter what my fears, I had no business contributing to the intellectual isolation of this community by hiding the truth about myself and about gays and lesbians everywhere.

Remembering how much at home I had felt on my many visits here, and yet how cautiously I had behaved, I wondered if my unwillingness to trust the people around me was a mark of my own still-partial vision. Was I still seeing what I had seen as a newcomer to the West: the frontier; the Wild West of the movies? Was I, perhaps, unwilling to see the people here as full human beings, intelligent women and men with infinite possibilities for change? Finally, as I clutched the quilt around me and stumbled into the kitchen to make tea, my head cleared: the people of Wallowa County, and other places where children were not exposed to the city's array of people and ideas, had a *right* to know who I was and what I thought. They deserved the chance to choose what to think, to grow into new attitudes, and to grapple with personal and collective change. They deserved the complexity and fullness that people acquire when they stretch to embrace a greater human diversity than they have previously known. I went back to bed, sipped my tea, and finally fell into a peaceful sleep.

In the morning I woke full of relief and resolve: relief that the class and the residency were over, and resolve to be braver, do better. Maybe one day, like William Stafford, I would look back in a poem on this time at Enterprise High School, and see it as a significant turning point. Refusing, for the moment, to grapple with the complexity of the lifelong coming-out process—one that I have sometimes experienced as two steps forward and one back—I vowed to make a difference. I would not forget the very real dangers I had felt around me in this community, but I would be bold; I would speak out; I would be myself.

A few days after returning to Portland that spring, I put together a set of informational articles about lesbians and gays for high school students and sent it off to Dan. Maybe he would use it in the class he had told me he taught each spring on diversity. I decided it was the best I could do under the circumstances, and that I should put the experience behind me. But it wasn't easy, and there were nights when I found myself having that conversation with Brad that had never happened—even nights when I considered going back to find him, so we could have it.

It was a relief to be back in the city where I felt relatively safe and accepted—where I didn't have to have my ears pricked, my defenses at the ready all the time. But the dream I had had that last night at Wallowa Lake stayed with me: I remembered the smell of that breeze and how it felt to sniff it for signs of the human predator. And Wallowa County stayed with me too, the extraordinary grandeur of its scenery etched into my mind and my poetry, while its people gradually came into focus. I struggled to stop seeing them as "the other"—they were, after all, no more a bunch of redneck loggers than I was a commie queer.

Mary Clearman Blew

M ary Clearman Blew grew up on a ranch in Montana, on the site of her great-grandfather's original homestead. The ranch was so isolated and far from school that her father eventually sold it and bought another, more marginal ranch close to town so the family could stay together while Blew and her two younger sisters attended high school. As Blew writes in her memoir, All But the Waltz, his hope was that his daughters would "become schoolteachers, like our mother and grandmothers, and that we would find country schools near home to teach during the winters (we'd have a little cash income, that way), and that we would live on the ranch during the summers and break horses and reclaim the hay meadows and even run a little stock again. But of course we did no such thing."

Instead, Blew graduated from the University of Montana and earned a doctorate at the University of Missouri, became a college professor and a writer—accomplishments achieved, to say the least, against great odds. Always, she has had to fight limited expectations for women, and not just from the rural communities in which she was raised. When her first short stories were accepted for publication, an editor suggested she write under her initials so no one would recognize that she was female.

Blew has published two collections of short stories, Lambing

Out and Other Stories *(1977) and* Runaway *(1990);* All But the
Waltz: Essays of a Montana Family *(1991); and* Balsamroot: A
Memoir *(1994). She is co-editor, with Kim Barnes, of* A Circle of
Women *(1994), an anthology of Western women's writing. This
essay, taken from* All But the Waltz, *captures her struggle to claim
for herself a life of the mind, a life of her own.*

"The Unwanted Child"
from *All But the Waltz*

DECEMBER 1958. I LIE ON MY BACK ON AN EXAMI-
nation table in a Missoula clinic while the middle-aged doctor
whose name I found in the Yellow Pages inserts his speculum and
takes a look. He turns to the sink and washes his hands.

"Yes, you're pregnant," he says. "Congratulations, Mommy."

His confirmation settles over me like a fog that won't lift. Myself I can manage for, but for myself and *it?*

After I get dressed, he says, "I'll want to see you again in a
month, Mommy."

If he calls me Mommy again, I will break his glasses and grind
them in his face, grind them until he has no face. I will kick him
right in his obscene fat paunch. I will bury my foot in his disgusting
flesh.

I walk through the glass doors and between the shoveled banks
of snow to the parking lot where my young husband waits in the
car.

"You're not, are you?" he says.

"Yes."

"Yes, you're not?"

"Yes, I am! Jeez!"

His feelings are hurt. But he persists: "I just don't think you are. I just don't see how you could be."

He has a theory on the correct use of condoms, a theory considerably more flexible than the one outlined by the doctor I visited just before our marriage three months ago, and which he has been arguing with increasing anxiety ever since I missed my second period. I stare out the car window at the back of the clinic while he expounds on his theory for the zillionth time. What difference does it make now? Why can't he shut up? If I have to listen to him much longer, I will kill him, too.

At last, even his arguments wear thin against the irrefutable fact. As he turns the key in the ignition his eyes are deep with fear.

"But I'll stand by you," he promises.

WHY GET MARRIED AT EIGHTEEN?

When you get married, you can move into married student housing. It's a shambles, it's a complex of converted World War II barracks known as the Strips, it's so sorry the wind blows through the cracks around the windows and it lacks hot-water heaters and electric stoves, but at least it's not the dormitory, which is otherwise the required residence of all women at the University of Montana. Although no such regulations apply to male students, single women must be signed in and ready for bed check by ten o'clock on weeknights and one on weekends. No alcohol, no phones in rooms. Women must not be reported on campus in slacks or shorts (unless they can prove they are on their way to a physical education class), and on Sundays they may not appear except in heels, hose, and hat. A curious side effect of marriage, however, is that the responsibility for one's virtue is automatically transferred from the dean of women to one's husband. Miss Maurine Clow never does bed checks or beer checks in the Strips.

When you get married, you can quit making out in the back seat of a parked car and go to bed in a bed. All young women in 1958 like sex. Maybe their mothers had headaches or hang-ups, but *they* are normal, healthy women with normal, healthy desires, and they know the joy they will find in their husbands' arms will—well, be better than making out, which, though none of us will admit it, is getting to be boring. We spend hours shivering with our clothes off in cars parked in Pattee Canyon in subzero weather, groping and being groped and feeling embarrassed when other cars crunch by in the snow, full of onlookers with craning necks, and worrying about the classes we're not attending because making out takes so much time. We are normal, healthy women with normal, healthy desires if we have to die to prove it. Nobody has ever said out loud that she would like to go to bed and *get it over with* and get on with something else.

There's another reason for getting married at eighteen, but it's more complicated.

BY GETTING MARRIED I have eluded Dean Maurine Clow only to fall into the hands of in-laws.

"We have to tell the folks," my husband insists. "They'll want to know."

His letter elicits the predictable long-distance phone call from them. I make him answer it. While he talks to them I rattle dishes in the kitchen, knowing exactly how they look, his momma and his daddy in their suffocating Helena living room hung with mounted elk antlers and religious calendars, their heads together over the phone, their faces wreathed in big grins at his news.

"They want to talk to you," he says finally. Then, "Come on!"

I take the phone with fear and hatred. "Hello?"

"Well!!!" My mother-in-law's voice carols over the miles. "I guess this is finally the end of college for you!"

A WEEK AFTER CHRISTMAS I lean against the sink in my mother's kitchen at the ranch and watch her wash clothes.

She uses a Maytag washing machine with a wringer and a monotonous, daylong chugging motor which, she often says, is a damn sight better than a washboard. She starts by filling the tub with boiling water and soap flakes. Then she agitates her whites for twenty minutes, fishes them out with her big fork, and feeds them sheet by sheet into the wringer. After she rinses them by hand, she reverses the wringer and feeds them back through, creased and steaming hot, and carries them out to the clothesline to freeze dry. By this time the water in the tub has cooled off enough for the coloreds. She'll keep running through her loads until she's down to the blue jeans and the water is thick and greasy. My mother has spent twenty-five years of Mondays on the washing.

I know I have to tell her I'm pregnant.

She's talking about college, she's quoting my grandmother, who believes that every woman should be self-sufficient. Even though I'm married now, even though I had finished only one year at the University of Montana before I got married, my grandmother has agreed to go on lending me what I need for tuition and books. Unlike my in-laws, who have not hesitated to tell me I should go to work as a typist or a waitress to support my husband through college (after all, he will be supporting me for the rest of my life), my grandmother believes I should get my own credentials.

My mother and grandmother talk about a teaching certificate as if it were a gold ring which, if I could just grab it, would entitle the two of them to draw a long breath of relief. Normally I hate to listen to their talk. They don't even know you can't get a two-year teaching certificate now, you have to go the full four years.

But beyond the certificate question, college has become something that I never expected and cannot explain: not something to grab and have done with but a door opening, a glimpse of an endless passage and professors who occasionally beckon from far ahead— like lovely, elderly Marguerite Ephron, who lately has been leading four or five of us through the *Aeneid*. Latin class has been my sanctuary for the past few months; Latin has been my solace from conflict that otherwise has left me as steamed and agitated as my mother's whites, now churning away in the Maytag; Latin in part because it is taught by Mrs. Ephron, always serene, endlessly patient, mercilessly thorough, who teaches at the university while Mr. Ephron works at home, in a basement full of typewriters with special keyboards, on the translations of obscure clay tablets.

So I've been accepting my grandmother's money under false pretenses. I'm not going to spend my life teaching around Fergus County the way she did, the way my mother would have if she hadn't married my father. I've married my husband under false pretenses, too; he's a good fly-fishing Helena boy who has no idea in the world of becoming a Mr. Ephron. But, subversive as a foundling in a fairy tale, I have tried to explain none of my new aspirations to my mother or grandmother or, least of all, my husband and his parents, who are mightily distressed as it is by my borrowing money for my own education.

"—and it's all got to be paid back, you'll be starting your lives in *debt!*"

"—the important thing is to get *him* through, *he's* the one who's got to go out and face the world!"

"—what on earth do you think you'll do with your education?"

And now all the argument is pointless, the question of teaching certificate over quest for identity, the importance of my husband's future over mine, the relentless struggle with the in-laws over what is most mine, my self. I'm done for, knocked out of the running by the application of a faulty condom theory.

"Mom," I blurt, "I'm pregnant."

She gasps. And before she can let out that breath, a frame of memory freezes with her in it, poised over her rinse tub, looking at me through the rising steam and the grinding wringer. Right now I'm much too miserable to wonder what she sees when she looks at me: her oldest daughter, her bookish child, the daydreamer, the one she usually can't stand, the one who takes everything too seriously, who will never learn to take no for an answer. Thin and strong and blue-jeaned, bespectacled and crop-haired, this girl could pass for fifteen right now and won't be able to buy beer in grocery stores for years without showing her driver's license. This girl who is too miserable to look her mother in the face, who otherwise might see in her mother's eyes the years of blight and disappointment. She does hear what her mother says:

"Oh, Mary, no!"

MY MOTHER WAS AN UNWANTED CHILD. The fourth daughter of a homesteading family racked by drought and debt, she was only a year old when the sister nearest her in age died of a cancerous tumor. She was only two years old when the fifth and last child, the cherished boy, was born. She was never studious like her older sisters nor, of course, was she a boy, and she was never able to find her own ground to stand on until she married.

Growing up, I heard her version often, for my mother was given to a kind of continuous oral interpretation of herself and her situation. Standing over the sink or stove, hoeing the garden, running her sewing machine with the permanent angry line deepening between her eyes, she talked. Unlike the stories our grandmothers told, which, like fairy tales, narrated the events of the past but avoided psychological speculation ("Great-great-aunt Somebody-or-other was home alone making soap when the Indians came, so she waited until they got close enough, and then she threw a ladle of lye on them . . ."), my mother's dwelt on the motives behind the darkest family impulses.

"Ma never should have had me. It was her own fault. She never should have had me if she didn't want me."

"But then you wouldn't have been born!" I interrupted, horrified at the thought of not being.

"Wouldn't have mattered to me," she said. "I'd never have known the difference."

What I cannot remember today is whom my mother was telling her story to. Our grandmothers told their stories to my little sisters and me, to entertain us, but my mother's bitter words flowed past us like a river current past small, ignored onlookers who eavesdropped from its shores. I remember her words, compulsive, repetitious, spilling out over her work—for she was always working—and I was awed by her courage. What could be less comprehensible than not wanting to be? More fearsome than annihilation?

Nor can I remember enough about the circumstances of my mother's life during the late 1940s and the early 1950s to know why she was so angry, why she was so compelled to deconstruct her childhood. Her lot was not easy. She had married into a close-knit family that kept to itself. She had her husband's mother on her hands all her life, and on top of the normal isolation and hard work of a ranch wife of those years, she had to provide home schooling for her children.

And my father's health was precarious, and the ranch was failing. The reality of that closed life along the river bottom became more and more attenuated by the outward reality of banks and interest rates and the shifting course of agribusiness. She was touchy with money worries. She saw the circumstances of her sisters' lives grow easier as her own grew harder. Perhaps these were reasons enough for rage.

I recall my mother in her middle thirties through the telescoped eye of the child which distorts the intentions of parents and enlarges them to giants. Of course she was larger than life. Unlike my father, with his spectrum of ailments, she was never sick. She was never hospitalized in her life for any reason but childbirth, never came down with anything worse than a cold. She lugged the armloads of wood and buckets of water and slops and ashes that came with cooking and washing and ironing in a kitchen with a wood range and no plumbing; she provided the endless starchy meals of roast meat and potatoes and gravy; she kept salads on her table and fresh or home-canned vegetables at a time when iceberg lettuce was a town affectation.

She was clear-skinned, with large gray eyes that often seemed fixed on some point far beyond our familiar slopes and cutbanks. And even allowing for the child's telescoped eye, she was a tall woman who thought of herself as oversized. She was the tallest of her sisters. *"As big as Doris* is what they used to say about me!"

Bigness to her was a curse. "You big ox!" she would fling at me over some altercation with my little sister. True to the imperative that is handed down through the generations, I in turn bought my clothes two sizes too large for years.

All adult ranch women were fat. I remember hardly a woman out of her teens in those years who was not fat. The few exceptions were the women who had, virtually, become a third sex by taking on men's work in the fields and corrals; they might stay as skinny and tough in their Levi's as hired hands.

But women who remained women baked cakes and cream pies and breads and sweet rolls with the eggs from their own chickens and the milk and butter and cream from the cows they milked, and they ate heavily from appetite and from fatigue and from the monotony of their isolation. They wore starched cotton print dresses and starched aprons and walked ponderously beside their whiplash husbands. My mother, unless she was going to be riding or helping in the hayfields, always wore those shapeless, starched dresses she sewed herself, always cut from the same pattern, always layered over with an apron.

What was she so angry about? Why was her forehead kneaded

permanently into a frown? It was a revelation for me one afternoon when she answered a knock at the screen door, and she smiled, and her voice lifted to greet an old friend of hers and my father's from their single days. Color rose in her face, and she looked pretty as she told him where he could find my father. Was that how outsiders always saw her?

Other ranch women seemed cheerful enough on the rare occasions when they came in out of the gumbo. Spying on them as they sat on benches in the shade outside the horticulture house at the county fair or visited in the cabs of trucks at rodeos, I wondered if these women, too, were angry when they were alone with only their children to observe them. What secrets lay behind those vast placid, smiling faces, and what stories could their children tell?

My mother believed that her mother had loved her brother best and her older sisters next best. "He was always The Boy and they were The Girls, and Ma was proud of how well they did in school," she explained again and again to the walls, the stove, the floor she was mopping, "and I was just Doris. I was average."

Knowing how my grandmother had misjudged my mother, I felt guilty about how much I longed for her visits. I loved my grandmother and her fresh supply of stories about the children who went to the schools she taught, the games they played, and the books they read. School for me was an emblem of the world outside our creek-bottom meadows and fenced mountain slopes. At eight, I was still being taught at home; our gumbo road was impassable for most of the school months, and my father preferred that we be kept safe from contact with "them damn town kids," as he called them. Subversively I begged my grandmother to repeat her stories again and again, and I tried to imagine what it must be like to see other children every day and to have a real desk and real lessons. Other than my little sister, my playmates were mostly cats. But my grandmother brought with her the breath of elsewhere.

My mother's resentment whitened in intensity during the

weeks before a visit from my grandmother, smoldered during the visit itself, and flared up again as soon as my grandmother was safely down the road to her next school. "I wonder if she ever realizes she wouldn't even have any grandchildren if I hadn't got married and had some kids! *The Girls* never had any kids! Some people should never have kids! Some people should never get married!"

With a child's logic, I thought she was talking about me. I thought I was responsible for her anger. I was preoccupied for a long time with a story I had read about a fisherman who was granted three wishes; he had used his wishes badly, but I was sure I could do better, given the chance. I thought a lot about how I would use three wishes, how I would use their potential for lifting me out of the present.

"What would you wish for, if you had three wishes?" I prodded my mother.

She turned her faraway gray eyes on me, as though she had not been ranting about The Girls the moment before. "I'd wish you'd be good," she said.

That was what she always said, no matter how often I asked her. With everything under the sun to wish for, that unfailing answer was a perplexity and a worry.

I was my grandmother's namesake, and I was a bookworm like my mother's older sisters. Nobody could pry my nose out of a book to do my chores, even though I was marked to be the outdoor-working child, even though I was supposed to be my father's boy.

Other signs that I was not a boy arose to trouble us both and account, I thought, for my mother's one wish.

"Mary's getting a butt on her just like a girl," she remarked one night as I climbed out of the tub. Alarmed, I craned my neck to see what had changed about my eight-year-old buttocks.

"Next thing, you'll be mooning in the mirror and wanting to pluck your eyebrows like the rest of 'em," she said.

"I will not," I said doubtfully.

I could find no way through the contradiction. On the one hand, I was a boy (except that I also was a bookworm), and my chores were always in the barns and corrals, never the kitchen. *You don't know how to cook on a wood stove?* my mother-in-law was to cry in disbelief. *And you grew up on a ranch?*

To act like a boy was approved; to cry or show fear was to invite ridicule. *Sissy! Big bellercalf!* On the other hand, I was scolded for hanging around the men, the way ranch boys did. I was not a boy (my buttocks, my vanity). What was I?

"Your dad's boy," my mother answered comfortingly when I asked her. She named a woman I knew. "Just like Hazel. Her dad can't get along without her."

Hazel was a tough, shy woman who rode fences and pulled calves and took no interest in the country dances or the "running around" her sisters did on weekends. Hazel never used lipstick or permed her hair; she wore it cut almost like a man's. Seen at the occasional rodeo or bull sale in her decently pressed pearl-button shirt and new Levi's, she stuck close to her dad. Like me, Hazel apparently was not permitted to hang around the men.

What Hazel did not seem interested in was any kind of fun, and a great resolve arose in me that, whatever I was, I was going to have . . . whatever it was. I would get married, even if I wasn't supposed to.

BUT MY MOTHER had another, darker reason to be angry with me, and I knew it. The reason had broken over me suddenly the summer I was seven and had been playing, on warm afternoons, in a rain barrel full of water. Splashing around, elbows and knees knocking against the side of the barrel, I enjoyed the rare sensation of being wet all over. My little sister, four, came and stood on tiptoe to watch. It occurred to me to boost her into the barrel with me.

My mother burst out of the kitchen door and snatched her back.

"What are you trying to do, kill her?" she shouted.

I stared back at her, wet, dumbfounded.

Her eyes blazed over me, her brows knotted at their worst. "And after you'd drowned her, I suppose you'd have slunk off to hide somewhere until it was all over!"

It had never crossed my mind to kill my sister, or that my mother might think I wanted to. (Although I had, once, drowned a setting of baby chicks in a rain barrel.) But that afternoon, dripping in my underpants, goose-bumped and ashamed, I watched her carry my sister into the house and then I did go off to hide until it was, somehow, all over, for she never mentioned it at dinner.

The chicks had been balls of yellow fuzz, and I had been three. I wanted them to swim. I can just remember catching a chick and holding it in the water until it stopped squirming and then laying it down to catch a fresh one. I didn't stop until I had drowned the whole dozen and laid them out in a sodden yellow row.

What the mind refuses to allow to surface is characterized by a suspicious absence. Of detail, of associations. Memories skirt the edge of nothing. There is for me about this incident that suspicious absence. What is being withheld?

Had I, for instance, given my mother cause to believe I might harm my sister? Children have done such harm, and worse. What can be submerged deeper, denied more vehemently, than the murderous impulse? At four, my sister was a tender, trusting little girl with my mother's wide gray eyes and brows. A younger sister of an older sister. A good girl. Mommy's girl.

What do I really know about my mother's feelings toward her own dead sister? Kathryn's dolls had been put away; my mother was never allowed to touch them.

"I'll never, never love one of my kids more than another!" she screamed at my father in one of her afternoons of white rage. The context is missing.

DURING THE GOOD YEARS, when cattle prices were high enough to pay the year's bills and a little extra, my mother bought wallpaper out of a catalog and stuck it to her lumpy walls. She enameled her kitchen white, and she sewed narrow strips of cloth she called "drapes" to hang at the sides of her windows. She bought a stiff tight cylinder of linoleum at Sears, Roebuck in town and hauled it home in the back of the pickup and unrolled it in a shiny flowered oblong in the middle of her splintery front room floor.

Occasionally I would find her sitting in her front room on her "davenport," which she had saved for and bought used, her lap full of sewing and her forehead relaxed out of its knot. For a moment there was her room around her as she wanted it to look: the clutter subdued, the new linoleum mopped and quivering under the chair legs that held down its corners, the tension of the opposing floral patterns of wallpaper, drapes, and slipcovers held in brief, illusory harmony by the force of her vision.

How hard she tried for her daughters! Over the slow thirty miles of gumbo and gravel we drove to town every summer for dentist appointments at a time when pulling teeth was still a more common remedy than filling them, when our own father and his mother wore false teeth before they were forty.

During the good years, we drove the thirty miles for piano lessons. An upright Kimball was purchased and hauled home in the back of the pickup. Its carved oak leaves and ivories dominated the front room, where she found time to "sit with us" every day as we practiced. With a pencil she pointed out the notes she had learned to read during her five scant quarters in normal school, and made us read them aloud. "F sharp!" she would scream over the throb of the Maytag in the kitchen as one of us pounded away.

She carped about bookworms, but she located the dim old Carnegie library in town and got library cards for us even though, as country kids, we weren't strictly entitled to them. After that, trips home from town with sacks of groceries included armloads of library books. Against certain strictures, she could be counted on. When, in my teens, I came home with my account of the new book the librarian kept in her desk drawer and refused to check out to me, my mother straightened her back as I knew she would. "She thinks she can tell one of my kids what she can read and what she can't read?"

On our next visit to the library, she marched up the stone steps and into the mote-filled sanctum with me.

The white-haired librarian glanced up inquiringly.

"You got *From Here to Eternity?*"

The librarian looked at me, then at my mother. Without a word she reached into her drawer and took out a heavy volume. She stamped it and handed it to my mother, who handed it to me.

How did she determine that books and dentistry and piano lessons were necessities for her daughters, and what battles did she fight for them as slipping cattle prices put even a gallon of white enamel paint or a sheet of new linoleum beyond her reach?

Disaster followed disaster on the ranch. An entire season's hay crop lost to a combination of ancient machinery that would not hold together and heavy rains that would not let up. A whole year's calf crop lost because the cows had been pastured in timber that had been logged, and when they ate the pine needles from the downed tops, they spontaneously aborted. As my father grew less and less able to face the reality of the downward spiral, what could she hope to hold together with her pathetic floral drapes and floral slipcovers?

BUNDLED IN COATS *and overshoes in the premature February dark, our white breaths as one, my mother and I huddle in the shadow of the chicken house. By moonlight we watch the white-tailed deer that have slipped down out of the timber to feed from the haystack a scant fifty yards away. Cautiously I raise my father's rifle to my shoulder. I'm not all that* good a marksman, I hate the inevitable explosive crack, but I brace myself on the corner of the chicken house and sight carefully and remember to squeeze. Ka-crack!

Eight taupe shapes shoot up their heads and spring for cover. A single mound remains in the snow near the haystack. By the time my mother and I have climbed through the fence and trudged up to the haystack, all movement from the doe is reflexive. "Nice and fat," says my mother.

Working together with our butcher knives, we lop off her scent glands and slit her and gut her and save the heart and liver in a bucket for breakfast. Then, each taking a leg, we drag her down the field, under the fence, around the chicken house, and into the kitchen, where we will skin her out and butcher her.

We are two mid-twentieth-century women putting meat on the table for the next few weeks. Neither of us has ever had a hunting license, and if we did, hunting season is long closed, but we're serene about what we're doing. "Eating our hay, aren't they?" says my mother. "We're entitled to a little venison. The main thing is not to tell anybody what we're doing."

AND THE PREGNANT EIGHTEEN-YEAR-OLD? What about her?

In June of 1959 she sits up in the hospital bed, holding in her arms a small warm scrap whose temples are deeply dented from the forceps. She cannot remember birthing him, only the long hours alone before the anesthetic took over. She feels little this morning, only a dull worry about the money, money, money for college in the fall.

The in-laws are a steady, insistent, increasingly frantic chorus of disapproval over her plans. *But, Mary! Tiny babies have to be kept warm!* her mother-in-law keeps repeating, pathetically, ever since she was told about Mary's plans for fall quarter.

But, Mary! How can you expect to go to college and take good care of a husband and a baby?

Finally, *We're going to put our foot down!*

She knows that somehow she has got to extricate herself from these sappy folks. About the baby, she feels only a mild curiosity. Life where there was none before. The rise and fall of his tiny chest. She has him on her hands now. She must take care of him.

Why not an abortion?

Because the thought never crossed her mind. Another suspicious absence, another void for memory to skirt. What she knew about abortion was passed around the midnight parties in the girls' dormitory: *You drink one part turpentine with two parts sugar. Or was it the other way around? . . . two parts turpentine to one part sugar. You drink gin in a hot bath . . .*

She has always hated the smell of gin. It reminds her of the pine needles her father's cattle ate, and how their calves were born shallow-breathed and shriveled, and how they died. She knows a young married woman who begged her husband to hit her in the stomach and abort their fourth child.

Once, in her eighth month, the doctor had shot her a look across his table. "If you don't want this baby," he said, "I know plenty of people who do."

"I want it," she lied.

No, but really. What is to become of this eighteen-year-old and her baby?

Well, she's read all the sentimental literature they shove on the high school girls. She knows how the plot is supposed to turn out.

Basically, she has two choices.

One, she can invest all her hopes for her own future in this sleeping scrap. *Son, it was always my dream to climb to the stars. Now the tears of joy spring at the sight of you with your college diploma . . .*

Even at eighteen, this lilylicking is enough to make her sick.

Or two, she can abandon the baby and the husband and become really successful and really evil. This is the more attractive version of the plot, but she doesn't really believe in it. Nobody she knows has tried it. It seems as out of reach from ordinary daylight Montana as Joan Crawford or the Duchess of Windsor or the moon. As she lies propped up in bed with the sleeping scrap in her arms, looking out over the dusty downtown rooftops settling into noon in the waning Eisenhower years, she knows very well that Joan Crawford will never play the story of her life.

What, then? What choice is left to her?

What outcome could possibly be worth all this uproar? Her husband is on the verge of tears these days; he's only twenty himself, and he had no idea what trouble he was marrying into, his parents pleading and arguing and threatening, even his brothers and their wives chiming in with their opinions, even the minister getting into it, even the neighbors; and meanwhile his wife's grandmother firing off red-hot letters from her side, meanwhile his wife's mother refusing to budge an inch—united, those two women are as formidable as a pair of rhinoceroses, though of course he has no idea in the world what it took to unite them.

All this widening emotional vortex over whether or not one Montana girl will finish college. What kind of genius would she have to be to justify it all? Will it be enough that, thirty years later, she will have read approximately 16,250 freshman English essays out of an estimated lifetime total of 32,000?

Will it be enough, over the years, that she remembers the frozen frame of her mother's face over the rinse tub that day after Christmas in 1958 and wonders whether she can do as much for her son as was done for her? Or that she often wonders whether she really lied when she said, *I want it?*

Will it be enough? What else is there?

Judy Blunt

J udy Blunt spent her first thirty-two years on wheat and cattle ranches in northeastern Montana. When her marriage broke up, she moved with her two children to Missoula to attend the University of Montana. She supported herself by sanding hardwood floors while she earned undergraduate degrees in English and journalism and an MFA in creative writing.

"Writers who are childless, who have a separate room and scheduled time to write, who have a spouse's income to help them through the lean times may well look upon my life in horror," writes Blunt. "For all things massive and minor, the buck stops right here—at a desk an arm's reach from the front door, two leaps from the telephone and the length of one sprawled child from the television set. I wear earplugs, the kind the cops use on the firing range. I write between bells and buzzers. I write while the house rocks on its springs like a loaded cattle truck. But if I write in spite of my children, even more I write because of them. Being a single parent has given me a drive, a reason why okay is not good enough, and my reward comes when this intensity and focus shine through a poem or an essay."

Blunt has published one book of poems, Not Quite Stone (1992), and a collection of essays is forthcoming from Little, Brown in 1996. Here, Blunt recalls her earliest experiences with racism.

"Lessons in Silence"

THAT FIRST WEEK OF SCHOOL THE INDOOR AIR was sultry with held-over August heat and farm kids too recently reined in and washed up. I was tall for my age and sat toward the back, looking down a row of raw necks and fresh haircuts. The sound of a pickup on the county road lured us like a bird's song. When it shifted down for the corner, we went along with it, anticipating each rev and crank of gears—some neighbor going to town, checking cattle, returning a borrowed tool somewhere up the road. In the next second the familiar pattern broke and we came to full attention. Instead of swelling, then fading into the distance, the noise grew steadily louder. Dust streamed through the open windows as a rust-colored pickup eased around the building to the east side and rattled to a stop by the front steps. The engine cut out, lugged a few times, and was still. Five heads lifted in the sudden quiet; five pairs of eyes fixed on our teacher's desk.

Mrs. Norby licked a gold foil star, tapped it into place, then squared the papers on her desk and rose to attend to this new business. I remember the tiny catch in her posture as she glanced out the window, not a motion or a movement exactly, but a slight drawing in as she smoothed her skirt. At the time I interpreted her sudden freezing as fear, and today, 400 miles and 27 years away from that moment, I believe my instinct was accurate. There was no reading her face as she left the classroom. I can think of nothing that would have kept the five of us from the front window when the door closed behind her.

MY OLDER BROTHER Russ, myself, the twins Guy and Greta, and a neighbor boy named Stevie made up the student population that year, filling four of the eight grades taught at our rural school.

Standing in the shadow of the drapes, we could see outside without being seen. The battered red pickup was not one of ours. The driver's door opened with a stiff pop and an old man eased slowly from behind the wheel. He stood with a red and black plaid cap in one hand as Mrs. Norby walked down the steps toward him. The cab rocked slightly to the passenger side as a woman got out and made her way around the dented nose of the pickup. At the steps she turned and produced a little boy from the shadow of her skirts, prodding him forward until he stood in front of her.

Mrs. Norby had her back to us, and through the window we could hear her sweet, modulated voice. The man spoke very politely in reply. "We didn't know the school had started," he said. His smile held as many gaps as teeth. The woman said nothing. Mrs. Norby spoke in her lecture voice, at ease now; there was nodding and smiling, a gentle laugh from the man. The boy turned to hide his face when Mrs. Norby bent over to talk to him, but when she straightened and held out her hand, he took it.

When the man raised his arm to put his cap back on, we flushed like grouse and were innocently at work by the time the second cloud of dust cleared and Mrs. Norby entered, towing a small dark-eyed boy with a mop of black hair. His name was Forest Walker, and he was starting first grade. He lived with his grandparents who were working for the Longs. These things she told us. The rest we saw in the formal tilt of her head, the blank smile, the way her hands cupped together at waist level. Our company manners appeared on cue. That he was an outsider goes without saying; we had cut our first teeth on each other, and we had never seen him before. But Forest was different in another way. Forest was Indian, and his presence in our world went beyond our experience, beyond our comprehension. We welcomed him to our school politely, as we had been taught to welcome the children of outsiders. But we would have been no less bewildered had we glanced up from our math drills and seen a grove of seedling pine take root in the hardpan outside.

FOREST WALKER. Even in fourth grade I was struck by the irony. We paid attention to names, and there wasn't a forest of note for hundreds of miles. Our community was identified by several layers of place names that signified ownership. The plains tribes who hunted that prairie had left hammers and arrowheads, tepee rings and medicine stones, but no names. Trappers and immigrant homesteaders had labeled the land as they pushed the Indians west, and by the time of my childhood, those earliest names belonged to the land alone. Carberrey, Whitcombe, Krumweide, Cruikshank— to say them aloud was to conjure a place long separated from a face or a family.

The chunk of short grass prairie we called Regina had been named by French-Canadians who drifted south out of Saskatchewan to trap beaver along the Missouri. The first homesteaders inherited a legacy of French place names that roll across the tongue like music, black-bottom draws and treacherous creeks and drainages identified by hisses and coos. The actual places seemed unrelated to the black letters and blue lines on the official Bureau of Land Management maps. We had little use for maps. Any rancher who wanted to see his land picked up a piece and rubbed it between his fingers. But the maps with their foreign spellings—Beauchamp, Fourchette, Peigneux, DuBuis—drew a solid line between insiders who knew the history of the land, and outsiders, who only knew maps and could not say the passwords. We all had our favorite stories.

"Had a guy up here yesterday, Government feller, asks me directions to Regina," a neighbor might say. We'd all grin and lean forward. The name "Regina" applied to some 2,500 square miles, but on the maps it appeared as a little gray circle, just like a town. "I tell him he's looking at it, but he ain't buying any of that. So we get to jawing and pretty soon he goes for his map and there she is." Here he'd pause and lift his eyebrows and hands in one gesture of innocence. "So hell, I give him directions."

Strangers who were rude or adamant enough about the little gray circle on the map were sent there, to the Regina Post Office. The best part of the story was imagining the driver's face when he pulled into our mail carrier's barnyard. A big official sign was nailed to the front of an old converted chicken house where Jake and Edie sorted the mail on Saturdays. The flag that waved over the Regina Post Office could have covered it like a pup tent.

We measured the wealth of our knowledge against the ignorance of outsiders, and judged ourselves superior. We pulled cars out of potholes, fed lost hunters at our kitchen table, sold gas from the big drums we kept behind the shop, and for the most part, we did so graciously. We could afford to be kind. But social or political upheaval going on outside seldom intruded, and families who managed to tuck themselves into a fold of flatland and hang on seldom went looking for something else to worry about. Their priorities were immediate—wind and heat and hoppers in summer, wind and snow and blizzards in winter. Our isolation was real. The nearest town lay an hour's drive north when the roads were good. To the south, the land plunged into rugged breaks and badlands, then dropped abruptly into a mile-wide stretch of water the maps called Fort Peck Lake. We still called it the Missouri River. In late summer a double row of dead cottonwoods reared out of the water where the original channel had been, and we could point to the site of submerged homesteads, name the families flooded out when the dam went in in the '30s. Halfway between the river and town, my parents bullied a hundred acres of winter wheat away from the silver sage and buffalo grass, and grazed cattle on the rest.

Our fences marched straight down the section lines, regiments of cedar posts and barbed wire strung so tight it hummed in a

strong wind. The corners were square and braced to meet the bor-
dering fields of neighbors just like us. Our families had home-
steaded, broken ground and survived into the third generation, and
we shared a set of beliefs so basic that they were seldom spoken
aloud. I remember them as adages: Hard work is the measure of a
man; A barn will build a house, but a house won't build a barn; Good
fences make good neighbors; That which belongs to everyone, belongs to no one. "This is no country for fools," my grandad said, and
these truths were what separated fools from survivors. They were
the only explanation I was ever given for the way we lived.

MRS. NORBY left Forest squirming in front of the class while she
and one of the boys fetched a small desk from the teacherage storeroom. A great deal more energy than necessary went into the shov-
ing and arranging of desks to make room for the new one, and a
haze of dust silted down around us by the time the sharp snap of our
teacher's fingers cut through the ruckus and settled us into them.
Throughout the process, Forest remained where she had left him,
staring back at us with eyes so dark I could not see the pupils. I
heard my sister's quick gasp and the teacher's weary voice in the
same instant, "Oh Forest!" A wet spot had appeared on the front of
his jeans and a puddle spread slowly along the uneven floor toward
the first row of desks.

Mrs. Norby handled this second disruption with cool efficiency, but there was an edge to her movements, and we dove back
into our books without being told. She rummaged through the box
of cast-offs we wore for art projects and came up with a pair of
bright cotton pedal-pushers and a large safety pin. These she
handed to my brother Russ with instructions. Most of us had been
in Forest's predicament at one time or other, and remembered our
own drawers draped across the oil stove or flapping on the barbed
wire fence outside. Russ took the little boy's hand with awkward
gentleness and led him away to the outhouse. They were gone a

long time. Mrs. Norby had finished mopping up and was back to grading papers, but she kept glancing at the door, clearly exasperated. Forest finally returned, still wearing his wet jeans, and went straight to his desk. From the doorway Russ met the teacher's raised eyebrows with a small shrug, empty-handed.

At recess, Russ withdrew into his grown-up persona and refused to tell us what had gone on in the outhouse. It was none of our business, he chided, and with his moral superiority established, he dropped the subject and organized a game of Annie High Over. He was thirteen and full of adolescent wisdom, infuriating. Later in the week we sat around the kitchen table after school, munching slabs of fresh bread we had buttered and sprinkled with brown sugar. Guy had captured our attention with stories about Forest. They had been paired up for a project, and Guy basked in the glory of inside knowledge.

"I had to show him everything," Guy bragged. "He didn't know nothing."

"Anything." Mom corrected him absently from the sink.

"I asked him stuff, but he don't know how to talk."

"Doesn't," Mom said, sliding more bread from the oven. Russ chewed and frowned at his little brother. Until moments ago, he had been the silent expert. "Can too," he said. In the two days Forest had spent at South First Creek, we had not heard him say one word. He would nod or shake his head, he would follow directions to get this or fetch that, but he had not spoken.

"I suppose *you* would know," Guy said, rolling his eyes. Russ responded to the challenge, telling us about the first day, the walk to the outhouse, Forest's stubborn refusal to be talked into the orange pedal-pushers. He would not undress himself.

"Then I thought maybe he was just bashful, so I gave him the pants and told him I'd wait outside," Ross said. Within seconds, Forest had pushed open the outhouse door and was walking toward

the schoolhouse. Russ made a hasty search for the dry pants. Forest
had thrown them down the toilet hole.

"So what did he say?" I asked eagerly, caught up in this drama.
Russ picked up his half-eaten bread.

"He said *No*," Russ replied. "When I tried to help him with the
button on his pants." He chewed thoughtfully. "He meant it, too.
He's tough."

Forest wet his pants on a regular basis, and we came to prefer
his damp earthy smell to the reek of bayberry Mrs. Norby left on
her after-the-fact rampages around the room with a can of Glade.
She never asked, and to my knowledge, no one told her the fate of
the orange pedal-pushers, but after the first day, Forest wore his
wet pants unchallenged.

TO HER CREDIT, Mrs. Norby never gave up on Forest, although his lessons soon resembled a series of skirmishes. She always began cheerfully enough, settling us to work by ourselves
then calling him up to her big desk where they would spend until
recess working on the big alphabet cards. Our first-grade year, we
all measured our progress and accomplishment by the growing row
of cards, memorized and thumbtacked to the wall above the blackboard. We adored them. On each card the stout black lines of upper
and lower case letters were incorporated into a picture and a story.
The letter C, I remember, was a profile of a mouth lined with teeth;
the sound of Mr. C coughing was the sound of the letter C. Lower-
case F was the tail of a frightened cat. Mr. D was a soldier, and
when he stood straight and beat his round drum it went duh-duh-
duh.

The first time Forest spoke, Mrs. Norby killed our reaction
with one remarkably vicious look, perhaps afraid that we would
frighten him back to silence. But Forest loved the stories, and his
soft, surprisingly deep voice became background music for our own

lessons. He learned the cards quickly, repeating the sounds, grandly embellishing the stories unless Mrs. Norby stopped him, and she must have expected him to take the next leap as effortlessly as we had. But he did not. He saw nothing in the shapes and sounds of the phonics cards that connected to the words written in a book. Mrs. Norby persisted like a trainer with a jump-shy colt, putting him through his paces, around the cards faster and faster, gaining momentum and then the book would appear and Forest would brace his feet and skid to a stop.

Against her decades of experience he had only endurance and a calm, sad stare that he seldom directed at the words she pointed out. After a few days he would have the words of Dick or Jane or Sally's exploits memorized and matched to the pictures on each page. Mrs. Norby would open to a page, he would look at it closely for a few seconds and then begin reciting the story that went with the pictures, sometimes adding bits from previous pages and often as not, reading with his eyes focused on his fingers as they twiddled with a paper clip or a bit of paper. When her voice grew clipped and brittle, he waited her out. Forest did not think in ABCs; for him the story was all.

FROM MY POSITION as third-row observer, I found Forest's academic failures neither surprising nor disappointing. Looking back, I can see it was his inability to read that kept him alive in my mind. From the first days I had attempted to find the mythical Red Man in Forest, and he had failed me on every other front. We had studied plains tribes in social studies. We had read the books, and when TV came to the county we were devoted to shows like "Wagon Train" and "Rawhide." The Indians we admired had no use for reading; they wore buckskin leggings and medicine pouches on leather thongs around their necks. They had eagle feathers and long braids, they danced and hunted and collected scalps. Forest showed little promise of living up to this exciting potential.

Greta and I were more given to fantasy than the boys, and we were the worst. It became a game. Every morning we all hung our coats and placed our lunch boxes in the hallway near the communal water crock. Every morning either Greta or I would ask permission to get a drink, using the few out-of-sight seconds to lift the catch on his lunch box or pat down the pockets of his jacket. His jacket held no crude weapons. His bologna sandwich was as boring as our own bologna sandwiches. No pemmican. No buffalo jerky. Obviously, we knew more about being Indian than Forest did.

My brothers, sister and I spent our childhood summers playing at myth. We made bows and arrows from green willow and cotton string and bounded barefoot through the creek bottoms, communicating with gestures and grunts like Tonto did on "The Lone Ranger." We had horses and could ride like cowboys, but my sister and I rebelled at the discipline of saddles and rules. We rode naked to the waist, hell-bent through the meadows on a palomino mare and a black, half-Shetland pony. We turned them out to pasture in late fall with heart-shaped bald spots where our butts had worn through the hair on their backs.

We had no bridge between make-believe and the reality of children like Forest. We knew our land and its people, every pore, every pothole and every heartache of a close, contained world. From that knowledge came identity and security. But we had only the vaguest sense of our place in the larger world. The Fort Belknap Reservation that lies 25 overland miles from my parents' ranch is no more real in my memory than New York City. What I knew about this place I learned indirectly—jokes overheard, fragments of conversation, phrases that slipped into dialogue sideways, in reference to other whites. Shiftless as a reservation buck. Stank like an Indian camp. Drunk-squaw mean. Wild as, lazy as, dirty as. Racial slurs discounted as harmless because they did not refer to anyone we knew. The people we knew were ranchers, neighbors who lived like we did. Indians were dark and dangerous and different. They got in bar fights and car wrecks; they hung around the Rez and took government handouts; they did not make good hired men. They were like the man we saw behind the rodeo arena pouring his horse a big feed of commodity oatmeal, U.S. Government stamped right on the sack. There was, my father said through clenched teeth, no goddamned excuse for that, no goddamned excuse in the world.

Forest and his grandparents were gone before Christmas. I never knew where they went or why they left. I suppose the extra desk got retired to the storeroom, but I don't remember that, either. What I do remember from that time is the lingering sense of nobility I felt for being kind to him. Tolerance was a gift I could have chosen not to give. I knew Forest would never belong to our school or to our community, just as I knew it wasn't proper to talk about it. These were things I knew without knowing why, things I learned as a child listening with half an ear to all that was said, and most intently to all that was not said. I remember the silence most of all.

THE TRIP TO HAVRE IS in my honor, my first trip to the dentist. He pulls four baby teeth to make room for the new ones sprouting through my gums at odd angles, and there is blood. When we leave the dentist's office I make it to the parking lot then vomit all I have swallowed and feel better. Breakfast happened before dawn, before dressing in our nicest clothes, before our three-hour drive. My father hands me a clean handkerchief to hold against my mouth and drives through downtown Havre in search of an inexpensive cafe. Afraid that misery is catching, my brothers and sisters crowd against the far side of the back seat. Under the stained hankie my cheeks feel heavy and pliant, like wet clay. My father swears at the traffic, a white-knuckled driver unaccustomed to stoplights, and I close my eyes to shut it out.

The cafe we pull up to is small but not crowded, and my stomach wakes to the perfume of hamburgers and french fries, a treat so rare that we could count their every appearance in our short lives, each event of "eating out." But when the food comes I am stunned to find a bowl of chicken soup set on the place mat in front of me, the kind my mother makes when she's too busy to cook. I stir noodles up from the bottom of the bowl and sulk, while the others take turns squeezing ketchup over hamburgers and fighting over split orders of fries. Even driven by hunger, I can't keep the soup from leaking through my numb lips, and when life becomes too unfair to stand, I slide to the floor under the table and begin to cry. My father drags me out by one arm and sends me to sit in the car until I can straighten up.

Outside, I lean against the bumper in pure defiance of direct orders. But the day is too warm and the wait too long. My attention wanders to the bench just outside the cafe door where an Indian woman sits holding a baby. I'm drawn to babies, and this one is a black-eyed beauty, her fat belly peeking out of a crocheted sweater, just big enough to sit upright on the old woman's knee. The woman sees me edging closer and smiles. "You like babies?" she asks, and I nod, my tongue still too thick to trust with words.

The woman is dressed in layers of bright color, wide skirts that brush the ground, a man's flannel shirt buttoned to the neck and a shawl that falls from her shoulders and drapes in folds around the baby. Thick gray braids coil at the nape of her neck. She bends her face near the baby's and clicks her tongue, tickling at the chubby brown chin, and the baby dissolves into giggles, her eyes fastened on the grandmother's face. The babies I have seen are next to bald, but this one has thick black hair standing up all over her head. I'm getting up the nerve to touch that hair when the cafe door opens and I leap back, scrambling toward our car, expecting my father. I turn, hand on the door handle, and an old man stands next to the woman and the baby. They are all looking at me, surprised.

The man hands the woman a wrapped hamburger and a paper cup of milk and walks back into the cafe. She lets the baby suck on the edge of the cup while she chews the sandwich, her lips disappearing with the motion of her jaw. She sets the cup aside, and I freeze against the car in wonder as she dips into her mouth with two fingers and pops a bit of chewed food into the baby's open mouth. The little girl works over the mashed hamburger and they rock gently on the bench, each gumming her own bite until it's swallowed. After a sip of milk, the baby leans forward comically, eyebrows arched, mouth and eyes round, ready for more. My own stomach shivers, squeamish, thrilled, but the process is done so gently that I can't be horrified. I watch the wonderful shuffle of food from mouth to fingers to baby, the easy sway between bites, until I'm full to bursting with news.

Back inside the cafe, I ignore the cold soup and dance against my mother's arm, conscious of slurring as I tell the story of what I've seen. Her nose wrinkles and her voice drops to a whisper as she hushes me.

"Did you talk to her?" she asks. Her voice is too flat and even, a trap I can't quite read. I nod, ready to work my lips and tongue around an explanation but her hand snakes out and grabs my ear before I can speak, twisting it, her knuckles pressing against my swollen cheek. Her eyes lock mine into full attention.

"You were told to get in the car." She says nothing else, but continues to glare, giving my ear another jerk for emphasis. Stunned, I walk with under-water steps out the door, straight without looking to the car and curl up on the back seat, heat thumping in my stomach.

It's a long ride home that night, late and dark, and the back seat is a crush of packages and sleeping children. My mouth has been awake for hours, throbbing. In the front seat my mother tells my story of the Indian woman feeding the baby. My father says "Jeezus Christ." My mother says it would be our luck if I caught something. I hear it in their voices and my belly fills with anger and shame. The old woman tricked me. On the outside nothing is what it seems, and I long for my own bed, the quilt my mother sewed from wool scraps

and old coats, the comfort of a sure thing. My father drives automatically now, slowing for ruts and cattle guards, banking the gentle curves of the county road. Lonesome Coulee. Jackson's Corner.
Taylor Hill. I press one cheek against the cool of the window and
close my eyes, drifting with the motion of the car. Almost home. I
can tell where we are by the feel.

Mary Crow Dog

"If you plan to be born," Mary Crow Dog says only half-jokingly in her autobiography, Lakota Woman *(1990)*, "make sure you are born white and male." Born Mary Brave Bird, she grew up fatherless in a one-room cabin, without running water or electricity, on the Rosebud reservation in South Dakota. On April 11, 1973, at the age of seventeen, she gave birth to her first child, Pedro, during a firefight in the seventy-one-day-long siege at the second battle of Wounded Knee. "It's hard being an Indian woman," she says. In 1976, her best friend, Annie Mae Aquash, "was found dead in the snow at the bottom of a ravine on the Pine Ridge Reservation." The police listed the cause of death as exposure, "but there was a .38 caliber slug in her head," Mary writes. "The FBI cut off her hands and sent them to Washington for fingerprint identification, hands that had helped my baby come into the world." By the time of Annie's death, Mary Brave Bird had become the wife of Leonard Crow Dog, the chief medicine man of the American Indian Movement, who revived the sacred but outlawed Ghost Dance. In fact, however, Mary Crow Dog's rebellion against the cruelties perpetrated against Indians over the last 500 years began much earlier, while she attended the mission boarding school at St. Francis. It was there, as we see in her account below, that she first became "a red panther."

"Civilize Them with a Stick"

from *Lakota Woman*

... Gathered from the cabin, the wickiup, and the tepee,
partly by cajolery and partly by threats;
partly by bribery and partly by force,
they are induced to leave their kindred
to enter these schools and take upon themselves
the outward appearance of civilized life.
—*Annual report of the Department of Interior, 1901*

IT IS ALMOST IMPOSSIBLE TO EXPLAIN TO A SYM-
pathetic white person what a typical old Indian boarding school was
like; how it affected the Indian child suddenly dumped into it like a
small creature from another world, helpless, defenseless, bewildered, trying desperately and instinctively to survive and sometimes not surviving at all. I think such children were like the victims of Nazi concentration camps trying to tell average,
middle-class Americans what their experience had been like. Even
now, when these schools are much improved, when the buildings
are new, all gleaming steel and glass, the food tolerable, the teachers well trained and well-intentioned, even trained in child psychology—unfortunately the psychology of white children, which is different from ours—the shock to the child upon arrival is still
tremendous. Some just seem to shrivel up, don't speak for days on
end, and have an empty look in their eyes. I know of an eleven-year-
old on another reservation who hanged herself, and in our school,
while I was there, a girl jumped out of the window, trying to kill
herself to escape an unbearable situation. That first shock is always
there.

Although the old tiyospaye [the extended family group] has been destroyed, in the traditional Sioux families, especially in those where there is no drinking, the child is never left alone. It is always surrounded by relatives, carried around, enveloped in warmth. It is treated with the respect due to any human being, even a small one. It is seldom forced to do anything against its will, seldom screamed at, and never beaten. That much, at least, is left of the old family group among full-bloods. And then suddenly a bus or car arrives, full of strangers, usually white strangers, who yank the child out of the arms of those who love it, taking it screaming to the boarding school. The only word I can think of for what is done to these children is kidnapping.

Even now, in a good school, there is impersonality instead of close human contact; a sterile, cold atmosphere, an unfamiliar routine, language problems, and above all the maza-skan-skan, that damn clock—white man's time as opposed to Indian time, which is natural time. Like eating when you are hungry and sleeping when you are tired, not when that damn clock says you must. But I was not taken to one of the better, modern schools. I was taken to the old-fashioned mission school at St. Francis, run by the nuns and Catholic fathers, built sometime around the turn of the century and not improved a bit when I arrived, not improved as far as the buildings, the food, the teachers, or their methods were concerned.

In the old days, nature was our people's only school and they needed no other. Girls had their toy tipis and dolls, boys their toy bows and arrows. Both rode and swam and played the rough Indian games together. Kids watched their peers and elders and naturally grew from children into adults. Life in the tipi circle was harmonious—until the whiskey peddlers arrived with their wagons and barrels of "Injun whiskey." I often wished I could have grown up in the old, before-whiskey days.

Oddly enough, we owed our unspeakable boarding schools to

the do-gooders, the white Indian-lovers. The schools were intended
as an alternative to the outright extermination seriously advocated
by generals Sherman and Sheridan, as well as by most settlers and
prospectors overrunning our land. "You don't have to kill those
poor benighted heathen," the do-gooders said, "in order to solve the
Indian Problem. Just give us a chance to turn them into useful farm-
hands, laborers, and chambermaids who will break their backs for
you at low wages." In that way the boarding schools were born. The
kids were taken away from their villages and pueblos, in their blankets and moccasins, kept completely isolated from their families—
sometimes for as long as ten years—suddenly coming back, their
short hair slick with pomade, their necks raw from stiff, high col-
lars, their thick jackets always short in the sleeves and pinching
under the arms, their tight patent leather shoes giving them corns,
the girls in starched white blouses and clumsy, high-buttoned
boots—caricatures of white people. When they found out—and
they found out quickly—that they were neither wanted by whites
nor by Indians, they got good and drunk, many of them staying
drunk for the rest of their lives. I still have a poster I found among
my grandfather's stuff, given to him by the missionaries to tack up
on his wall. It reads:

1. Let Jesus save you.
2. Come out of your blanket, cut your hair, and dress like a
   white man.
3. Have a Christian family with one wife for life only.
4. Live in a house like your white brother. Work hard and
   wash often.
5. Learn the value of a hard-earned dollar. Do not waste your
   money on giveaways. Be punctual.
6. Believe that property and wealth are signs of divine approval.

7. Keep away from saloons and strong spirits.
8. Speak the language of your white brother. Send your children to school to do likewise.
9. Go to church often and regularly.
10. Do not go to Indian dances or to the medicine men.

The people who were stuck upon "solving the Indian Problem" by making us into whites retreated from this position only step by step in the wake of Indian protests.

The mission school at St. Francis was a curse for our family for generations. My grandmother went there, then my mother, then my sisters and I. At one time or other every one of us tried to run away. Grandma told me once about the bad times she had experienced at St. Francis. In those days they let students go home only for one week every year. Two days were used up for transportation, which meant spending just five days out of three hundred and sixty-five with her family. And that was an improvement. Before grandma's time, on many reservations they did not let the students go home at all until they had finished school. Anybody who disobeyed the nuns was severely punished. The building in which my grandmother stayed had three floors, for girls only. Way up in the attic were little cells, about five by five by ten feet. One time she was in church and instead of praying she was playing jacks. As punishment they took her to one of those little cubicles where she stayed in darkness because the windows had been boarded up. They left her there for a whole week with only bread and water for nourishment. After she came out she promptly ran away, together with three other girls. They were found and brought back. The nuns stripped them naked and whipped them. They used a horse buggy whip on my grandmother. Then she was put back into the attic—for two weeks.

My mother had much the same experiences but never wanted to talk about them, and then there I was, in the same place. The school is now run by the BIA—the Bureau of Indian Affairs—but only since about fifteen years ago. When I was there, during the 1960s, it was still run by the Church. The Jesuit fathers ran the boys' wing and the Sisters of the Sacred Heart ran us—with the help of the strap. Nothing had changed since my grandmother's days. I have been told recently that even in the '70s they were still beating children at that school. All I got out of school was being taught how to pray. I learned quickly that I would be beaten if I failed in my devotions or, God forbid, prayed the wrong way, especially prayed in Indian to Wakan Tanka, the Indian Creator.

The girls' wing was built like an F and was run like a penal institution. Every morning at five o'clock the sisters would come into our large dormitory to wake us up, and immediately we had to kneel down at the sides of our beds and recite the prayers. At six o'clock we were herded into the church for more of the same. I did not take kindly to the discipline and to marching by the clock, left-right, left-right. I was never one to like being forced to do something. I do something because I feel like doing it. I felt this way always, as far as I can remember, and my sister Barbara felt the same way. An old medicine man once told me: "Us Lakotas are not like dogs who can be trained, who can be beaten and keep on wagging their tails, licking the hand that whipped them. We are like cats, little cats, big cats, wildcats, bobcats, mountain lions. It doesn't matter what kind, but cats who can't be tamed, who scratch if you step on their tails." But I was only a kitten and my claws were still small.

Barbara was still in the school when I arrived and during my first year or two she could still protect me a little bit. When Barb was a seventh-grader she ran away together with five other girls, early in the morning before sunrise. They brought them back in the evening. The girls had to wait for two hours in front of the mother superior's office. They were hungry and cold, frozen through. It was wintertime and they had been running the whole day without food, trying to make good their escape. The mother superior asked each girl, "Would you do this again?" She told them that as punishment they would not be allowed to visit home for a month and that she'd keep them busy on work details until the skin on their knees and elbows had worn off. At the end of her speech she told each girl, "Get up from this chair and lean over it." She then lifted the girls' skirts and pulled down their underpants. Not little girls either, but teenagers. She had a leather strap about a foot long and four inches wide fastened to a stick, and beat the girls, one after another, until they cried. Barb did not give her that satisfaction but just clenched her teeth. There was one girl, Barb told me, the nun kept on beating and beating until her arm got tired.

I did not escape my share of the strap. Once, when I was thirteen years old, I refused to go to Mass. I did not want to go to church because I did not feel well. A nun grabbed me by the hair, dragged me upstairs, made me stoop over, pulled my dress up (we were not allowed at the time to wear jeans), pulled my panties down, and gave me what they called "swats"—twenty-five swats with a board around which Scotch tape had been wound. She hurt me badly.

My classroom was right next to the principal's office and almost every day I could hear him swatting the boys. Beating was the common punishment for not doing one's homework, or for being late to school. It had such a bad effect upon me that I hated and mistrusted every white person on sight, because I met only one kind. It was not until much later that I met sincere white people I could relate to and be friends with. Racism breeds racism in reverse.

The routine at St. Francis was dreary. Six A.M., kneeling in church for an hour or so; seven o'clock, breakfast; eight o'clock, scrub the floor, peel spuds, make classes. We had to mop the dining room twice every day and scrub the tables. If you were caught taking a rest, doodling on the bench with a fingernail or knife, or just rapping, the nun would come up with a dish towel and just slap it across your face, saying, "You're not supposed to be talking, you're supposed to be working!" Monday mornings we had corn-meal mush, Tuesday oatmeal, Wednesday rice and raisins, Thursday cornflakes, and Friday all the leftovers mixed together or sometimes fish. Frequently the food had bugs or rocks in it. We were eating hot dogs that were weeks old, while the nuns were dining on ham, whipped potatoes, sweet peas, and cranberry sauce. In winter our dorm was icy cold while the nuns' rooms were always warm.

I have seen little girls arrive at the school, first-graders, just fresh from home and totally unprepared for what awaited them, little girls with pretty braids, and the first thing the nuns did was chop their hair off and tie up what was left behind their ears. Next they would dump the children into tubs of alcohol, a sort of rubbing alcohol, "to get the germs off." Many of the nuns were German immigrants, some from Bavaria, so that we sometimes speculated whether Bavaria was some sort of Dracula country inhabited by monsters. For the sake of objectivity I ought to mention that two of the German fathers were great linguists and that the only Lakota-English dictionaries and grammars which are worth anything were put together by them.

At night some of the girls would huddle in bed together for comfort and reassurance. Then the nun in charge of the dorm would come in and say, "What are the two of you doing in bed together? I smell evil in this room. You girls are evil incarnate. You are sinning. You are going to hell and burn forever. You can act that way in the devil's frying pan." She would get them out of bed in the middle of the night, making them kneel and pray until morning. We had not the slightest idea what it was all about. At home we slept two and three in a bed for animal warmth and a feeling of security.

The nuns and the girls in the two top grades were constantly battling it out physically with fists, nails, and hair-pulling. I myself was growing from a kitten into an undersized cat. My claws were getting bigger and were itching for action. About 1969 or 1970 a strange young white girl appeared on the reservation. She looked about eighteen or twenty years old. She was pretty and had long, blond hair down to her waist, patched jeans, boots, and a backpack. She was different from any other white person we had met before. I think her name was Wise. I do not know how she managed to overcome our reluctance and distrust, getting us into a corner, making us listen to her, asking us how we were treated. She told us that she was from New York. She was the first real hippie or Yippie we had come across. She told us of people called the Black Panthers, Young Lords, and Weathermen. She said, "Black people are getting it on. Indians are getting it on in St. Paul and California. How about you?" She also said, "Why don't you put out an underground paper, mimeograph it. It's easy. Tell it like it is. Let it all hang out." She spoke a strange lingo but we caught on fast.

Charlene Left Hand Bull and Gina One Star were two full-blood girls I used to hang out with. We did everything together. They were willing to join me in a Sioux uprising. We put together a newspaper which we called the *Red Panther*. In it we wrote how bad the school was, what kind of slop we had to eat—slimy, rotten, blackened potatoes for two weeks—the way we were beaten. I think I was the one who wrote the worst article about our principal of the moment, Father Keeler. I put all my anger and venom into it. I called him a goddam wasičun son of a bitch. I wrote that he knew nothing about Indians and should go back to where he came from, teaching white children whom he could relate to. I wrote that we knew which priests slept with which nuns and that all they ever could think about was filling their bellies and buying a new car. It was the kind of writing which foamed at the mouth, but which also lifted a great deal of weight from one's soul.

On Saint Patrick's Day, when everybody was at the big pow-wow, we distributed our newspapers. We put them on windshields and bulletin boards, in desks and pews, in dorms and toilets. But someone saw us and snitched on us. The shit hit the fan. The three of us were taken before a board meeting. Our parents, in my case my mother, had to come. They were told that ours was a most serious matter, the worst thing that had ever happened in the school's long history. One of the nuns told my mother, "Your daughter really needs to be talked to." "What's wrong with my daughter?" my mother asked. She was given one of our *Red Panther* newspapers. The nun pointed out its name to her and then my piece, waiting for mom's reaction. After a while she asked, "Well, what have you got to say to this? What do you think?"

My mother said, "Well, when I went to school here, some years back, I was treated a lot worse than these kids are. I really can't see how they can have any complaints, because we was treated a lot stricter. We could not even wear skirts halfway up our knees. These girls have it made. But you should forgive them because they are young. And it's supposed to be a free country, free speech and all that. I don't believe what they done is wrong." So all I got out of it was scrubbing six flights of stairs on my hands and knees, every day. And no boy-side privileges.

The boys and girls were still pretty much separated. The only time one could meet a member of the opposite sex was during free time, between four and five-thirty, in the study hall or on benches or the volleyball court outside, and that was strictly supervised. One day Charlene and I went over to the boys' side. We were on the ball team and they had to let us practice. We played three extra minutes, only three minutes more than we were supposed to. Here was the nuns' opportunity for revenge. We got twenty-five swats. I told Charlene, "We are getting too old to have our bare asses whipped that way. We are old enough to have babies. Enough of this shit. Next time we fight back." Charlene only said, "Hoka-hay!"

We had to take showers every evening. One little girl did not want to take her panties off and one of the nuns told her, "You take those underpants off—or else!" But the child was ashamed to do it. The nun was getting her swat to threaten the girl. I went up to the sister, pushed her veil off, and knocked her down. I told her that if she wanted to hit a little girl she should pick on me, pick one her own size. She got herself transferred out of the dorm a week later.

In a school like this there is always a lot of favoritism. At St. Francis it was strongly tinged with racism. Girls who were near-white, who came from what the nuns called "nice families," got preferential treatment. They waited on the faculty and got to eat ham or eggs and bacon in the morning. They got the easy jobs while the skins, who did not have the right kind of background—myself among them—always wound up in the laundry room sorting out ten bushel baskets of dirty boys' socks every day. Or we wound up scrubbing the floors and doing all the dishes. The school therefore fostered fights and antagonism between whites and breeds, and between breeds and skins. At one time Charlene and I had to iron all the robes and vestments the priests wore when saying Mass. We had to fold them up and put them into a chest in the back of the church. In a corner, looking over our shoulders, was a statue of the crucified Savior, all bloody and beaten up. Charlene looked up and said, "Look at that poor Indian. The pigs sure worked him over." That was the closest I ever came to seeing Jesus.

I was held up as a bad example and didn't mind. I was old enough to have a boyfriend and promptly got one. At the school we had an hour and a half for ourselves. Between the boys' and the girls' wings were some benches where one could sit. My boyfriend and I used to go there just to hold hands and talk. The nuns were very uptight about any boy-girl stuff. They had an exaggerated fear of anything having even the faintest connection with sex. One day in religion class, an all-girl class, Sister Bernard singled me out for some remarks, pointing me out as a bad example, an example that should be shown. She said that I was too free with my body. That I was holding hands which meant that I was not a good example to follow. She also said that I wore unchaste dresses, skirts which were too short, too suggestive, shorter than regulations permitted, and for that I would be punished. She dressed me down before the whole class, carrying on and on about my unchastity.

I stood up and told her, "You shouldn't say any of those things, miss. You people are a lot worse than us Indians. I know all about you, because my grandmother and my aunt told me about you. Maybe twelve, thirteen years ago you had a water stoppage here in St. Francis. No water could get through the pipes. There are water lines right under the mission, underground tunnels and passages where in my grandmother's time only the nuns and priests could go, which were off-limits to everybody else. When the water backed up they had to go through all the water lines and clean them out. And in those huge pipes they found the bodies of newborn babies. And they were white babies. They weren't Indian babies. At least when our girls have babies, they don't do away with them that way, like flushing them down the toilet, almost.

"And that priest they sent here from Holy Rosary in Pine Ridge because he molested a little girl. You couldn't think of anything better than dump him on us. All he does is watch young women and girls with that funny smile on his face. Why don't you point him out for an example?"

Charlene and I worked on the school newspaper. After all we had some practice. Every day we went down to Publications. One of the priests acted as the photographer, doing the enlarging and developing. He smelled of chemicals which had stained his hands yellow. One day he invited Charlene into the darkroom. He was going to teach her developing. She was developed already. She was a big girl compared to him, taller too. Charlene was nicely built, not fat, just rounded. No sharp edges anywhere. All of a sudden she rushed out of the darkroom, yelling to me, "Let's get out of here! He's trying to feel me up. That priest is nasty." So there was this too to contend with—sexual harassment. We complained to the student body. The nuns said we just had a dirty mind.

We got a new priest in English. During one of his first classes he asked one of the boys a certain question. The boy was shy. He spoke poor English, but he had the right answer. The priest told him, "You did not say it right. Correct yourself. Say it over again." The boy got flustered and stammered. He could hardly get out a word. But the priest kept after him: "Didn't you hear? I told you to do the whole thing over. Get it right this time." He kept on and on.

I stood up and said, "Father, don't be doing that. If you go into an Indian's home and try to talk Indian, they might laugh at you and say, 'Do it over correctly. Get it right this time!' "

He shouted at me, "Mary, you stay after class. Sit down right now!"

I stayed after class, until after the bell. He told me, "Get over here!" He grabbed me by the arm, pushing me against the blackboard, shouting, "Why are you always mocking us? You have no reason to do this."

I said, "Sure I do. You were making fun of him. You embarrassed him. He needs strengthening, not weakening. You hurt him. I did not hurt you."

He twisted my arm and pushed real hard. I turned around and hit him in the face, giving him a bloody nose. After that I ran out of the room, slamming the door behind me. He and I went to Sister Bernard's office. I told her, "Today I quit school. I'm not taking any more of this, none of this shit anymore. None of this treatment. Better give me my diploma. I can't waste any more time on you people."

Sister Bernard looked at me for a long, long time. She said, "All right, Mary Ellen, go home today. Come back in a few days and get your diploma." And that was that. Oddly enough, that priest turned out okay. He taught a class in grammar, orthography, composition, things like that. I think he wanted more respect in class. He was still young and unsure of himself. But I was in there too long. I didn't feel like hearing it. Later he became a good friend of the Indians, a personal friend of myself and my husband. He stood up for us during Wounded Knee and after. He stood up to his superiors, stuck his neck way out, became a real people's priest. He even learned our language. He died prematurely of cancer. It is not only the good Indians who die young, but the good whites, too. It is the timid ones who know how to take care of themselves who grow old. I am still grateful to that priest for what he did for us later and for the quarrel he picked with me—or did I pick it with him?—because it ended a situation which had become unendurable for me. The day of my fight with him was my last day in school.

Judith Freeman

W hen Judith Freeman was a child, she never imagined that she would become a writer. The daughter of a large Mormon family in Utah, she thought she might work for a short time as a stewardess or a nurse; she knew she would get married and have children. She did get married—at the age of seventeen—and went with her husband and infant child to a college in the Midwest where a literature course set her mind on fire. This was the first step toward discovering who she really was, and what she most wanted to do. It took years before she could allow her storyteller heart free rein; when she did, she had to brave the familial and cultural taboos that conspired to silence the stories that were most intimately hers to tell.

Freeman is the author of Family Attractions (1988), a collection of short stories, and two novels, The Chinchilla Farm (1989) and Set for Life (1991). She is currently at work on a new novel, A Body of Water, forthcoming from Pantheon, and her first book of nonfiction, India Journal, in collaboration with the photographer Tina Barney.

How Does the Dance Begin?

JUST A LITTLE OVER THREE YEARS AGO, ON A gray December morning a few days before Christmas, I got a phone call—a call which I had been both expecting and dreading. I was staying in the house of a friend in the hills of Topanga Canyon above the Pacific Ocean. The house had no heat, only a fireplace, and I remember starting a fire early that day. The call came while I was in the shower. My husband answered the phone, and when I finished my shower, he said to me, "Your father called. He wants you to call him back."

A certain moment in my life as a writer, a woman, a daughter, had arrived, and I knew it. I had just published my first novel, *The Chinchilla Farm*, and had sent my parents a copy a few weeks earlier. I had done nothing to prepare them for the contents, because I didn't know how to. I knew this was what my father was calling about. He'd read my book, and I was pretty sure he was upset.

About twenty years ago my father had told my younger brother, who had announced his intention of becoming a writer, that he could write about anything he wanted to except two things: he was forbidden to write about our family, or our religion. In the long run, my brother didn't write about anything. He became a bus driver. I became the writer, and no one was more surprised than myself. Although I had not been directly forbidden to write about my family or our religion, I knew what my father had told my brother, and all the years I worked to become a writer, to find a way to give expression to the stories I had to tell, I didn't forget that comment. I also knew that I would someday violate my father's rule.

As I picked up the phone to call my father back, I felt fear, anxiety, a sense of dread and impending doom, and I wished very much that I didn't have to make that call. But there arose amid the fear a faint feeling of defiance, and an equally timid sense of pride in having, against considerable odds, become a writer at all. Cling to these things, I told myself. I had written about forbidden subjects—family, childhood, memory, and above all, Mormonism, a religion which has been almost totally neglected in mainstream American literature because it has produced so few writers. I had described the rituals and practices of this religion as only an insider could, mentioned things I'd been forbidden to ever speak about. And here I was, over forty years old, having long since left the church myself, now about to face my father, the patriarch of my clan, and I felt terrified. There was nothing to say to Anthony, my husband, nothing he could say to me before I made that call, although I do remember muttering something like, "Well, this is it," and going to the phone, which sat in a cold little cubicle surrounded by windows looking out onto a leaf-scattered lawn and winter-bare trees.

As I dialed the number, I could imagine my father, sitting by the phone in the little house trailer in southern Utah where he and my mother spend the winters, surrounded by the red clay hills which border the Temple View RV Court. My father is eighty years old. He's blind in one eye. A series of seizures has left him thin as a child, and almost as small. He's shrinking with age. Each year, his blind eye grows smaller, his limbs thinner. He stoops, his balance is poor, and his heart is bad. Yet he's still alert, a strong, formidable man who when I was growing up had the distinction of being the only Democrat in our ward—an uneducated man with an inquiring mind and sharp opinions. In the seventies, he supported the Equal Rights Amendment, and not many people did in Ogden, Utah. He wore an ERA button around town, and put the same message on his car bumper. I think local people thought he was a baseball fan, that ERA stood for earned run average. From him I got my liberal political views. But his is a peculiar brand of liberalism, more like renegade Western Populism mixed with a class consciousness born of his own painful experiences, all combined with his deep religious beliefs.

I'm not sure I've ever understood my father, or known who he is. I have an image of him from my childhood, dressed in dark clothes, leaving the house early in the morning to go to his job. He worked for the Kennecott Copper Company, at the Bingham mine, not far from the Great Salt Lake. At night when he came home, wordlessly he changed his clothes and went straight to the garden where, until called for dinner, he worked steadily among his beds of tall roses and brambly raspberry bushes. His garden was his buffer between the world of the copper mine, which he came to hate, and the eight children and wife who waited at the table, about whom he had the most complicated feelings. "I never should have had eight children," he said to me when I was older. "I didn't have the temperament for it." He did have eight children, though, and between them and the mine, he was trapped, with only the earth and light of the garden to escape to in the hours between when he came home and dinner was set out on the table.

When I returned my father's call that morning several years ago, I heard the tone of his voice—cold, serious, methodical—and I knew there was trouble. "I have a few things I'd like to discuss with you, having read this book you've written," he said. No greeting. No preliminaries. No emotion. "For one thing, it says here . . ."

I heard a paper rattling. I knew he'd made a list.

And then he began. Did I realize I had written about things I never should have? Did I understand I had made the Mormons look bad? Did I know how I had pictured them in a very unfavorable light? I had made them look like racists. I remember interrupting him and saying I didn't think I had done that at all. But I added, didn't he think that a church that had barred blacks from holding the priesthood for nearly 150 years had a problem with racism? No answer. The paper rattled again. "What about the passage," he said, "where you call religion a 'cruel and beautiful deception'? Is this the way you feel?" I said, "First of all, it's the character in the book, Verna, who says that, and even if I did feel that way, what would be wrong with us disagreeing on this issue?" He didn't respond, because we weren't having a conversation. I saw that clearly. Did I have to describe the holy underwear worn by Mormons? he wanted to know. Did I suppose I could sell a lot of books by having them everywhere in the book, described in such detail, flapping from clotheslines, hanging in basements? I believed, I said, that it wouldn't hurt to tell the truth about these things. It might demystify Mormonism, make it more comprehensible to the world. A church with too many secrets, I said, is like a man with too many secrets: he is vulnerable, he can be easily frightened, easily intimidated and misunderstood. Why had I written a novel, anyway? he wanted to know. Why hadn't I the "courage" to write an autobiography? "Because I write fiction," I said. "I'm a fiction writer." He said he supposed that I thought I wouldn't be held accountable. Did I even know the meaning of the word "accountable"? He thought I probably didn't, but he'd looked it up for me in the dictionary, and he wanted to read me the definition. The paper rattled again. " 'Liable to be called to account,' " he said, " 'to make satisfactory amends for something, to give satisfactory reasons for, to explain, to be responsible.' " I could only respond by saying I did feel accountable, accountable to myself.

The conversation went on for a while longer. More painful accusations were leveled, eliciting increasingly dull responses. It didn't become easier. In fact, it got worse, and later, when I tried to find the words to describe what had happened, I would say, rather stunned, "My father really raked me over the coals," or "My father took me to task over my novel," or "My father was so angry he really gave it to me." But what did it really feel like, that conversation with him? Failure? Betrayal? Rejection? How is a writer to accept such a thing as the wrath of a father? Righteous, terrible, almost biblical wrath, for doing nothing more than what the writer is compelled to do? I didn't know then, and I still don't know.

The last part of the phone call was the worst. He said the family—my family—was very angry with me, my older brothers, my sister were upset. Many of my siblings are still Mormons, still active in the church. Apparently, I had offended them too. "I'm afraid the family is against you on this one," my father said. It wasn't as a writer so much that I felt this comment, but as a daughter, a sister, a woman. I suddenly felt cast out, banished by the patriarch who spoke for the whole family, spoke in a powerful male voice, much the way a powerful male leader will speak for a whole country. It was a horrible thing, the idea that my family had turned against me, that they could do such a thing, and allow him to be the instrument of my punishment. Then, my father administered the coup de grâce: "Your book . . . ?" he said. "It isn't even very good. It's boring. There's nothing there."

I hung up on my father then, and it's probably a good thing I did. It could only have gotten worse. Under those circumstances, I realized I couldn't "account" for myself. I couldn't give an explanation, justify, or defend myself, because pain had short-circuited reason. Certain people recognize the truth when they read it. I felt for my father, seeing parts of his life on a page, perhaps clumsily or inaccurately rendered by his daughter. Maybe he had been devastated. But not once during that phone call had he talked about the family stories I had told. Instead, he'd focused on religion, and I felt religion was perhaps a smoke screen for his deeper feelings, his real hurts. I felt for him, but not enough to pull myself together and stay on the line. I bailed out. It was the best I could do. And then I spent the rest of that day immobile, sitting quietly by the fire, thinking deeply about many things. Didn't I have the right to become a writer and write about my own life? Whose life was really on those pages, anyway?

I NEVER INTENDED to become a writer. I wasn't one of those kids who wrote stories at an early age. I hardly even read as a child, or was read to. There were few books in our house, and those that were there had titles like *A Marvelous Work and a Wonder* and *Answers to Gospel Questions*. I do remember an anthology of pioneer stories with the remarkable title of *Heart Throbs of the West*, published by the Daughters of the Utah Pioneers, and I liked those stories; they seemed true to me. I had, in fact, no idea what I wanted to do when I grew up but I remember answering a questionnaire in our church youth group about what I wanted to be: I wrote, "I'd like to be either a secretary or a stewardess and then get married and be a mother." I still have that questionnaire, and when I read it, it astonishes me, and I feel something like embarrassment, that I would see such narrow choices for myself. Was that me speaking? Or was this the child of meticulous conditioning? In fact, I got married when I was seventeen, the day after I graduated from high school, as if blindly fulfilling that future foreshadowed for me.

BY THE TIME I WAS EIGHTEEN, I had a baby. My son was born with a serious congenital heart problem. I came home from the hospital without him. He had emergency surgery at three weeks and afterwards spent months in an incubator in a hospital on a hill above Salt Lake City. Sometimes his chances looked good, and sometimes they didn't. I remember sitting next to that incubator in that children's hospital in Salt Lake City and feeling trapped, as though my life had suddenly veered out of control. Things had not gone as I imagined they would. When I got married, I had dreamed of the Peace Corps, Africa, adventures. I thought I'd found an "out," a way to free myself to move into the world. Instead, I found myself burdened with painful responsibilities as the mother of a very sick child, and I remember thinking: my life is set on a course and I'm powerless to alter it. I felt swept up by events, very young and frightened, with a future that no longer looked promising at all. I've written about these feelings in a story called "Going Out to Sea."

"Going Out to Sea" is one of the most autobiographical stories I've ever written. In it, I tried to describe what it was like being a teenaged mother with a sick child and the experience of taking that child to Minnesota in order for him to have open-heart surgery, which in 1967 was still a pretty big deal. What I didn't tell in that story, and what I've yet to write about, was what else happened to me in Minnesota . . . the wonderful part, the part that changed my life. It was in Minnesota, at the age of twenty, that I discovered literature and reading.

My husband, who was by then studying psychology, landed a job on the campus of a small university in St. Paul called Macalester College, as director of a dormitory that had just become coeducational. It was the first time the college had allowed men and women to live together, segregated by floor. At the age of twenty, I became a dorm mother in a dorm where half the kids were older than I was. These students seemed vastly more educated, sophisticated, and experienced than me. One girl, a theological student named Mary, had just returned from Prague and told us of the Russian tanks that rolled into the city that spring. I remember Parents' Visiting Day and the surprise on the parents' faces when I was introduced as the dorm mother—I must have seemed more immature than their own sons and daughters. I had never been outside Utah, except for short car trips in neighboring states. Now I found myself thrust into a tumultuous world. Within a year or two of moving, Robert Kennedy was dead, and Martin Luther King. Kent State erupted in violence, and the Democratic Convention in Chicago became a strained testing ground for opposing forces. Cities were burning. And of course, there was Vietnam, and the daily protest vigils on campus.

I felt almost everyone at Macalester knew more about the world than I did. But the important thing was, as a faculty wife I could take courses on campus for free, and I enrolled in a literature course taught by a man named Roger Blakely. There, I discovered writers—D. H. Lawrence, Hardy and Joyce, Willa Cather, Sherwood Anderson, and Virginia Woolf. I discovered reading.

I took another class over the summer, a writing class also taught by Mr. Blakely, and I wrote my first short story. It won first prize in the class. It was the story of a girl who falls in love in kindergarten with another little girl and waits for her in the coat closet in order to wrestle her to the floor and give her kisses among the galoshes. I think even then I knew I had discovered what I wanted to do: I wanted to write, to give expression to feeling and experience. I dreamed of writing. Instead, my marriage fell apart, I moved back to Utah, and I spent the next twelve years raising my son, working odd jobs—as a secretary, a sales clerk at a church-owned department store, wrangling horses and running a dude string in Idaho, and teaching skiing. Not until much later, when I was nearing my mid-thirties and my son went to live with his father, did I decide to move to Los Angeles and devote myself to writing.

SINCE THAT TIME, it's all I've wanted to do. It sounds odd, just sitting down to write one day, imagining such a thing might be possible. It was hard, trying to figure out how to make stories from scratch. I wanted to write about the world I knew, the world that had formed me—the West, Utah, Mormonism—the strange and exotic yet so terribly ordinary and very American experience I had gone through being raised the way I was. I wanted to tell family stories. These things, I felt, were mine, my landscape, both physical and emotional.

As I struggled to create those first stories, I spent a lot of time worrying about how people close to me might feel if I wrote about them. I made false starts. I tried to tell the truth, I tried to distort it. I attempted to do as Faulkner suggests, and turn the actual into the apocryphal. Eventually, I followed my deepest instincts, which is what a writer must do. I listened to the Muse. I allowed the spirit of pure creativity to move me. I wrote the novel that I knew I must write, and once it was finished, I sat back and waited, with an uneasy feeling that everything was at once lost, and gained.

FOR A LONG WHILE after that phone call with my father, we didn't speak. There's a banished place, Plato's cave, the shack in the ice, and I think it's not only writers who come to know that place quite well, it's anyone who wants to spend some time seriously contemplating the nature of existence. Although it was terribly painful to receive the wrath of my father, to feel misunderstood and rejected by my family, to be banished to a very solitary place, I also felt liberated in some way by that phone call. I stepped more fully into myself, as a woman, and a writer. I entered a landscape so private and singular I knew I could never again be terrorized in the same way.

After months of silence, I finally heard from my father again. His letter was still full of anger and accusatory statements. My mother tried to play the peacemaker, as mothers often do. She wrote that it had been very painful for her to read my book, and she was especially dismayed that I had chosen to reveal certain sacred temple rituals practiced by Mormons. Yet she said she would defend my right to express myself over any objection she might have to what I wrote. She ended her letter by quoting Shakespeare to me: "To thine own self be true."

Months went by. I thought about my father, that frail old man, nearing the end of his life, and I grieved. There are times, I saw, when it is possible to get so far outside ourselves we can see someone else's plight very clearly, and for a moment feel their pain more acutely than our own.

Then something happened. One day, a few months after my novel came out, I got a call from a professor at Brigham Young University, who said he represented an organization called the Association for Mormon Letters, a group of academics, historians, readers, and booksellers who each year evaluate any novels that deal with the subject of Mormonism. He was calling, he said, to inform me that my novel had been chosen to receive the award for literature— an award that came with a small cash prize and certificate. I was astonished, and deeply pleased. Of course, in the back of my mind, I was thinking of my father and how this award would certainly prove to him that my book was not anti-Mormon. Here it was, receiving a prize from a group of Mormons!

I sent my father a copy of the award thinking it might change his view of things. It didn't. In a letter to my brother, he wrote that there must have been a mistake. The award must have come from the Methodists, he said, not the Mormons. He also set out, much to my embarrassment, to track down the person who had given me the award, and through a series of phone calls and letters to this person, managed to get him to write a letter stating that this award in no way was officially sanctioned by the church. My father then wrote to me: "Sadly, I have to inform you that your award doesn't come from the church, and therefore does not indicate any approval of your book. I have been assured that the only books officially sanctioned by the church are the Book of Mormon, The Pearl of Great Price, and The Doctrine and Covenants, and *not* The Chinchilla Farm."

IN TIME, MY father wrote to me again, this time with less anger, and I responded. I wrote back to him and tried to explain what it felt like to have become a writer. I talked about how I made my stories, how I worked each day. I wanted to try and help him understand how subjective an activity writing is, how memory and imagination become almost indistinguishable, like lovers whose bodies are inseparably pressed together in a dizzying dance. Slowly, we began corresponding: Dear Judith Ann, he wrote, your recent letter was appreciated. How I hope you'll be the correspondent you were before our unfortunate phone escapade . . .

Phone escapade. I looked at those two words. It seemed remarkable to me that what we'd been through could be reduced to this.

"Now a word about our misunderstanding," he continued. "What you penned in your letter is so true. It's so difficult to write about people we know—without the risk of someone becoming offended. Ninety percent of the trouble in the world stems from misunderstanding. Someone doesn't know the facts—or in pursuing a form of art, is dealing with too many uninformed people. I hope you will continue to try to educate me. We may not always see eye to eye on some issues, however, we should attempt to stay in the same 'camp'." He went on to discuss the recent turmoil surrounding the NEA, and how he thought they were practicing censorship, and how he believed this was wrong. It was better, he wrote, to promote artistic freedom in the world than to staunch the flow of true creativity.

Not too long afterward, I received another letter, which began this way: "My dear Judith: You must fill a void in my heart for I find myself thinking of you. I've written books to you . . ."

I am very touched by the capacity human beings have to endure, to go on, to forgive and attempt to understand, and especially, to write opening lines to a letter like those, at the age of eighty, after a life spent working as a truck driver, a shoe salesman, a mine employee and civil servant. I believe that at night, in his bed in the little trailer nestled among the red hills of southern Utah, my father probably did write books to me in his mind, books which I will never read, and unfortunately never understand.

Once I had a dream in which I saw clearly all the Time available in the universe; I saw just how much Time there was, and it was astonishing—so much Time, and then I became aware of what a tiny bit, what an infinitesimal amount was allotted to human beings, and it made me very sad. It was no Time at all, really, this human time, and it seemed immeasurably tragic that that's all we got, out of all the Time I could sense in the universe, just this little bit for us. Still, it's ours—whether it's sweeping forward, going back in memory, or standing still in the present, and I suppose that what I wish now, for myself, for every reader, and every writer, is that we make it as rich, as good a time, as possible.

I DIDN'T REALIZE just how short my father's remaining time would be. A few months after his last letter to me, during a particularly cool and pleasant July, my mother called to say my father was ill. He was no longer eating, and growing weaker by the day. "Come," she said, "if you can. He would like to see you."

I drove two days to be with him. The moment I walked into his room and saw him lying in his bed I saw the change in him, how much frailer, how very thin he'd become. He greeted me with more love than I could have imagined. "This is what I've been waiting for," he said.

There was much we needed to say to each other, and we talked a lot over the next few days. He asked two things of me, that I forgive him his anger and help keep his family strong and unified when he was gone. That was all that mattered to him, that his family would go on undivided by petty grievances.

He died a few days later on the night of a full moon, an auspicious passing. In the end, he got his wish: reconciled, we found ourselves in that same "camp" he'd spoken of, the place where families huddle, unprotected, weathering with often fragile capacity the inevitable emotional storms.

Laurie Gunst

P erhaps because she was raised as something of an outsider—a
Jew in the South—Laurie Gunst has always identified with
the mythic desperados in American Westerns. As a graduate
student in Caribbean history at Harvard, she started spending time
in Jamaica, and was fascinated to learn that members of the country's violent political gangs also identified with these Western heroes
and anti-heroes.

In time, the real life of the "sufferers" in Jamaica's shanty-
towns fascinated her more than the ivory tower; she realized she was
cut out to be a journalist rather than a scholar. She finished her doctorate but went on to spend a total of eight years of "immersion-
journalism" in Kingston and New York, studying the posses that
migrated north as part of the cocaine trade. Her work has cul-
minated in a book, Born Fi' Dead: A Journey through the Jamaican Posse Underworld, which was published by Henry Holt in
1995. Here, she meditates on the connections between the romantic
myth of the frontier desperado and the contemporary violence in
what is deemed by some the new frontier: the inner cities.

"The Harder They Fall"

from *Born Fi' Dead: A Journey through the Jamaican Posse Underworld*

ON A SWELTERING TROPICAL AFTERNOON IN THE spring of 1986, when I was living in Kingston, Jamaica, I went out to a shantytown called Homestead near the city to interview a gunman nicknamed Billy the Kid. Billy was an outlaw-prince in Homestead; he had procured a shipment of guns for some local mercenaries just before the crucial Jamaican election of 1980, a bloodbath in which almost a thousand people died in warfare between the island's rival political gangs. These gangs had started calling themselves "posses," an inverted homage to the Wild West desperados whose bravura style they loved.

I was then taking the first steps along the posses' outlaw trail, following an underground railroad that began in the ghettos of Kingston but would soon lead me to New York, Miami, and a dozen other cities where the Jamaican gangs shed their island political vendettas and became cocaine traffickers. Like all outlaw trails, it had no maps. But it was marked by a cultural resonance between the legendary bandits of the American frontier and Jamaica's own Johnny-Too-Bad desperados. The outlaws called themselves such names as Billy the Kid or Bucky Marshall, and the reggae stars took their cue from these ghetto heroes and adopted stage names like "Dillinger" and "the Outlaw Josey Wales." They were latter-day gunslingers with a certain cinematic panache.

My afternoon with Billy did not begin well. He was taciturn and evasive, hedging about his role in the 1980 gunplay. We were sitting in a tiny rumshop with a scratchy jukebox that played old

ballads by Marty Robbins and Tex Ritter—Jamaicans love country
music—when the friend who'd brought me to meet the Kid had a
sudden inspiration about how to put him at ease.

"Billy," said my friend Brambles, "this-here is one serious
daughter, you know. Is Wyoming she a' come from."

Billy's eyes lit up as he considered me with fresh respect.

"Whoy," he breathed in a reverent whisper. "I know 'bout that
place! Yeah, mon. I hear 'bout Hole-in-the-Wall, Butch Cassidy an'
the Sundance Kid. You ever see that flim?" (That is how Jamaicans
pronounce it.) "Bwoy, that was a great flim! So you know 'bout the
Wild West, eh? Well, is pure Wild West we have here in Jamaica."

And then Billy started to talk, with the engaging blend of mod-
esty and braggadocio common to outlaws everywhere. He figured
that if I came from Wyoming, I could understand the thrill of the
gunslinger's life.

THE JAMAICAN POSSES are the bastard offspring of their
country's own tortured political history and a Hollywood ethos that
glorified the banditry that many Jamaicans must take up in order to
survive. The poverty in their ghettos is so dire that Jamaicans bestow an honorific title, "the sufferers," upon the men and women
with the courage and resourcefulness to endure it.

The gangs of Kingston were spawned in the 1960s, when
Jamaica gained its independence from England and the island's
politicians began their fierce struggle for electoral power in the
city's thronged ghettos. The leaders knew that they could never
hope to control the slums without help from the top-ranking outlaws who had earned the sufferers' respect, so they started paying
and arming these gunmen as mercenary vigilantes. The criminals
became bagmen, labor brokers and terrorists for the politicians.
This was Jamaica's dirty little secret, the reality behind the island's
polite parliamentary facade. Everyone knew about it and lamented

its vicious results, but no one was willing to expose or dismantle this shadowy symbiosis between the politicians and their hired guns.

Although these downtown paladins worked for their uptown politician-patrons, they were also freelance bandits who robbed banks and the homes of the wealthy; they were Robin Hoods in a time-honored tradition. There was one notorious bandit of the 1970s, nicknamed Copper, who routinely raided the Kingston flour mill and distributed flour to the poor. There was the legendary Claudie Massop, a West Kingston gunman with a strong resemblance to Che Guevara, who had the courage to stand up to the politician for whom he worked and accuse this man of being nothing but a warlord. Claudie's bravery cost him his life: a few months after he dared to confront his patron, the police gunned him down in cold blood. Such men were dangerous desperados, but they had a bravura and proud rebelliousness that earned them an honored place in the sufferers' pantheon. Their exploits became the stuff of reggae legend, stories told again and again by the light of kerosene lanterns in the rumshops and tenement yards of downtown Kingston. These were the legends I heard when I began going to Jamaica in the 1970s, and it was this aspect of the island's outlaw underworld that first captured my heart and mind. Despite the abyss that yawned between their experience and mine, the same movies had given us our myths and shaped our vision of the world.

This confluence of the West Indies and the Wild West flashed before my eyes for the first time in 1975, as I sat in a Cambridge, Massachusetts, movie theater watching *The Harder They Come*. It is the saga of a real-life Jamaican desperado, a famous gunman from the 1950s named Ivan O. Martin. As played by the reggae singer Jimmy Cliff, Ivan is a country boy who comes to Kingston with big dreams of making it as a musician, only to get sucked down into the ghetto world of marijuana-dealing gangsterism. Just after Ivan gets to town, he goes with some friends to see a spaghetti Western,

Django, starring Franco Nero. Ivan sits in the audience of shining black faces lit by the glow from the screen and watches, transfixed, while Nero crouches behind a log on the muddy main street of some nameless Western town, facing down a posse of white-hooded vigilantes who stalk toward him with rifles.

Ivan holds his breath until one of his friends whispers that this isn't the end yet: "Hero can't dead till the las' reel!" The savvy kids from Kingston know the rules of this game. And then Nero leaps up from behind the log with a Gatling gun and mows down the entire posse. The audience howls with delight.

At the end of his own last reel, Ivan is on the run and cornered by a squadron of soldiers on a deserted beach near Kingston. Seriously wounded and hopelessly outgunned, he flashes back to that scene from *Django*. He staggers out from cover, a six-gun in each hand, and shouts for a chance to shoot it out in a fair fight.

"Jus' send out one mon!" he dares. "One mon who can draw!"

The soldiers cut him down in a barrage of machine-gun fire, a Jamaican replay of the Bolivian endgame for Butch Cassidy and the Sundance Kid.

I WAS LIVING two thousand miles from Kingston when I saw *The Harder They Come*, working on my doctorate in Caribbean history at Harvard. But I was already beginning to shuttle back and forth between the contemporary turbulence of Jamaica and the cool, battleship-gray stacks of Widener Library. This culture straddling was turning me into an alienated misfit with a divided heart, something I shared with one of my favorite professors, John Womack. He was the youngest tenured member of the history department, an Oklahoma-born Marxist who had written the definitive biography of the Mexican revolutionary Emiliano Zapata, and he came to lectures wearing jeans and cowboy boots. With his years of living in Mexico, he knew something about the confusion engendered by shuttling between Harvard's unquestioned privilege and the Third

World, and he told me something one night that later became a kind of valediction for me.

"I can paint the scenario for the next ten years of your life," he said. "You'll keep going back and forth to Jamaica. But the place will never be anything else to you than what it is now, a loved mystery. And neither will you ever be really comfortable here again. Eventually, you'll become a full-fledged exile in both places."

The idea of exile was terrifying, but it was familiar, too, because I had grown up as a kind of self-proclaimed outsider. I came of age in the South during the civil-rights movement, in a family of liberal Jews; we were therefore on the perimeters of Virginia's established conservatism. I grew up seeing the abundant heroism of black southerners and the cowardice of too many whites, and I was constantly trying to make sense of a moral universe where there was a clear line between right and wrong but tremendous pressure to fit in: the legacy of being an assimilated minority. So I took my child's deep longing for certainty and righteousness to the movies, and the movies were almost always Westerns.

I remember two that changed me forever. The first was *The Magnificent Seven*, with Yul Brynner leading a posse of gunfighters to defend a tiny Mexican village against marauding bandits. It was about fighting back against injustice, something I was thinking a lot about then because my older sister had recently taken me along to a sit-in at the Woolworth's lunch counter downtown, where we were menaced by a tribe of shouting segregationists. This was nothing compared to the firebombings and Klan murders that were then going down all across the South, but it still taught me a lesson in fear. So the character in *The Magnificent Seven* who won my heart was the posse's coward, played by Robert Vaughn. His was a classic Western role—the gunfighter who has lost his nerve—but I knew that he was going to find it again in a blaze of courage before he died in the climactic shootout.

The second movie was *Lonely Are the Brave*, which I saw at the

ripe age of ten. Although I didn't know it then, this was my first
brush with Edward Abbey, who wrote the novel on which that film
was based. It was also about civil disobedience, played out against
the backdrop of a contemporary West I had never imagined. Kirk
Douglas plays a modern-day cowboy who runs afoul of the law after
he tries to spring a friend from jail, a man who landed behind bars
because he smuggled Mexican illegals across the Rio Grande.
Douglas is paired not with a woman, but with a horse named Whiskey, whom he will not leave behind even when the mountainous terrain into which he flees makes the going impossible for his horse.
They are both under siege from the modern West, a landscape that
would once have sheltered a valiant rebel but in which this horse
and rider no longer have a place. Trying to cross a rainy highway,
they are hit by a truck and Whiskey dies. I was so stunned by this
bitter ending that I failed to even cry. I think this movie was my
first taste of the twentieth-century West, with all its grandeur and
sorrow.

I took these movies not so much as lessons about machismo
and violence, but as metaphors for my own loneliness. They taught
me about alienation and the inevitability of loss. They were mirrors
held up to my girl-child's universe, and I never thought to question
their absence of heroines. I just did a shape-shift and identified completely with the men: outlaws, misfits and rebels with whom I discovered an affinity that I never quite gave up.

I grew up to become a historian, someone who finds her bear-
ings by delving into the past. That journey eventually took me to
Harvard, although I never could bring myself to feel entirely comfortable within that bastion of male power. And in the midst of my
doctoral thrashings, at the same time that Jamaica and its pica-
resque outlaws were entering my life through one door, the West
was coming in through another. In the summer of 1976, I went to
Wyoming for the first time. Like so many women, I followed a man:
in this case, a Harvard law student whose family had settled in Wy-

oming and who rather casually invited me to come see the place
where he lived. My marriage had crumbled the year before, and I
was feeling adventurous.

The little town where I spent that summer was in Wind River
Valley, at the western end of a region that starts in the Red Desert
country around Lander and breaks along the Continental Divide on
the way to the Teton range. The area is a mother lode of history,
part of the territory where outlaws from the Hole-in-the-Wall gang
sometimes laid low when they were on the run from the law. There
were ranchers still living in the valley whose parents had wintered
Butch Cassidy like any other cowboy who rode the grub line. Cassidy was friendly with a Lander freight driver, Eugene Amoretti,
who had a spread near town where the outlaw spent the winter of
1892. There were stories about Butch's riding down to Fort Wa-
shakie through a blizzard to fetch a doctor for a sick child at a
neighboring ranch. Old men in Lander thought they had seen Butch
long after he was supposedly killed in Bolivia, and they told apocryphal tales about his Robin Hood kindness: how he robbed banks and
then gave some of the money back to the widows of men whom the
banks had evicted from their homesteads.

"I have often given some of the victims back their part," Butch
said once to no less a figure than Ethelbert Talbot, the Episcopal
bishop of Wyoming, whom he met one day on a lonely road where
the bishop's stagecoach broke down. "I know how you feel, bishop,"
the outlaw said, "that a man should obey the law. That is the law of
the Almighty God, and God did not order that families should be
turned out of their homes and go hungry so [some banker's] bank-
roll should grow fatter. An animal will leave a carcass after he gets
his belly full, but you never see a banker do that."

It was not just the stories of long-gone desperados that made
me feel at home in Wyoming; it was the present-day plethora of
remarkable women who gave this little town so much of its life.
They were female ranchers and horse wranglers, newspaper editors

and environmental activists who astonished me with their independence and sense of place. They taught me lessons about self-
acceptance that somehow began healing wounds I did not even
know I had, the lesions from a Southern girlhood in which I had
always felt scrutinized and spurned for being too much myself. Like
thousands of Eastern misfits before me, I discovered a territory that
set no limits on self-definition, and it beckoned me into a freedom I
had not known.

I went back to this town every summer. In 1983 I summoned
enough nerve to "prove up" by buying a place of my own there. By
then I had earned my doctorate; along with that came the necessity
of kicking myself out of Harvard's treacherously safe nest. I was
still mesmerized by Jamaica and its violent politics, and I decided to
move to Kingston and take a teaching job at the University of the
West Indies. But my real purpose was to write the secret history of
the island's outlaw gangs. For Jamaica was still the "loved mystery"
that my teacher John Womack had long ago called it. That tiny island had been my "teachment," the place that kept yanking me out
of the safety and removal I came to despise at Harvard, into that
place that academics so blithely call "the real world." For although I
did not know it, I was already turning from a historian into a journalist. I had buried myself for ten years in the archives; it was time
to leave the land of the dead for that of the living, with all the risks
that such a move entailed.

In Kingston, I befriended and slowly earned the trust of men
and women in the ghettos downtown, sufferers who were the true
and only experts on the history of the gangs. The man called Brambles became my closest friend, and with him I moved for the better
part of a year through the downtown labyrinth of gunmen and
posses.

I met men who'd fought Jamaica's undeclared civil war between the two parties, black paladins on a tropical frontier who
drew whatever sense they had of life's scarce meaning from the leg-

ends they saw on the silver screen. I got to know an aging gang leader named Dixie who wept whenever we played "Ghost Riders in the Sky" on the jukebox at the rumshop where we drank. I met children who already knew the difference between the sound of a single-shot revolver and the rapid-fire assault rifles that had become the weapon of choice among right-wing gunmen, courtesy of the CIA. I got to know the top cop on the Kingston police force, a killer in uniform who earned his nickname, "Trinity," from a spaghetti Western with an anti-hero of the same name. Trinity was fond of going to downtown Kingston's dancehalls dressed all in black, like a gunfighter. By his own reckoning, he'd been in some 97 shootouts with Kingston's desperados, but he modestly pretended to have stopped counting years ago.

But the person I loved best was Brambles, perhaps because he and I both lived in multiple worlds. He was born and raised in the waterfront ghetto where he still lived, but he was also a superb photojournalist who dedicated his skills to picturing this world, and he let me know how limited my own vision of it often was.

"You take things for granted," he said one night as we sat in his yard downtown, "for you are very pampered. But these people who you talk with are professors in their own right. Let's call them the professors of poverty. And regardless of your education, you could not survive one week in this ghetto without prostituting yourself. These people don't have any protection. They are strong. They are resilient. Yet they are only the victims of circumstance, the pawns in the game of power politics."

I had learned the viciousness of that game by then, so well that my early, naive preference for Jamaica's leftist politicians had evaporated in the fearsome recognition that the left was every bit as corrupted by political thuggery as the right. Brambles had presided over my sorrowful disillusionment; it mirrored his own coming to terms with Jamaica's grim truths, and he was gentle about this teachment.

"You are not here to say who is good and who is bad," he offered. "You should only be committed to reality."

Despite the violence of this gang underworld, I was drawn to its outlaws by their Wild West vision of themselves. Like the cowboy heroes and anti-heroes I had fallen for as a girl, they taught me about endurance and survival. But by the end of my two years in Kingston, as I was getting ready to leave that city for New York and to follow the outlaw trail north, I had come to recognize that this Jamaican underworld was no frontier fantasy. My criminal compañeros were not turn-of-the-century bandits: they, and their enthusiastic use of excessive force, belonged to the twentieth century with a vengeance. They sold cocaine and heroin instead of stolen cattle; they killed police in cold blood instead of defending their homesteads from bankers or cattle barons. And when they lit out for territory, it wasn't Monument Valley. It was the inner cities of the American promised land that became their turf, a hellish landscape where they made their stand.

The right-wing regime that was installed after Jamaica's brutal 1980 election had used the gunmen during the campaign, but afterwards it had no more use for their services. The ruling politicians gave Jamaica's police a free rein in the ghettos, letting them execute as many gunmen as they could. Meanwhile, the island simmered back into an ominous quiet, locked down tighter than a sardine can by its own ruthless government and the International Monetary Fund, which laid siege to the island's threadbare, debt-ridden economy and devastated what was left of its social infrastructure. So the gunmen read the handwriting on the wall and left Kingston by the thousands, moving to the United States where the inner-city crack epidemic was just beginning. The Latino cocaine bosses who controlled the trade needed street-level black dealers to sell their product; the Jamaican gangsters, hardened by years of fighting the island's police and each other, were excellent candidates. By the time I left Jamaica and began following the posses into their American hegira, these gangs had killed over two thousand people in this country, and they were becoming the deadliest cocaine syndicates in the United States.

I knew some of the posse leaders from Kingston; others I met on the streets or in the prisons of New York. Some were hardened criminals who took their murderous style from the violent movies of the post-Vietnam era, the rotgut deathfests and Rambo fantasies that Hollywood churns out to satisfy this country's appetite for carnage. One posse youth who had grown up on a steady diet of cinematic cruelty told me how the Westerns had influenced his friends and the leader of their gang, a killer named Delroy Edwards.

"Even before I killed somebody," this young man said, "I felt like I killed before. I think maybe Hollywood had a part in the posse thing, with the movies they put out. Like certain Westerns. Jamaicans act out a lot of that stuff, want to be tough like outlaws. Even Delroy. Every time he would shoot somebody we would say, 'Hey! You just got another notch in your gun.' "

But most of the gang members and street-level dealers I came to know had never killed anyone; they were caught in the drug trade's web simply because there was no other work on the streets where they lived. Uneducated and unskilled, they were marginalized by the legal economy and desperate for money. I got to know a Jamaican crack dealer named Luke only a month before he was killed by his cocaine supplier, to whom he owed $2,000.

"I'm not thinking about sitting up here and selling drugs for the rest of my life," Luke said. "I try to get legal jobs here but I don't succeed, and I have a family to feed down in Jamaica. Someday, though, I'm going home."

I listened to the tape of our conversation after Luke was already dead; I had not found the time to transcribe our interview until a friend on the street called to tell me that he had been gunned down the night before. When I listened to his voice, I thought about the legends that still follow many a Western outlaw: how they never intended to take up that life but were delivered into it by poverty and need. As Butch Cassidy once said, "I never feared no man and I would not take a life, but they have pushed me in this situation."

It took five years of immersion-journalism on the streets of New York before I became close enough with some of these men to enter their lives and bring to a close the story that began in Kingston. By the end of my journey through this underworld, I came to wonder if, as Brambles had long ago advised me, I had been able to keep my commitment to reality. And I also began to wonder if, in the cities where most of us live and where millions of marginalized people are struggling to survive, drug dealing has not taken the place that cattle rustling and bank robbery once held on the Western frontier. There are many sociologists who speak of urban America itself as the twentieth-century frontier, a theater of danger and risk. Now, living partly in Wyoming but mostly in New York, I still treasure the hard questions that were put before me by the time I've spent with people who dwell on the other side of the law.

I remind myself these days of the nervous journalist in Clint Eastwood's *Unforgiven*, the bowler-hatted author of penny-dreadfuls who trails the gunfighter English Bob from one shootout to another, vainly trying to get the straight story on assorted mythic episodes. The time comes when this little man gets to see a real-life gunfight, and that's the end of his fantasies about killing. Yet he stays with English Bob. And I have stuck by the friends I made in the posse world. But unlike the journalist from *Unforgiven*, I have a modern-day agenda: to understand the violence that has become the signal pathology of our time. And I am still riding into the West, looking there for clues to the twentieth century.

Janet Campbell Hale

J anet Campbell Hale is the author of two novels, The Owl's Song (1974) and The Jailing of Cecilia Capture (1985), and a personal history, Bloodlines: Odyssey of a Native Daughter (1993). Born in Los Angeles in 1946, she spent the majority of her first ten years with her parents on the Coeur d'Alene Indian reservation in northern Idaho. Growing up, she attended twenty-one schools in three western states. She has a B.A. from the University of California at Berkeley and an M.A. from the University of California at Davis. Like tens of thousands of other Native Americans, much of Hale's experience is that of being an urban Indian, cut off, and, in her case, even estranged, from her ancestral lands. She now resides in New York.

Her maternal great-great-grandfather was a white man, Dr. John McLoughlin, better known in history books as chief factor for the Hudson's Bay Company (1821–42) and the official "Father of Oregon." His wife was a Chippewa. As she observes in Bloodlines, however, the family's name, Campbell, is derived from the Indian name of her paternal great-grandfather, Col-man-nee, who was born about 1820, and she descends from a long line of full-bloods on both sides of her family. Regretfully, the Campbells are "the last remaining family of what was once the powerful, but now little re-

membered, Turtle clan." As Nobel Prize winner Toni Morrison puts it, "Janet Campbell Hale's gifts are genuine and deeply felt." In this essay she writes about her life as a teenaged single mother on the run from an abusive husband while living on $145 per month in the Haight-Ashbury district of San Francisco during the late 1960s.

"Transitions"

from *Bloodlines*

THE SONG THAT ALWAYS REMINDS ME OF THE SUM-mer I was nineteen is the old Simon and Garfunkel hit, "I Am a Rock." I lived in San Francisco then in a room with a view (and little else), and "I Am a Rock" played several times an hour throughout the day on the Top 40 radio station I listened to.

A young man named Derek, a student who lived in my building, loaned me (and would later give me when my baby son and I moved on) that radio. It was all I had in my room at the top of the stairs, a little furnished attic room in a renovated Victorian on Haight Street near Ashbury. I was virtually penniless, though I got enough welfare to pay the rent and buy enough groceries to keep us going. I had nothing left over for such luxuries as bus fare or to buy a can of soda pop or an ice-cream bar, let alone to pay the price of admission at the movies. My neighborhood was full of people, some young, some not so young, who were dropping out, turning on and tuning in. I didn't have the wherewithal for any of that, though.

Derek loaned me books, whatever was left from his humanities and social sciences courses that couldn't be resold. I read a lot of these books. I had to wash diapers every day by hand and I vomited every time I did. I never did get used to soiled diapers, and my son would not be toilet trained for over a year.

"I am a rock . . . I am an I-I-Island!" played in the background all that summer.

My son, then a year old, had no playthings. He made do with cardboard boxes and books and other little odds and ends. The single mother who lived on the floor below us gave him some plastic toys for his bath. The weather was always nice, and we had a park nearby that we went to often. My son was healthy, strong, beautiful. And, the important thing, I kept reminding myself, besides having a roof over our heads and food to eat, was this: We were safe. Safe at last. I had successfully left my husband, and so far he didn't know where we were. (Though I knew that he eventually would. The welfare office would force him to make child-support payments to them, and in exchange he would have "visitation rights." But I would cross that bridge when I came to it. For right then we were safe.)

The last time I'd left him, after a beating, he'd tracked me down. I don't know how he found me. Maybe someone he knew had seen me go into the welfare hotel. Maybe he himself had seen me. Maybe he had seen me one day in the vicinity and followed me. What he told me, though, he who was then a psychiatric social worker at San Francisco General Hospital, was that he had guessed that I had gone to welfare and gotten on Aid to the Indigent (he knew I didn't have any money) and that I would be using my own (maiden) name, not his. He had called welfare, he said, identified himself as a social worker, told the records clerk that I had been admitted as a patient to San Francisco General and he needed to know my address and other pertinent information for his files. She gave him my address over the phone. Whether or not this was true, I have no way of knowing. But this was what he told me. He had ways of finding me. At any rate, he did find me and came knocking at my door.

"Who is it?" No answer. Silence. Then more knocking. "Who's there?" Again no answer. I'd been there a week, almost. The only visitors I ever got were the hotel manager's daughters, who were about twelve and thirteen. Who else could it be? Possibly someone from welfare. I opened my door.

He had a big, heavy ashtray from the hotel lobby (though I didn't know what it was at first; I just felt the blow that knocked me to the floor), the kind that isn't meant to go anywhere, with sharp metal handles on each side. This is what he hit me with. The wound near my eye spurted blood like a geyser. It left a scar, an indentation about a quarter of an inch from my right eye.

I also had a bump on one eyelid (I can't remember which one) left over from a black eye inflicted by him. The doctors told me this lump was "an organized blood clot" and could not be removed. They said I would probably have it all of my life. People were always asking me how I got it (salesclerks, people at bus stops, people who interviewed me for jobs). Anyone. Everyone. "How did you get that lump on your eyelid?" they would ask, even though it was only visible when I closed my eyes or glanced down. Or to one side. The lump went away of its own accord about three years after I left the room at the top of the stairs.

I have no fond memories of my first brief marriage to a white man who clearly looked down on me. I was barely eighteen. He was the first person I ever knew, aside from schoolteachers, who had a college education. Was I impressed with that? Maybe I was. Maybe I was impressed because he and his similarly white and college-educated friends marched against U.S. involvement in Vietnam and picketed Bank of America in protest of its discriminatory hiring practices, because they listened to K-Jazz radio and owned expensive stereo equipment to play their jazz and classical records on and they read Jack Kerouac and Henry Miller and Ken Kesey. They were hip. I was not. They rejected the values of their parents' generation. All I knew about was getting by from one day to the next.

Clearly this was not a marriage of equals.

Once he handed me a matchbook cover in front of his hip, jazz-buff friends that advertised "Earn Your High School Diploma at Home by Mail" and said, "This is what you should do!" But had I not dropped out of school I *still* wouldn't have been out of high school yet. I wasn't his age, after all. I was just a kid. But he and his friends got a good laugh out of the matchbook cover "joke."

One day when I was seven or eight months pregnant we went over to Berkeley to see the police haul away the Free Speech demonstrators from Sproul Hall. I had no idea then that this great university would one day be *my* university, that this would be the place that would open a new world to me and lead me back into active involvement in an Indian community. I never thought of a future for myself in those days.

When I had a baby things changed. For his sake, I told myself, I *can* imagine a future. I can be more than I was. I can be strong. I can be a rock.

That was how I came to spend the summer of '66 in a plain, white-walled attic room in the Haight-Ashbury all alone except for my son, and flat broke, making do, waiting for time to pass, for a better day, bored and unspeakably lonely, but safe at last and free, with a lump on one eyelid and a scar by my right eye, listening to Simon and Garfunkel singing about emotional and social isolation.

AS THE SUMMER WORE ON, I spent more evenings with Derek, whose room, like himself, was impeccably neat and clean. He was from Jamaica, was a graduate student in physics at San Francisco State College, worked full-time at Bank of America, budgeted every dime. He was one serious, hard-working (and, I thought, uptight) boy. He thought I was aimless, though he didn't say so in as many words.

"Why don't you do something? Go to school? Get a job?"

"I can't, Derek."

"Ain't no such word as *can't*."

"Hey, Mon," I said, trying to sound sort of like him, "can't you see I've got a little baby and nothing else? I'm all alone. How am I supposed to do something?"

"So . . . you got some plans?"

I didn't, not yet, but if I did, I wouldn't tell him. He told me he came from such wretched poverty, I could not imagine. No American could, he said. When he was a boy, he used to dive for silver coins tourists would toss from ships. But he had become educated. Now he had a future. Once or twice I went out to eat and to a movie with Derek, conscious every minute of the hard-earned money he was spending, uncomfortable because of this and because I knew he thought me lazy. Looking back some years later, I wondered if Derek realized then how young I was or if he imagined I was near his age, which was twenty-three or twenty-four.

A few months later I moved into an apartment in another building in another neighborhood at the end of Castro Street. Derek helped me move, told me to keep the radio and surprised me with a gift of twenty dollars. He told me to call him if I "needed anything." He would drop by once in a while when I lived on Castro Street. I was always glad to see him (and glad to see him leave).

My new apartment was cheaper, larger, better, much better, and there were other young welfare mothers and their babies living in that building, people, in other words, like ourselves. New friends. We welfare girls traded babysitting. Sometimes I worked as an office temp and brought home a few dollars. I bought an ancient console television for twenty dollars (I hadn't watched TV in years, since my ex was too intellectual for TV). I got a goldfish. I had girlfriends my own age at last, with babies and no husbands. I wasn't so lonely anymore. I was passably happy then. My little son and I used to dance to the radio (no more "I Am a Rock") to "Wild Thing" and the one that goes "Hot time, summer in the city," and to Bob Dylan singing, "How does it feeeeeeeellll . . . to be on your own . . . like a rollin' stone . . ."

My son used to like to hear about an incident that occurred when we lived on Castro Street. "Tell me about the time I went out on the edge of the roof of a high building and you got me to come back by tricking me."

HE WAS A FAST-MOVING, rambunctious, full-of-the-devil toddler at the time. He liked to run away from me, now that he could run.

We went up on the roof of our building, which was eight stories tall, one warm, sunshiny day for a little outing. I'd brought a blanket to lie on and a *Cosmopolitan* magazine (which was full of stories about sex and the single girl), the radio Derek had given me, and a few toys for my son. The roof was all safely fenced in with a chain-link fence.

In one corner was a large chicken-wire cage of some sort. Maybe pigeons had been kept there once.

I lay down and began reading my magazine while my son played nearby. Once in a while he would stop playing to dance around a bit if he heard some danceable music playing on our radio. He went inside the cage in the corner. I dozed off a little.

Then suddenly I was wide awake. I sat up and looked around. There was my son standing on the narrow ledge of the roof (about four feet wide) outside the fence. He'd gone through the pigeon cage (if that's what it was) and through a small hole in the wire I hadn't seen.

First I told him to come back in a very stern voice. "You come back here right now!" A wide grin spread across his face. Running-away time. He was about to start running, clumsy little toddler that he was, on that narrow strip of tar and gravel that was all there was between him and eternity.

I dropped to my knees then and held my face in my hands and began to pretend to cry, sobbing loudly. He seemed to give up the idea of running away, at least for the moment, and began to inch back towards the hole in the wire, back towards me and safety. But he seemed to sense a trick and didn't climb through. (As an older child he would remember how I had pretended to cry sometimes to get him to do what I wanted when he was little. I was "shamelessly manipulative," he said. Sometimes I had to be.)

Finally I picked up the paper bag that had contained his toys and my magazine and began pretending to take pieces of candy from it and pop them into my mouth.

"Yum," I said, pretending to chew, "this candy sure is good. Yum, yum."

In no time at all he climbed through the hole in the wire, back into the cage and out of it, and was in my arms, asking for candy.

MY EX-HUSBAND found us again on Castro Street, but he didn't physically threaten me anymore. I had no phone. No car. No job. No future. I was such a mess, he would say, nothing but a no-class welfare bum. I didn't have a pot to pee in, he would sneer . . . and look at the dump I lived in, what a loser I was. Then I would feel downhearted for a while. My ex had money (not really a lot, but it seemed like a lot to me), drove a nice car, wore good clothes. What did I have? Well, I had my boy. And now that I was rid of my ex, I had myself.

By Christmas I had a boyfriend (a friend of a friend who lived in my building) from England. He was as poor as Derek but was not uptight and hardworking . . . he was a rolling stone (wherever he hung his hat was his home). He was not critical of me. He would play his guitar and sing to me. He would tell me of his travels. Of course he'd been to Paris and Rome. And he had seen the Taj Mahal, too, and the pyramids in Egypt. He was company and, when my ex found out about him, he didn't exercise his visitation rights as often. Then my ex got a better job, which required him to move to a city far from San Francisco. Before he left, he warned me that I had better not ask for more than fifty dollars per month child support when I got the divorce. Fifty dollars was all I asked for.

My boyfriend took me to see *Doctor Zhivago* on my twentieth birthday. Then he was gone. To Australia, I think.

ONCE, I APPLIED TO A PROGRAM at the Youth Opportunity Center that was for unmarried mothers under the age of twenty-one who were on welfare and didn't have any job skills and were lacking a high school diploma. The federally funded program ran for something like five or six months. Participants were provided money for child care, bus fare, books and supplies, and even a small clothing allowance. Participants would receive training as clerk-typists while earning a high school diploma (in those days I didn't know about the GED, the high school equivalency exam, and I didn't think it was possible for a person to go to college without first finishing high school). I was very excited about the program at the Youth Opportunity Center. I was all set. But on the day I went in to begin my training, I was stopped short by my counselor. She had received my high school transcripts. "You weren't honest with us," she said to me in an angry tone. "You lied to us."

"How did I lie?"

"You said you were sure you could handle our program. Your transcripts are very, very poor. A D in math, a D in English . . . an F in social studies. You hardly even went to school at all. You know as well as I do you don't have what it takes to either become a clerk-typist or to earn a high school diploma." She had already made an appointment for me to interview for a job as a domestic. She handed me the referral card I was to give to my prospective employer. My interview would be in an hour, "so you'll have to hurry." I took the referral card from her and, right in front of her face, I tore it into little pieces and dropped it in the wastebasket.

I HAD SOME FULL-TIME JOBS. One, as a clerk-typist at Southern Pacific Hospital, I lost because they found out I had lied about being twenty-four and about having attended college for two years. Another, at the post office, I had to quit because of the irregular hours I had to work and problems finding a reliable sitter.

Then I found out, from a neighbor, that I could go to open-admissions, tuition-free City College of San Francisco without having finished high school if I were twenty-one, which I soon would be. I took the entrance exam at City College and passed with scores so high I wouldn't have to take any remedial courses at all but could begin a program of university-parallel courses that were transferable to any four-year college or university in California. (My ex, who was not only white but who lived in one place all of his growing-up years and always knew he would be going to college—the man who had so looked down on me—had had to take a remedial English course when he began college. Ah, how sweet it was!)

I put my son on a waiting list at a beautiful state-subsidized child-care center. For just seven dollars per week they would keep him all day, five days a week, and they would give him a hot breakfast and lunch and late-afternoon snack.

We had to move again—this time to a ratty suite above a bar between Mission and South Van Ness. (I didn't know my rights as a tenant in those days . . . and even if I had known them, I don't think I would have been able to stand up to a much older, more powerful landlord and assert them. I tended to let myself get pushed around, as poor people do.) There were cigarette burns all over the carpet in my new place. It was the former apartment of a prostitute before she got busted on drug-related charges. (My new neighbors told me all about it. It had caused a lot of excitement in the building. They were all concerned about what had happened to her sweet little poodle after the bust when she was carted off to jail.) Men were always coming there when I first moved in, ringing the doorbell at all hours. I would stick my head out the window and ask them what they wanted and tell them she was gone. A few of them asked me if I was "a working girl" too. Not likely.

I bought a bicycle at the Purple Heart Thrift Store and had a passenger seat put on the back. That was where my son rode when we went tooling around the city. We would race down the steep hill at Mission Dolores Park on that bike and cruise around Golden Gate Park on it. We would go out to Playland at the Beach and go down the giant wooden indoor slides. Sometimes we would go to Powell and Market and ride the cable cars for fun. It only cost fifteen cents for adults in those days, and children rode free. The most exciting part of the ride would be when a car would slip from its cable and coast wildly down one of those steep San Francisco hills. We liked that. I heard that doesn't happen anymore.

Shortly before my twenty-first birthday, I was informed by the day-care center that there would be a space for my son, provided he was fully toilet trained (he was), in time for the coming semester at City College. I used one of my old Wapato girlfriends' Youth Fare Card (for people nineteen and under) and took the airplane home for a visit. My son's passage was free. It was cheaper flying than it would have been taking the Greyhound bus.

We had a good visit with my parents (they had settled once and for all in Wapato by this time). My mother had just begun to use a wheelchair (this was the first time I saw her in a wheelchair), but she was still able to get herself in and out of bed and into the bathroom. She still liked to cook. She didn't seem to be suffering much anymore . . . or at least she didn't for the few days we were there.

MY SON AND I went with my father to Idaho, to our reservation during that time, about a twelve-hour round-trip by car. He had business to attend to regarding his land and tribal politics, and he was taking me to talk to the tribal chairman, his lifelong friend, regarding an education grant to attend college.

Without some kind of help I didn't know how I could make it. Welfare only gave me $145 per month (my ex sent his $50 child-support payments directly to welfare) and out of that, $95 had to go for rent. After paying the day-care center $7 per week, I would have $28 per month. That $28 would have to cover everything. (Food stamps in those days were not free. You were required to purchase a certain minimum, I think $25 per month for $100 worth of stamps. I had never been able to purchase this minimum.) Food, clothing, and laundry for the two of us and bus fare, books and supplies for myself had to come out of that $28. It just wasn't possible, or so I thought, without some kind of help. My father felt confident that I would get a grant from the tribe. I remember our trip to the Coeur d'Alene Reservation as very pleasant, despite the cold, overcast day, and, in Idaho, a light snow. I'd made that same trip with my father or with both parents many times, but this was the first time I'd gone home as an adult. I didn't know it then, but this was the last few days I'd ever spend with Dad, as he would die suddenly, of a heart attack, in March of the following year.

My son had a very good singing voice, even at a very young age (a special gift, I always thought, but he said I just thought so because he was my kid). He began, as we sailed along the highway heading east, to sing like a flute. Dad told him his flute sounded beautiful, and it did. Dad had never heard anything like it. My little boy kept up his flute for a long while, an hour or more. It was a happy flute, but subtle, too, and full of emotional intensity.

THIS WAS THE FIRST TIME I thought about connections to people who had come before, connections to the land—about ancestral roots that predated the white society that had superimposed itself onto North America. And this was the first time I thought about my own posterity . . . of the possibility of my own bloodline continuing down through the ages.

I had taken my camera along and I took pictures of what seemed like nothing much when I got them developed and got a look at them: my home, my first home. The wild hills. The tall trees. The snow. I took a picture of Dad too. I insisted. In this photo he's standing under a pine tree, its branches behind his head and the snow is falling lightly. He's still handsome at seventy-five, still looks strong and vital and at least ten years younger than he really is. This was the last picture that would ever be taken of him. I have it still. We went to the agency and saw the tribal chairman. He assured me that the tribe would send me six hundred dollars as soon as I sent proof of my enrollment at City College.

TWO DAYS LATER, when my son and I were all packed and ready to go to the Yakima airport for our flight back to San Francisco International (my father would drive us—Mom was staying home), my parents, smiling and looking very proud of themselves, presented me with a surprise, two going-to-college presents: a little old Smith Corona typewriter made during World War II but in perfect condition, and one hundred dollars cash. I was overwhelmed. I could tell that they'd planned their surprise together. I knew, too, that for them the purchase of that typewriter and the hundred dollars was a huge outlay. It represented a big sacrifice on their part.

The last time I saw my father, he was standing at the fence at the airport in the snow. We were in the airplane and we could see Dad, but he couldn't see us. My son waved to him and called good-bye. As the small plane began to taxi down the field, Dad waved to us—which made my son think he saw us. I felt like crying, but controlled myself. I didn't want to set a bad (crybaby) example.

BACK IN SAN FRANCISCO, my first year of college was most difficult, to say the least. Sometimes non-Indians would say things to me like, "The government pays for your education, doesn't it, since you're an Indian," or "Your tribe helped you out, didn't it?"

My tribe did help me during that first horrible year, but not the way you might think, not in a conventional way. I say "horrible" because some horrible things happened. We had to move twice, for instance. Once I got the Hong Kong flu and was so sick, I had to crawl on my hands and knees to get to the bathroom. But that was during Christmas break, and somehow we managed, and my boy didn't get the flu. The worst, or one of the worst, the scariest thing that happened was my little boy got sick one night, very, very sick. He ran a high fever and had chills and was delirious. I had no way of getting him to a hospital. I left him alone in our apartment and went out to a pay phone about three blocks away and called the emergency room of the nearest hospital and asked to speak with a physician. The doctor told me that there was no time to bring him in; if I didn't act very quickly, he would soon go into convulsions. He instructed me to give him aspirin (I had to knock on the doors of ten neighbors before I got one answer that time of night and borrowed some aspirin) and to stand him in a tub, ankle-deep, of cool water and to sponge him all over for about twenty minutes . . . and then to do it again ten minutes later if he weren't much better. I only had to do it once. He was much better. By the next day his temperature was back down to normal and he was as lively as could be. I had no idea what had caused his illness.

We had a lot of rough times. The tribe never did send any money, but they never said they wouldn't, and that was how they helped. They kept accepting my long-distance calls, kept telling me my money would be coming soon. "Now it has to be approved by another committee," or "Now it has to be sent to Lapwai (the Bureau of Indian Affairs office for northern Idaho) for final approval," or "Your check will be issued from the Portland Area Office. This will take a little time." My money would always be coming soon.

If I had known that all I would have while I went to college was $145 per month—$28 after rent and child care—I wouldn't even have attempted it. But that $600 check was always on its way. I can hang on until the first of the month, I would tell myself. Or, I can do it for just two more weeks. Not long now. And I would dream of the food and clothes I was going to buy, and all the textbooks and pens. Maybe we would take in a movie. Somehow I made it through my first year. And I passed all of my courses.

Then I spoke with my father's old friend who had assured me the tribe would be sending me a six-hundred-dollar education grant that day in Idaho, and he told me he was really sorry, but they had had no more money at the time I applied. They approved my application, though, and they thought maybe they would get some more money during the school year. They didn't want to tell me there wasn't any money. They didn't want me to give up hope. I told him I would never have made it without that hope.

I TOOK THE SAT and applied for admission to the University of California at Berkeley. I was accepted. And I was granted tuition waivers and scholarships and educational loans. I would be a welfare mother no more. I was twenty-two years old.

Linda Hasselstrom

L inda Hasselstrom is the author of two books of poetry and three
books of nonfiction. Like other women in this anthology, she
lives where she works: on a cattle ranch in western South Dakota. For her, such experiences as climbing alone into a corral with
an angry bull or pitching hay to cattle in thirty-degree-below-zero
weather are commonplace. She graduated from the University of
South Dakota at Vermillion. After graduate school in American
literature at the University of Missouri, she and her first husband
moved back to South Dakota to ranch in 1973. There they founded a
literary magazine, Sunday Clothes, and Lame Johnny Press
(named after a horse thief). Although the couple divorced, Hasselstrom continued to publish the magazine and Lame Johnny Books
for eleven years. While teaching at Black Hills State College during
the 1974–75 academic year, she met George R. Snell. They were
married in 1979. Although George had already survived two battles
with Hodgkin's disease when Linda met him, he was still under
treatment. At one point, his doctors told him that he was completely
free of the disease and that it might never come back, but George died
from the side effects of his treatments in 1988. In 1991, Hasselstrom
published Land Circle, a hefty collection of thirty-three poems and
thirty-three essays. Few books in American literature have successfully sustained such an ambitious design, and of those that have, even

fewer have found as many readers among both ordinary people and scholars. In this essay taken from the book, we can easily see why.

"Why One Peaceful Woman Carries a Pistol"

from *Land Circle*

I'M A PEACE-LOVING WOMAN. I ALSO CARRY A PIStol. For years, I've written about my decision in an effort to help other women make intelligent choices about gun ownership, but editors rejected the articles. Between 1983 and 1986, however, when gun sales to men held steady, gun ownership among women rose fifty-three percent, to more than twelve million. We learned that any female over the age of twelve can expect to be criminally assaulted some time in her life, that women aged thirty have a fifty-fifty chance of being raped, robbed, or attacked, and that many police officials say flatly that they cannot protect citizens from crime. During the same period, the number of women considering gun ownership quadrupled to nearly two million. Manufacturers began showing lightweight weapons with small grips, and purses with built-in holsters. A new magazine is called *Guns and Women,* and more than eight thousand copies of the video *A Woman's Guide to Firearms* were sold by 1988. Experts say female gun buyers are not limited to any particular age group, profession, social class, or area of the country, and most are buying guns to protect themselves. Shooting instructors say women view guns with more caution than do men, and may make better shots.

I decided to buy a handgun for several reasons. During one

four-year period, I drove more than a hundred thousand miles alone, giving speeches, readings, and workshops. A woman is advised, usually by men, to protect herself by avoiding bars, by approaching her car like an Indian scout, by locking doors and windows. But these precautions aren't always enough. And the logic angers me: *because* I am female, it is my responsibility to be extra careful.

As a responsible environmentalist, I choose to recycle, avoid chemicals on my land, minimize waste. As an informed woman alone, I choose to be as responsible for my own safety as possible: I keep my car running well, use caution in where I go and what I do. And I learned about self-protection—not an easy or quick decision. I developed a strategy of protection that includes handgun possession. The following incidents, chosen from a larger number because I think they could happen to anyone, helped make up my mind.

When I camped with another woman for several weeks, she didn't want to carry a pistol, and police told us Mace was illegal. We tucked spray deodorant into our sleeping bags, theorizing that any man crawling into our tent at night would be nervous anyway; anything sprayed in his face would slow him down until we could hit him with a frying pan, or escape. We never used our improvised weapon, because we were lucky enough to camp beside people who came to our aid when we needed them. I returned from that trip determined to reconsider.

At that time, I lived alone and taught night classes in town. Along a city street I often traveled, a woman had a flat tire, called for help on her CB, and got a rapist; he didn't fix the tire either. She was afraid to call for help again and stayed in her car until morning. Also, CBs work best along line-of-sight; I ruled them out.

As I drove home one night, a car followed me, lights bright. It passed on a narrow bridge, while a passenger flashed a spotlight in my face, blinding me. I braked sharply. The car stopped, angled across the bridge, and four men jumped out. I realized the locked doors were useless if they broke my car windows. I started forward, hoping to knock their car aside so I could pass. Just then, another car appeared, and the men got back in their car, but continued to follow me, passing and repassing. I dared not go home. I passed no lighted houses. Finally, they pulled to the roadside, and I decided to use their tactic: fear. I roared past them inches away, horn blaring. It worked; they turned off the highway. But it was desperate and foolish, and I was frightened and angry. Even in my vehicle I was too vulnerable.

Other incidents followed. One day I saw a man in the field near my house, carrying a shotgun and heading for a pond full of ducks. I drove to meet him, and politely explained that the land was posted. He stared at me, and the muzzle of his shotgun rose. I realized that if he simply shot me and drove away, I would be a statistic. The moment passed; the man left.

One night, I returned home from class to find deep tire ruts on the lawn, a large gas tank empty, garbage in the driveway. A light shone in the house; I couldn't remember leaving it on. I was too embarrassed to wake the neighbors. An hour of cautious exploration convinced me the house was safe, but once inside, with the doors locked, I was still afraid. I put a .22 rifle by my bed, but I kept thinking of how naked I felt, prowling around my own house in the dark.

It was time to consider self-defense. I took a kung fu class and learned to define the distance to maintain between myself and a stranger. Once someone enters that space without permission, kung fu teaches appropriate evasive or protective action. I learned to move confidently, scanning for possible attack. I learned how to assess danger, and techniques for avoiding it without combat.

I also learned that one must practice several hours every day to be good at king fu. By that time I had married George; when I practiced with him, I learned how *close* you must be to your attacker to use martial arts, and decided a 120-pound woman dare not let a six-foot, 220-pound attacker get that close unless she is very, very good at self-defense. Some women who are well trained in martial arts have been raped and beaten anyway.

Reluctantly I decided to carry a pistol. George helped me practice with his .357 and .22. I disliked the .357's recoil, though I later became comfortable with it. I bought a .22 at a pawn shop. A standard .22 bullet, fired at close range, can kill, but news reports tell of attackers advancing with five such bullets in them. I bought magnum shells, with more power, and practiced until I could hit someone close enough to endanger me. Then I bought a license making it legal for me to carry the gun concealed.

George taught me that the most important preparation was mental: convincing myself I could shoot someone. Few of us really wish to hurt or kill another human being. But there is no point in having a gun—in fact, gun possession might increase your danger—unless you know you can use it against another human being. A good training course includes mental preparation, as well as training in safety. As I drive or walk, I often rehearse the conditions which would cause me to shoot. Men grow up handling firearms, and learn controlled violence in contact sports, but women grow up learning to be subservient and vulnerable. To make ourselves comfortable with the idea that we are capable of protecting ourselves requires effort. But it need not turn us into macho, gun-fighting broads. We must simply learn to do as men do from an early age: believe in, and rely on, *ourselves* for protection. The pistol only adds an extra edge, an attention-getter; it is a weapon of last resort.

Because shooting at another person means shooting to kill. It's impossible even for seasoned police officers to be sure of only wounding an assailant. If I shot an attacking man, I would aim at the largest target, the chest. This is not an easy choice, but for me it would be better than rape.

In my car, my pistol is within instant reach. When I enter a deserted rest stop at night, it's in my purse, my hand on the grip.

When I walk from a dark parking lot into a motel, it's in my hand, under a coat. When I walk my dog in the deserted lots around most motels, the pistol is in a shoulder holster, and I am always aware of my surroundings. In my motel room, it lies on the bedside table. At home, it's on the headboard.

Just carrying a pistol is not protection. Avoidance is still the best approach to trouble; watch for danger signs, and practice avoiding them. Develop your instinct for danger.

One day while driving to the highway mailbox, I saw a vehicle parked about halfway to the house. Several men were standing in the ditch, relieving themselves. I have no objection to emergency urination; we always need moisture. But they'd also dumped several dozen beer cans, which blow into pastures and can slash a cow's legs or stomach.

As I slowly drove closer, the men zipped their trousers ostentatiously while walking toward me. Four men gathered around my small foreign car, making remarks they wouldn't make to their mothers, and one of them demanded what the hell I wanted.

"This is private land; I'd like you to pick up the beer cans."

"What beer cans?" said the belligerent one, putting both hands on the car door, and leaning in my window. His face was inches from mine, the beer fumes were strong, and he looked angry. The others laughed. One tried the passenger door, locked; another put his foot on the hood and rocked the car. They circled, lightly thumping the roof, discussing my good fortune in meeting them, and the benefits they were likely to bestow upon me. I felt small and trapped; they knew it.

"The ones you just threw out," I said politely.

"I don't see no beer cans. Why don't you get out here and show them to me, honey?" said the belligerent one, reaching for the handle inside my door.

"Right over there," I said, still being polite, "there and over there." I pointed with the pistol, which had been under my thigh.

Within one minute the cans and the men were back in the car, and headed down the road.

I believe this small incident illustrates several principles. The men were trespassing and knew it; their judgment may have been impaired by alcohol. Their response to the polite request of a woman alone was to use their size and numbers to inspire fear. The pistol was a response in the same language. Politeness didn't work; I couldn't intimidate them. Out of the car, I'd have been more vulnerable. The pistol just changed the balance of power.

My husband, George, asked one question when I told him. "What would you have done if he'd grabbed for the pistol?"

"I had the car in reverse; I'd have hit the accelerator, and backed up; if he'd kept coming, I'd have fired straight at him." He nodded.

In fact, the sight of the pistol made the man straighten up; he cracked his head on the door frame. He and the two in front of the car stepped backward, catching the attention of the fourth, who joined them. They were all in front of me then, and as the car was still running and in reverse gear, my options had multiplied. If they'd advanced again, I'd have backed away, turning to keep the open window toward them. Given time, I'd have put the first shot into the ground in front of them, the second into the belligerent leader. It might have been better to wait until they were gone, pick up the beer cans, and avoid confrontation, but I believed it was reasonable and my right to make a polite request to strangers littering my property. Showing the pistol worked on another occasion when I was driving in a desolate part of Wyoming. A man played cat-and-mouse with me for thirty miles, ultimately trying to run my car off the road. When his car was only two inches from mine, I pointed my pistol at him, and he disappeared.

I believe that a handgun is like a car; both are tools for specific purposes; both can be lethal if used improperly. Both require a license, training, and alertness. Both require you to be aware of what

is happening before and behind you. Driving becomes almost in-
stinctive; so does handgun use. When I've drawn my gun for protection, I simply found it in my hand. Instinct told me a situation
was dangerous before my conscious mind reacted; I've felt the same
while driving. Most good drivers react to emergencies by instinct.

Women didn't always have jobs, or drive cars or heavy equipment, though western women did many of those things almost as
soon as they arrived here. Men in authority argued that their attempt to do so would unravel the fabric of society. Women, they
said, would become less feminine; they hadn't the intelligence to
cope with the mechanics of a car, or the judgment to cope with
emergencies. Since these ideas were so wrong, perhaps it is time
women brought a new dimension to the wise use of handguns as
well.

We can and should educate ourselves in how to travel safely,
take self-defense courses, reason, plead, or avoid trouble in other
ways. But some men cannot be stopped by those methods; they understand only power. A man who is committing an attack already
knows he's breaking laws; he has no concern for someone else's
rights. A pistol is a woman's answer to his greater power. It makes
her equally frightening. I have thought of revising the old Colt slo-
gan "God made man, but Sam Colt made them equal" to read "God
made men *and women* but Sam Colt made them equal." Recently I
have seen an ad for a popular gunmaker with a similar sentiment;
perhaps this is an idea whose time has come, though the pacifist inside me will be saddened if the only way women can achieve equality is by carrying a weapon.

As a society, we were shocked in early 1989 when a female jog-
ger in New York's Central Park was beaten and raped savagely and
left in a coma. I was even more shocked when reporters interviewed
children who lived near the victim and quoted a twelve-year-old as
saying, "She had nothing to guard herself; she didn't have no man
with her; she didn't have no Mace." And another sixth-grader said,

"It is like she committed suicide." Surely this is not a majority opinion, but I think it is not so unusual, either, even in this liberated age. Yet there is no city or county in the nation where law officers can relax because all the criminals are in jail. Some authorities say citizens armed with handguns stop almost as many crimes annually as armed criminals succeed in committing, and that people defending themselves kill three times more attackers and robbers than police do. I don't suggest all criminals should be killed, but some can be stopped only by death or permanent incarceration. Law enforcement officials can't prevent crimes; later punishment may be of little comfort to the victim. A society so controlled that no crime existed would probably be too confined for most of us, and is not likely to exist any time soon. Therefore, many of us should be ready and able to protect ourselves, and the intelligent use of firearms is one way.

We must treat a firearm's power with caution. "Power tends to corrupt, and absolute power corrupts absolutely," as a man (Lord Acton) once said. A pistol is not the only way to avoid being raped or murdered in today's world, but a firearm, intelligently wielded, can shift the balance and provide a measure of safety.

Jeanne Wakatsuki Houston

J eanne Wakatsuki Houston was born in California on September 26, 1934, to Ko Wakatsuki (a farmer and fisherman) and Riku Sugai Wakatsuki (a nurse and dietitian from a farming family in eastern Washington State). The youngest in a family of ten children, Jeanne was only seven years old in December 1941, when, two weeks after the Japanese surprise attack on Pearl Harbor, the FBI arrested her father on the grounds that he was potentially disloyal. Less than two months later President Roosevelt signed Executive Order 9066, authorizing the War Department "to define military areas in the western states and to exclude from them anyone who might threaten the war effort." Thus, with a single penstroke, Roosevelt opened the way for the forced removal of 110,000 Americans of Japanese ancestry to ten inland camps. Of these, the Manzanar Camp in Owens Valley, California, which was the first to open, has become the most notorious, thanks largely to Jeanne Wakatsuki Houston's superb chronicle of those years. Her book, Farewell to Manzanar (1973), co-authored with her novelist husband, James D. Houston, documents an extraordinary episode in Western American history. As the Houstons note, at its peak in the summer of 1942, "Manzanar was the biggest city between Reno and Los Angeles, a special kind of western boom town that sprang from the sand, flour-

ished, had its day, and now has all but disappeared." For more than three years, however, the barracks, guard towers, mess halls, shower rooms, school, hospital, tea and rock gardens, and pear orchards surrounded by a square mile of barbed wire were "home" for the Wakatsukis and sometimes as many as 10,000 other Japanese-Americans. (Despite their extensive researches, historians have been unable to record even a single case of disloyalty or sabotage on the part of Japanese-Americans during the entire war.) In the following three episodes from her book, Jeanne Wakatsuki Houston re-creates her experience with sensitivity, light humor, affection, and subtle irony. It wouldn't be until June 1952, with the congressional passage of Public Law 414, that Japanese-Americans would acquire the legal right to become naturalized citizens. The events described below all take place between March and September of 1942.

Episodes from
Farewell to Manzanar

IN DECEMBER OF 1941 PAPA'S DISAPPEARANCE didn't bother me nearly so much as the world I soon found myself in.

He had been a jack-of-all-trades. When I was born he was farming near Inglewood. Later, when he started fishing, we moved to Ocean Park, near Santa Monica, and until they picked him up, that's where we lived, in a big frame house with a brick fireplace, a block back from the beach. We were the only Japanese family in the neighborhood. Papa liked it that way. He didn't want to be labeled or grouped by anyone. But with him gone and no way of knowing what to expect, my mother moved all of us down to Terminal Island. Woody already lived there, and one of my older sisters had married a Terminal Island boy. Mama's first concern now was to keep the family together; and once the war began, she felt safer there than isolated racially in Ocean Park. But for me, at age seven, the island was a country as foreign as India or Arabia would have been. It was the first time I had lived among other Japanese, or gone to school with them, and I was terrified all the time.

This was partly Papa's fault. One of his threats to keep us younger kids in line was "I'm going to sell you to the Chinaman." When I had entered kindergarten two years earlier, I was the only Oriental in the class. They sat me next to a Caucasian girl who happened to have very slanted eyes. I looked at her and began to scream, certain Papa had sold me out at last. My fear of her ran so deep I could not speak of it, even to Mama, couldn't explain why I was screaming. For two weeks I had nightmares about this girl, until the teachers finally moved me to the other side of the room. And it was still with me, this fear of Oriental faces, when we moved to Terminal Island.

In those days it was a company town, a ghetto owned and controlled by the canneries. The men went after fish, and whenever the boats came back—day or night—the women would be called to process the catch while it was fresh. One in the afternoon or four in the morning, it made no difference. My mother had to go to work right after we moved there. I can still hear the whistle—two toots for French's, three for Van Kamp's—and she and Chizu would be out of bed in the middle of the night, heading for the cannery.

The house we lived in was nothing more than a shack, a barracks with single plank walls and rough wooden floors, like the cheapest kind of migrant workers' housing. The people around us were hardworking, boisterous, a little proud of their nickname, *yo-go-re*, which meant literally *uncouth one*, or roughneck, or dead-end kid. They not only spoke Japanese exclusively, they spoke a dialect peculiar to Kyushu, where their families had come from in Japan, a rough, fisherman's language, full of oaths and insults. Instead of saying *ba-ka-ta-re,* a common insult meaning *stupid,* Terminal Islanders would say *ba-ka-ya-ro,* a coarser and exclusively masculine use of the word, which implies gross stupidity. They would swagger and pick on outsiders and persecute anyone who didn't speak as they did. That was what made my own time there so hateful. I had never spoken anything but English, and the other kids in the second grade despised me for it. They were tough and mean, like ghetto kids anywhere. Each day after school I dreaded their ambush. My brother Kiyo, three years older, would wait for me at the door, where we would decide whether to run straight home together, or split up, or try a new and unexpected route.

None of these kids ever actually attacked. It was the threat that frightened us, their fearful looks, and the noises they would make, like miniature Samurai, in a language we couldn't understand.

At the time it seemed we had been living under this reign of fear for years. In fact, we lived there about two months. Late in February the navy decided to clear Terminal Island completely. Even though most of us were American-born, it was dangerous having that many Orientals so close to the Long Beach Naval Station, on the opposite end of the island. We had known something like this was coming. But, like Papa's arrest, not much could be done ahead of time. There were four of us kids still young enough to be living with Mama, plus Granny, her mother, sixty-five then, speaking no English, and nearly blind. Mama didn't know where else she could get work, and we had nowhere else to move *to.* On February 25 the choice was made for us. We were given forty-eight hours to clear out.

The secondhand dealers had been prowling around for weeks, like wolves, offering humiliating prices for goods and furniture they knew many of us would have to sell sooner or later. Mama had left all but her most valuable possessions in Ocean Park, simply because she had nowhere to put them. She had brought along her pottery, her silver, heirlooms like the kimonos Granny had brought from Japan, tea sets, lacquered tables, and one fine old set of china, blue and white porcelain, almost translucent. On the day we were leaving, Woody's car was so crammed with boxes and luggage and kids we had just run out of room. Mama had to sell this china.

One of the dealers offered her fifteen dollars for it. She said it was a full setting for twelve and worth at least two hundred. He said fifteen was his top price. Mama started to quiver. Her eyes blazed up at him. She had been packing all night and trying to calm down Granny, who didn't understand why we were moving again and what all the rush was about. Mama's nerves were shot, and now navy jeeps were patrolling the streets. She didn't say another word. She just glared at this man, all the rage and frustration channeled at him through her eyes.

He watched her for a moment and said he was sure he couldn't pay more than seventeen fifty for that china. She reached into the red velvet case, took out a dinner plate and hurled it at the floor right in front of his feet.

The man leaped back shouting, "Hey! Hey, don't do that! Those are valuable dishes!"

Mama took out another dinner plate and hurled it at the floor, then another and another, never moving, never opening her mouth, just quivering and glaring at the retreating dealer, with tears streaming down her cheeks. He finally turned and scuttled out the door, heading for the next house. When he was gone she stood there smashing cups and bowls and platters until the whole set lay in scattered blue and white fragments across the wooden floor.

THE AMERICAN FRIENDS SERVICE helped us find a small house in Boyle Heights, another minority ghetto, in downtown Los Angeles, now inhabited briefly by a few hundred Terminal Island

refugees. Executive Order 9066 had been signed by President
Roosevelt, giving the War Department authority to define military
areas in the western states and to exclude from them anyone who
might threaten the war effort. There was a lot of talk about internment, or moving inland, or something like that in store for all
Japanese Americans. I remember my brothers sitting around the
table talking very intently about what we were going to do, how we
would keep the family together. They had seen how quickly Papa
was removed, and they knew now that he would not be back for
quite a while. Just before leaving Terminal Island Mama had received her first letter, from Bismarck, North Dakota. He had been
imprisoned at Fort Lincoln, in an all-male camp for enemy aliens.

Papa had been the patriarch. He had always decided everything
in the family. With him gone, my brothers, like councilors in the
absence of a chief, worried about what should be done. The ironic
thing is, there wasn't much left to decide. These were mainly days of
quiet, desperate waiting for what seemed at the time to be inevitable. There is a phrase the Japanese use in such situations, when
something difficult must be endured. You would hear the older
heads, the Issei, telling others very quietly, *"Shikata ga nai"* (It cannot be helped). *"Shikata ga nai"* (It must be done).

Mama and Woody went to work packing celery for a Japanese
produce dealer. Kiyo and my sister May and I enrolled in the local
school, and what sticks in my memory from those few weeks is the
teacher—not her looks, her remoteness. In Ocean Park my teacher
had been a kind, grandmotherly woman who used to sail with us in
Papa's boat from time to time and who wept the day we had to leave.
In Boyle Heights the teacher felt cold and distant. I was confused by
all the moving and was having trouble with the classwork, but she
would never help me out. She would have nothing to do with me.

This was the first time I had felt outright hostility from a Caucasian. Looking back, it is easy enough to explain. Public attitudes
toward the Japanese in California were shifting rapidly. In the first

few months of the Pacific war, America was on the run. Tolerance had turned to distrust and irrational fear. The hundred-year-old tradition of anti-Orientalism on the west coast soon resurfaced, more vicious than ever. Its result became clear about a month later, when we were told to make our third and final move.

The name Manzanar meant nothing to us when we left Boyle Heights. We didn't know where it was or what it was. We went because the government ordered us to. And, in the case of my older brothers and sisters, we went with a certain amount of relief. They had all heard stories of Japanese homes being attacked, of beatings in the streets of California towns. They were as frightened of the Caucasians as Caucasians were of us. Moving, under what appeared to be government protection, to an area less directly threatened by the war seemed not such a bad idea at all. For some it actually sounded like a fine adventure.

Our pickup point was a Buddhist church in Los Angeles. It was very early, and misty, when we got there with our luggage. Mama had bought heavy coats for all of us. She grew up in eastern Washington and knew that anywhere inland in early April would be cold. I was proud of my new coat, and I remember sitting on a duffel bag trying to be friendly with the Greyhound driver. I smiled at him. He didn't smile back. He was befriending no one. Someone tied a numbered tag to my collar and to the duffel bag (each family was given a number, and that became our official designation until the camps were closed), someone else passed out box lunches for the trip, and we climbed aboard.

I had never been outside Los Angeles County, never traveled more than ten miles from the coast, had never even ridden on a bus. I was full of excitement, the way any kid would be, and wanted to look out the window. But for the first few hours the shades were drawn. Around me other people played cards, read magazines, dozed, waiting. I settled back, waiting too, and finally fell asleep.

The bus felt very secure to me. Almost half its passengers were immediate relatives. Mama and my older brothers had succeeded in keeping most of us together, on the same bus, headed for the same camp. I didn't realize until much later what a job that was. The strategy had been, first, to have everyone living in the same district when the evacuation began, and then to get all of us included under the same family number, even though names had been changed by marriage. Many families weren't as lucky as ours and suffered months of anguish while trying to arrange transfers from one camp to another.

We rode all day. By the time we reached our destination, the shades were up. It was late afternoon. The first thing I saw was a yellow swirl across a blurred, reddish setting sun. The bus was being pelted by what sounded like splattering rain. It wasn't rain. This was my first look at something I would soon know very well, a billowing flurry of dust and sand churned up by the wind through Owens Valley.

We drove past a barbed-wire fence, through a gate, and into an open space where trunks and sacks and packages had been dumped from the baggage trucks that drove out ahead of us. I could see a few tents set up, the first rows of black barracks, and beyond them, blurred by sand, rows of barracks that seemed to spread for miles across this plain. People were sitting on cartons or milling around, with their backs to the wind, waiting to see which friends or relatives might be on this bus. As we approached, they turned or stood up, and some moved toward us expectantly. But inside the bus no one stirred. No one waved or spoke. They just stared out the windows, ominously silent. I didn't understand this. Hadn't we finally arrived, our whole family intact? I opened a window, leaned out, and yelled happily. "Hey! This whole bus is full of Wakatsukis!"

Outside, the greeters smiled. Inside there was an explosion of laughter, hysterical, tension-breaking laughter that left my brothers choking and whacking each other across the shoulders.

WE HAD PULLED UP just in time for dinner. The mess halls weren't completed yet. An outdoor chow line snaked around a half-finished building that broke a good part of the wind. They issued us army mess kits, the round metal kind that fold over, and plopped in scoops of canned Vienna sausage, canned string beans, steamed rice that had been cooked too long, and on top of the rice a serving of canned apricots. The Caucasian servers were thinking that the fruit poured over rice would make a good dessert. Among the Japanese, of course, rice is never eaten with sweet foods, only with salty or savory foods. Few of us could eat such a mixture. But at this point no one dared protest. It would have been impolite. I was horrified when I saw the apricot syrup seeping through my little mound of rice. I opened my mouth to complain. My mother jabbed me in the back to keep quiet. We moved on through the line and joined the others squatting in the lee of half-raised walls, dabbing courteously at what was, for almost everyone there, an inedible concoction.

After dinner we were taken to Block 16, a cluster of fifteen barracks that had just been finished a day or so earlier—although finished was hardly the word for it. The shacks were built of one thickness of pine planking covered with tarpaper. They sat on concrete footings, with about two feet of open space between the floorboards and the ground. Gaps showed between the planks, and as the weeks passed and the green wood dried out, the gaps widened. Knotholes gaped in the uncovered floor.

Each barracks was divided into six units, sixteen by twenty feet, about the size of a living room, with one bare bulb hanging from the ceiling and an oil stove for heat. We were assigned two of these for the twelve people in our family group; and our official family "number" was enlarged by three digits—16 plus the number of this barracks. We were issued steel army cots, two brown army blankets each, and some mattress covers, which my brothers stuffed with straw.

The first task was to divide up what space we had for sleeping. Bill and Woody contributed a blanket each and partitioned off the first room: one side for Bill and Tomi, one side for Woody and Chizu and their baby girl. Woody also got the stove, for heating formulas.

The people who had it hardest during the first few months were young couples like these, many of whom had married just before the evacuation began, in order not to be separated and sent to different camps. Our two rooms were crowded, but at least it was all in the family. My oldest sister and her husband were shoved into one of those sixteen-by-twenty-foot compartments with six people they had never seen before—two other couples, one recently married like themselves, the other with two teenage boys. Partitioning off a room like that wasn't easy. It was bitter cold when we arrived, and the wind did not abate. All they had to use for room dividers were those army blankets, two of which were barely enough to keep one person warm. They argued over whose blanket should be sacrificed and later argued about noise at night—the parents wanted their boys asleep by 9:00 P.M.—and they continued arguing over matters like that for six months, until my sister and her husband left to harvest sugar beets in Idaho. It was grueling work up there, and wages were pitiful, but when the call came through camp for workers to alleviate the wartime labor shortage, it sounded better than their life at Manzanar. They knew they'd have, if nothing else, a room, perhaps a cabin of their own.

That first night in Block 16, the rest of us squeezed into the second room—Granny, Lillian, age fourteen, Ray, thirteen, May, eleven, Kiyo, ten, Mama, and me. I didn't mind this at all at the time. Being youngest meant I got to sleep with Mama. And before we went to bed I had a great time jumping up and down on the mattress. The boys had stuffed so much straw into hers, we had to flatten it some so we wouldn't slide off. I slept with her every night after that until Papa came back.

◆ ◆ ◆

I DON'T REMEMBER what we ate that first morning. I know we stood for half an hour in cutting wind waiting to get our food. Then we took it back to the cubicle and ate huddled around the stove. Inside, it was warmer than when we left, because Woody was already making good his promise to Mama, tacking up some ends of lath he'd found, stuffing rolled paper around the door frame.

Trouble was, he had almost nothing to work with. Beyond this temporary weather stripping, there was little else he could do. Months went by, in fact, before our "home" changed much at all from what it was the day we moved in—bare floors, blanket partitions, one bulb in each compartment dangling from a roof beam, and open ceilings overhead so that mischievous boys like Ray and Kiyo could climb up into the rafters and peek into anyone's life.

The simple truth is the camp was no more ready for us when we got there than we were ready for it. We had only the dimmest ideas of what to expect. Most of the families, like us, had moved out from southern California with as much luggage as each person could carry. Some old men left Los Angeles wearing Hawaiian shirts and Panama hats and stepped off the bus at an altitude of 4000 feet, with nothing available but sagebrush and tarpaper to stop the April winds pouring down off the back side of the Sierras.

The War Department was in charge of all the camps at this point. They began to issue military surplus from the First World War—olive-drab knit caps, earmuffs, peacoats, canvas leggings. Later on, sewing machines were shipped in, and one barracks was turned into a clothing factory. An old seamstress took a peacoat of mine, tore the lining out, opened and flattened the sleeves, added a collar, put arm holes in and handed me back a beautiful cape. By fall dozens of seamstresses were working full-time transforming thousands of these old army clothes into capes, slacks and stylish coats. But until that factory got going and packages from friends outside began to fill out our wardrobes, warmth was more important than style. I couldn't help laughing at Mama walking around in army earmuffs and a pair of wide-cuffed, khaki-colored wool trousers several sizes too big for her. Japanese are generally smaller than Caucasians, and almost all these clothes were oversized. They flopped, they dangled, they hung.

It seems comical, looking back; we were a band of Charlie Chaplins marooned in the California desert. But at the time, it was pure chaos. That's the only way to describe it. The evacuation had been so hurriedly planned, the camps so hastily thrown together, nothing was completed when we got there, and almost nothing worked.

I was sick continually, with stomach cramps and diarrhea. At first it was from the shots they gave us for typhoid, in very heavy doses and in assembly-line fashion: swab, jab, swab, *Move along now*, swab, jab, swab, *Keep it moving*. That knocked all of us younger kids down at once, with fevers and vomiting. Later, it was the food that made us sick, young and old alike. The kitchens were too small and badly ventilated. Food would spoil from being left out too long. That summer, when the heat got fierce, it would spoil faster. The refrigeration kept breaking down. The cooks, in many cases, had never cooked before. Each block had to provide its own volunteers. Some were lucky and had a professional or two in their midst. But the first chef in our block had been a gardener all his life and suddenly found himself preparing three meals a day for 250 people.

"The Manzanar runs" became a condition of life, and you only hoped that when you rushed to the latrine, one would be in working order.

That first morning, on our way to the chow line, Mama and I

tried to use the women's latrine in our block. The smell of it spoiled what little appetite we had. Outside, men were working in an open trench, up to their knees in muck—a common sight in the months to come. Inside, the floor was covered with excrement, and all twelve bowls were erupting like a row of tiny volcanoes.

Mama stopped a kimono-wrapped woman stepping past us with her sleeve pushed up against her nose and asked, "What do you do?"

"Try Block Twelve," the woman said, grimacing. "They have just finished repairing the pipes."

It was about two city blocks away. We followed her over there and found a line of women waiting in the wind outside the latrine. We had no choice but to join the line and wait with them.

Inside it was like all the other latrines. Each block was built to the same design, just as each of the ten camps, from California to Arkansas, was built to a common master plan. It was an open room, over a concrete slab. The sink was a long metal trough against one wall, with a row of spigots for hot and cold water. Down the center of the room twelve toilet bowls were arranged in six pairs, back to back, with no partitions. My mother was a very modest person, and this was going to be agony for her, sitting down in public, among strangers.

One old woman had already solved the problem for herself by dragging in a large cardboard carton. She set it up around one of the bowls, like a three-sided screen. OXYDOL was printed in large black letters down the front. I remember this well, because that was the soap we were issued for laundry; later on, the smell of it would permeate these rooms. The upended carton was about four feet high. The old woman behind it wasn't much taller. When she stood, only her head showed over the top.

She was about Granny's age. With great effort she was trying to fold the sides of the screen together. Mama happened to be at the head of the line now. As she approached the vacant bowl, she and the old woman bowed to each other from the waist. Mama then moved to help her with the carton, and the old woman said very graciously, in Japanese, "Would you like to use it?"

Happily, gratefully, Mama bowed again and said, *"Arigato"* (Thank you). *"Arigato gozaimas"* (Thank you very much). "I will return it to your barracks."

"Oh, no. It is not necessary. I will be glad to wait."

The old woman unfolded one side of the cardboard, while Mama opened the other; then she bowed again and scurried out the door.

Those big cartons were a common sight in the spring of 1942. Eventually sturdier partitions appeared, one or two at a time. The first were built of scrap lumber. Word would get around that Block such and such had partitions now, and Mama and my older sisters would walk halfway across the camp to use them. Even after every latrine in camp was screened, this quest for privacy continued. Many would wait until late at night. Ironically, because of this, midnight was often the most crowded time of all.

Like so many of the women there, Mama never did get used to the latrines. It was a humiliation she just learned to endure: *shikata ga nai*, this cannot be helped. She would quickly subordinate her own desires to those of the family or the community, because she knew cooperation was the only way to survive. At the same time she placed a high premium on personal privacy, respected it in others and insisted upon it for herself. Almost everyone at Manzanar had inherited this pair of traits from the generations before them who had learned to live in a small, crowded country like Japan. Because of the first they were able to take a desolate stretch of wasteland and gradually make it livable. But the entire situation there, especially in the beginning—the packed sleeping quarters, the communal mess halls, the open toilets—all this was an open insult to that other, private self, a slap in the face you were powerless to challenge.

◆ ◆ ◆

AT SEVEN I was too young to be insulted. The camp worked on me in a much different way. I wasn't aware of this at the time, of course. No one was, except maybe Mama, and there was little she could have done to change what happened.

It began in the mess hall. Before Manzanar, mealtime had always been the center of our family scene. In camp, and afterward, I would often recall with deep yearning the old round wooden table in our dining room in Ocean Park, the biggest piece of furniture we owned, large enough to seat twelve or thirteen of us at once. A tall row of elegant, lathe-turned spindles separated this table from the kitchen, allowing talk to pass from one room to the other. Dinners were always noisy, and they were always abundant with great pots of boiled rice, platters of home-grown vegetables, fish Papa caught.

He would sit at the head of this table, with Mama next to him serving and the rest of us arranged around the edges according to age, down to where Kiyo and I sat, so far away from our parents, it seemed at the time, we had our own enclosed nook inside this world. The grownups would be talking down at their end, while we two played our secret games, making eyes at each other when Papa gave the order to begin to eat, racing with chopsticks to scrape the last grain from our rice bowls, eyeing Papa to see if he had noticed who won.

Now, in the mess halls, after a few weeks had passed, we stopped eating as a family. Mama tried to hold us together for a while, but it was hopeless. Granny was too feeble to walk across the block three times a day, especially during heavy weather, so May brought food to her in the barracks. My older brothers and sisters, meanwhile, began eating with their friends, or eating somewhere blocks away, in the hope of finding better food. The word would get around that the cook over in Block 22, say, really knew his stuff, and they would eat a few meals over there, to test the rumor. Camp authorities frowned on mess hall hopping and tried to stop it, but the good cooks liked it. They liked to see long lines outside their kitchens and would work overtime to attract a crowd.

Younger boys, like Ray, would make a game of seeing how many mess halls they could hit in one meal period—be the first in line at Block 16, gobble down your food, run to 17 by the middle of the dinner hour, gulp another helping, and hurry to 18 to make the end of that chow line and stuff in the third meal of the evening. They didn't *need* to do that. No matter how bad the food might be, you could always eat till you were full.

Kiyo and I were too young to run around, but often we would eat in gangs with other kids, while the grownups sat at another table. I confess I enjoyed this part of it at the time. We all did. A couple of years after the camps opened, sociologists studying the life noticed what had happened to the families. They made some recommendations, and edicts went out that families *must* start eating together again. Most people resented this; they griped and grumbled. They were in the habit of eating with their friends. And until the mess hall system itself could be changed, not much could really be done. It was too late.

My own family, after three years of mess hall living, collapsed as an integrated unit. Whatever dignity or feeling of filial strength we may have known before December 1941 was lost, and we did not recover it until many years after the war, not until after Papa died and we began to come together, trying to fill the vacuum his passing left in all our lives.

The closing of the camps, in the fall of 1945, only aggravated what had begun inside. Papa had no money then and could not get work. Half of our family had already moved to the east coast, where jobs had opened up for them. The rest of us were relocated into a former defense workers' housing project in Long Beach. In that small apartment there never was enough room for all of us to sit down for a meal. We ate in shifts, and I yearned all the more for our huge round table in Ocean Park.

Soon after we were released I wrote a paper for a seventh-grade journalism class, describing how we used to hunt grunion before the war. The whole family would go down to Ocean Park Beach after dark, when the grunion were running, and build a big fire on the sand. I would watch Papa and my older brothers splash through the moonlit surf to scoop out the fish, then we'd rush back to the house where Mama would fry them up and set the sizzling pan on the table, with soy sauce and horseradish, for a midnight meal. I ended the paper with this sentence: "The reason I want to remember this is because I know we'll never be able to do it again."

YOU MIGHT SAY it would have happened sooner or later anyway, this sliding apart of such a large family, in postwar California. People get married; their interests shift. But there is no escaping the fact that our internment accelerated the process, made it happen so suddenly it was almost tangible.

Not only did we stop eating at home, there was no longer a home to eat in. The cubicles we had were too small for anything you might call "living." Mama couldn't cook meals there. It was impossible to find any privacy there. We slept there and spent most of our waking hours elsewhere.

Mama had gone to work again soon after we arrived. The call went out for people with any kind of skill to offer their services. Thousands were responding, with great surges of community spirit, sometimes with outright patriotism, wanting "to do their part." Woody signed on as a carpenter. One of my brothers-in-law was a roofing foreman. Another ran a reservoir crew. Mama had worked as a dietician in Washington after she was married. In camp this was high-priority training. In addition to the daily multitude, those amateur cooks were faced with allergy cases, diabetics, nurs-

ing mothers, infants who required special feedings. For Mama it
was also a way to make a little money. Nineteen dollars a month.
This was top wage for an internee. Unskilled labor started at eight.
All volunteer of course. You didn't have to get out of bed in the
morning if you didn't want to. Mama wanted the work. She had a
monthly fee to pay the warehouse in Los Angeles where she had
stored what remained of our furniture and silver just before we
evacuated. She worried about this constantly.

She worried about Papa too. Letters from him trickled in, once
or twice a month, with half the words blacked out, calling her
"Sweetheart" for the first time in fifteen years. She was always distracted, staring at things I could never see. I would try to get her
attention, grab her around the legs. At night, in bed, she would hug
me close. But during the day she never seemed to notice me.

Adrift, I began to look elsewhere for attention and thus took
the first steps out of my child's realm toward a world of grownups
other than my parents. Though I was only seven, my images of certain people from this period are very precise, because I had begun to
see adults for the first time. On Terminal Island I first *saw* Orientals,
those demon-children who had terrorized me. At Manzanar, past
the fear of slanted eyes and high cheekbones, I watched with fresh
amazement the variety of faces and bodies and costumes all around
me. This may have resulted, in part, from the life Manzanar had
forced upon us all. Once the weather warmed up, it was an out-of-
doors life, where you only went "home" at night, when you finally
had to: 10,000 people on an endless promenade inside the square
mile of barbed wire that was the wall around our city.

One of our neighbors was a tall, broad woman, taller than anyone in camp, as far as I recall. She walked erectly and wore an Aunt
Jemima scarf around her head. She was married to a Japanese man,
and they had adopted a little Japanese girl I sometimes played with.
But this woman, I realized much later, was half-black, with light
mulatto skin, passing as a Japanese in order to remain with her hus-

band. She wore scarfs everywhere to cover her give-away hair.

In the barracks facing ours there lived an elegant woman who astounded me each time I saw her. She and her husband both came from Japan, and her long aristocratic face was always a ghastly white. In traditional fashion she powdered it with rice flour every morning. By old-country standards this made her more beautiful. For a long time I thought she was diseased.

Two more white faces stand out in my memory, a pair of nurses I saw from time to time in the clinic. They wore white shoes, white hose, and white dresses. Above their bleached faces their foreheads had been shaved halfway over their scalp's curve to make a sharp widow's peak where starched black hair began to arch upward, reminding me of a cobra's hood. Their lips were gone. Their brows were plucked. They were always together, a pair of reptilian kabuki creatures at loose in the camp hospital.

You might say they were the negatives for two other women I soon began to see almost every day and, in fact, saw more of for a while than I did my mother. Their robes were black, their heads were hooded in white. Sister Mary Suzanne was about forty then, a frail, gentle woman from Japan who could speak no English. Sister Mary Bernadette was a feisty, robust little Canadian Japanese who spoke both languages fluently.

They were Maryknoll nuns, members of that missionary order whose special task is to go into a country, with knowledge of its language, and convert its people to the Catholic faith. Before the war they had run an orphanage in Los Angeles for children of Japanese ancestry. Evacuated to Manzanar and given the job of caring for some fifty orphans interned there, they set up what came to be known as "Children's Village," and they had one barracks turned into a chapel. They were joined by Father Steinback, one of the few Caucasians to live among us inside the compound and eat in our mess halls. He was greatly admired for this, and many internees converted to Catholicism before the camp was closed.

I was almost one of them. Papa stepped in just before my baptism day. If he had been there during those early months I probably would never have started spending time with the Maryknolls. He was always suspicious of organized religions. I think he had already tried to scare me away from Catholics. That was one of his prime methods of instruction: fear. On my way home from school each day in Ocean Park I would break into a run as I passed the local Catholic church. The nuns I glimpsed were robed and ghostly figures I wanted no part of.

Culturally we were like those Jews who observe certain traditions but never visit a synagogue. We kept a little Buddhist shrine in the house, and we celebrated a few Japanese holidays that were religiously connected—the way Christmas is. But we never said prayers. I had never been inside a Buddhist church. And as for Christianity, I had not heard the word God until we reached Terminal Island. I first heard about Jesus when the one friend I made there—another Japanese girl—took me to a Baptist Sunday School on the island, where a Caucasian teacher bewildered me with pictures of lambs and donkeys and golden-domed pavilions.

For some reason these did not appeal to me nearly as much as the stories of the saints and martyrs I heard a few months later when I began to study catechism with the Maryknolls. Soon I was over there every afternoon and most of Sunday. With no regular school to attend and no home to spend time in, it's no mystery that I should have been drawn to these two kind and generous women. They had organized a recreation program. They passed out candy. But what kept me coming back, once I started, were the tales of the unfortunate women like Saint Agatha, whose breasts were cut off when she refused to renounce her faith.

I had to walk nearly a mile to reach their chapel, and walk a mile back. That summer it was miserably hot, over one hundred degrees most days. Yet I made the trip gladly. A big homely girl about twenty years old who wore boys' shoes and an Eisenhower jacket taught catechism to the younger kids. She loved to sit us down and fix us with the eye of a mother superior and tell us about Saint Agatha, or Saint Juliana, who was boiled alive, or Saint Marcella, who was whipped to death by the Goths.

I was fascinated with the miseries of women who had suffered and borne such afflictions. On my way home, I would hike past row upon row of black barracks, watching mountains waver through that desert heat, with the sun trying to dry up my very blood, and imagine in some childish way that I was among them, that I too was up there on the screen of history, in a white lace catechism dress, sweating and grimy, yet selflessly carrying my load.

I fulfilled this little fantasy one blistering afternoon when the heat finally got me. Sunstroke. While crossing one of the wide sandy firebreaks that separated some of the blocks, I passed out.

This put me in bed for a week. After I recovered, several months went by before I resumed my catechism. For one thing, Papa discouraged me. It was just before this happened that he had returned from Fort Lincoln. He was back among us, making decisions, giving commands. For a while it seemed we would almost be a family again. But it didn't turn out that way. He was not the same man. Something terrible had happened to him in North Dakota.

HE ARRIVED AT MANZANAR on a Greyhound bus. We all went down to the main gate to meet him, everyone but Woody's wife, Chizu, who was in the camp hospital. The previous day she'd given birth to Papa's first grandson. She named him George, in honor of Papa's return. Two of my sisters were pregnant at the time, and they were there at the gate in hot-weather smocks, along with Woody, who had left the hospital long enough to welcome Papa back, and Granny and Mama and the rest of the family, a dozen of us standing in the glare, excited, yet very reverent as the bus pulled in.

The door whished open, and the first thing we saw was a

cane—I will never forget it—poking from the shaded interior into sunlight, a straight, polished maple limb spotted with dark lidded eyes where small knotholes had been stained and polished.

Then Papa stepped out, wearing a fedora hat and a wilted white shirt. This was September 1942. He had been gone nine months. He had aged ten years. He looked over sixty, gaunt, wilted as his shirt, underweight, leaning on that cane and favoring his right leg. He stood there surveying his clan, and nobody moved, not even Mama, waiting to see what he would do or say, waiting for some cue from him as to how we should deal with this.

I was the only one who approached him. I had not thought of him much at all after he was taken away. He was simply gone. Now I was so happy to see him that I ran up and threw my arms around his waist and buried my face in his belt. I thought I should be laughing and welcoming him home. But I started to cry. By this time everyone was crying. No one else had moved yet to touch him. It was as if the youngest, the least experienced, had been appointed to display what the others, held back by awe or fear, or some old-country notion of respect for the patriarch, could not. I hugged him tighter, wanting to be happy that my father had come back. Yet I hurt so inside I could only welcome him with convulsive tears.

Teresa Jordan

Teresa Jordan grew up as part of the fourth generation on a ranch in the Iron Mountain country of southeastern Wyoming. The ranch was sold in 1978, the year after she graduated from college, and she has written about ranching and rural culture ever since. "Writing," she once told an interviewer, "has given me a way to hold to the land." Jordan's work has focused on issues of family and community, and much of it has been driven by a desire to understand why, when the rural people she grew up with were so strong, they were often not, in the end, flexible enough to endure. "My family was not alone when we left ranching," Jordan wrote in Riding the White Horse Home. "We were part of an exodus of over thirteen million people who have left the land during my lifetime."

Jordan is the author of Cowgirls: Women of the American West (1982; second edition 1992), distilled from interviews with nearly a hundred women on ranches and in the rodeo; and a memoir, Riding the White Horse Home: A Western Family Album (1993). She is the editor of Graining the Mare: The Poetry of Ranch Women (1994).

"Bones"

from *Riding the White Horse Home*

At Laguna, when someone dies, you don't "get over it" by
forgetting; you "get over it" by *remembering*.
—*Leslie Marmon Silko*

IT IS HOT AUGUST, HIGH NOON UNDER AN AIRLESS
sky, and my father and a hired hand have brought in a sick bull for
doctoring. I am four years old, maybe five, and I sit on a corral rail
to watch. I smell horse sweat and the black, watery manure that the
bull swipes with his tail in an arc across his ass. Dust cakes in my
nostrils and around the edges of my mouth. I want to go back to the
coolness of the house, but I also want to watch. I rub my mouth
with the back of my hand and stay.

The bull is on the fight and he paws the ground. His eyes are
dull and green with sickness, and when he throws his head and bellers, long strands of snot stream from his mouth and fly back across
his shoulders, raising a few of the flies that blanket his rump.

When my father rides into the corral, the bull tries to take him.
My father pivots his horse out of the way and ropes the bull, pulls
him up short to the snubbing post and dallies around. He passes the
end of the rope to the hired man, who has come into the corral on
foot. Once the bull is secure, my father dismounts, ties his horse to a
fence post, and returns with boluses and a syringe full of antibiotic.

The bull grumbles, fights the rope, snorts. But he is sick and he
grows calmer with fatigue. My father jabs the needle into the animal's thigh. The bull rears back against the rope. The wraps on the
post slip. The bull breaks loose, snot flying in an arc, his beller blue
and loud.

From the fence I watch as he takes my daddy down. The world erupts in dust and blood. The bull is roaring, groaning, grinding, someone is yelling, my father is a tiny spider of flailing arms and legs.

I hear the hired hand crying over and over, "Oh my God, oh my God, oh my God." He tries to snub the bull again but he might as well attempt to drag a mountain from its plain. Finally, he gains a wrap of rope and my father rolls free. I watch as he crawls across the corral, climbs the fence hand over hand, his heavy legs dangling uselessly beneath him. He casts himself over the top rail, crashes in a grunt of dust on the other side. The bull bellers and falls silent. The dust settles. Everything is perfectly still.

My father was loaded onto a door and taken to town in the back of a pickup. A few weeks later he came back, and though he walked with a limp, he took up his regular chores. The bull, too, recovered. He was a quality bull and we kept him until he was too old to service cows. Then we shipped him to the packers.

We. A few weeks ago, I learned that this happened before I was born. I have carried it like a memory, but it's not a memory; it's a story I've heard, fleshed out by details told down through the years. I'm amazed. I cannot imagine this event without also imagining myself within it, watching.

FEW OCCUPATIONS are as physically threatening as arid-country cattle ranching. Professional football is; roughnecking on an oil rig; logging. And like other occupations that depend on the body yet place it constantly in peril, cattle ranching breeds an attitude toward danger of both reverence and disdain.

Our neighbor Buddy Hirsig always helped us brand. One time his horse fell on him and broke his ankle as we brought cattle into the corral. "Do you mind if I rope today?" he asked my father. "I can't walk so good and I'd rather stay horseback."

"Oh hell," my father answered. "We have plenty of help. Go on home." But Buddy insisted on staying, and no one was surprised. He roped calf after calf and only when the day's work was finished did he cut off his boot and head to town to get his ankle casted.

I remember a term: major plaster. Minor injuries—a broken wrist, a sprained ankle, a cut requiring stitches—were too insignificant to mention. Major plaster meant serious injury, something that would take months, even years, to heal. A cast on an arm didn't count. One from toe to ass did. So did body casts or almost anything requiring traction. Community gatherings nearly always found someone in major plaster, and Iron Mountain was not a large community. If everyone came together at the same time, they might have numbered sixty.

Each new badge of plaster met with predictable banter. "You *needed* a vacation." "That's one way to get sympathy." "It's about time you broke something. The doc's youngest son just graduated high school." (Dr. Klein was the bone doctor in Cheyenne and we were convinced our debilities paid for his children's Ivy League educations.)

The quips and wisecracks were a lie, a safe way to say "I'm sorry." Injury meant doctors' bills—huge doctors' bills—often in a time of high interest rates, low cattle prices, and drought. Injury meant one less person to do the work. Injury meant more strain on the marriage. Injury meant new insult to a body already prematurely old. And injury meant pain, acute pain for a while and then chronic pain that flared each time the barometer fell. But injury also promised resurrection. If you were injured, at least you weren't dead.

ANOTHER MEMORY. I am eight years old and wearing a lime-green tutu when Harold, our foreman, comes through the door from the thunderstorm outside to tell my mother that Dad has broken his leg. His horse slipped on a bridge. I am to be in a ballet recital that night in town. "What about me?" I ask.

"We'll try to make it on time," she says.

A hired hand's smashed thumb a few days before has wiped us out of codeine, so she gives my father aspirin before they load him on the door. This time they put him in the back of our station wagon. During the two-hour ride through mud and rain to town, he calls me his ballerina cowgirl and recites Kipling to pass the time:

Yes, Din! Din! Din!
You Lazarushian-leather Gunga Din!
Though I've belted you and flayed you,
By the living Gawd that made you,
You're a better man than I am, Gunga Din!

I danced that night, though my father didn't see me. Both bones in his lower leg had been crushed and four hours of surgery left him with a three-inch pin in his calf. The bones had been broken so many times before, they wouldn't knit. He wore a hip cast for a year and a half, and a brace for another year. With the cast, he couldn't ride, he couldn't drive, and he couldn't climb our narrow stairway, so he slept on the Hide-A-Bed in the living room.

He could weld and he worked long hours in the shop, the plastered leg stretched out in front of him. We accused him of welding every piece of metal on the ranch together, and in fact he soon ran out of work. He bought a Heathkit and built an FM radio. Diagrams, tiny wires, and transistors were scattered across the dining-room table for weeks and he soldered patiently. When he finished, the radio worked fine, but we were too far out in the country to pick up any signals.

Once the cast came off, he bought a therapeutic boot to which weights could be attached. Each night he sat in his shorts on the island in the kitchen and strapped it on. He'd straighten the leg again and again until his T-shirt was soaked with sweat. I remem-

ber the grind of his teeth as he worked at the weights, and the way
tears squeezed out of the corners of his eyes.

YOU DID WHAT YOU HAD TO and went on. Accommoda-
tion, not much talked about, was key. People in Iron Mountain still
talk of Mrs. Steele, who ran a nearby ranch by herself after her
husband went crazy. A horse fell on her and broke her arm. The arm
never bent right after that, and she had trouble combing her hair, so
she wore it cropped short, like a man's.

A cowhand's walk, shaped by years of damage and recovery, is
a study in accommodation. The body cants forward from the waits,
the lower back fuses, the hips stiffen, the walk becomes awkward,
the head seems to settle into the shoulders. "It's a kink in the neck,"
one old-timer told me, trying to describe his own gait, "and a limp
in all four limbs."

Not all accommodation is physical. One night, when my father
was rehabilitating his leg and had finished eighty repetitions with
fifty pounds, he joked to my mother, "See that? It's almost good
enough to break again." Through two and a half years, she had been
calm, caring, full of humor. She had chauffeured him to the fields
each morning and waited until frustration made him ask to go back
home. She had arranged her work in the house around his presence.
She had made up his bed on the sofa. She had carted the things he
couldn't carry, accomplished the chores he couldn't do. All this
without complaint. But that night she turned to him. "Larry," she
said without a smile, "break it again and I'll treat you like a horse."

The psychology of accommodation is letting things go.
"Sooner or later," one woman told me, "the other boot is going to
drop. No sense worryin' until you hear the crash." Then, she might
have added, you pick up the pieces. Buddy Hirsig bought a dirt bike
to use around the ranch. The first time he chased a cow, the bike hit
a rock and he catapulted over the top. He was traveling fifteen or
twenty miles an hour when he lit on his hands. They swelled up like

hams. He couldn't hold a fork, turn a doorknob, work a button. Glenna, his wife, didn't mind dressing him or feeding him or even attending to his personal needs. What she minded, she said, was helping him smoke.

IT NEVER OCCURRED TO ME that the men and women I grew up with were courageous. Israeli writer and war correspondent Yaël Dayan, the daughter of General Moshe Dayan, once wrote that her father could not be called courageous because he had no fears to overcome. As a child, it seemed to me that my people were similarly fearless, and being fearless, they were invulnerable. I was not alone in this illusion. Carol Horn, a rancher in North Park, Colorado, told me about watching her grandmother thrown off a hay rake by a runaway team. "Here she was," Carol recalled, "in her sixties, being rolled around under the rake. I wasn't even concerned about it, because it was Grandma. Grandma took care of everything. She had that much control."

In this world of bashed and battered bodies, I felt safe. Injury was real, but it didn't seem to matter much. The injured could rise, phoenixlike, from the ashes of catastrophe, and their feats of recuperation still amaze me. When a horse fell on my seventy-two-year-old Great-aunt Marie and broke her pelvis in three places, the doctors told her she would never ride again. Two months later, she proved them wrong. Merrill Farthing was in his eighties when he fell on a fence spike and punctured his lung. When he finally agreed to go to town, he had double pneumonia and the doctors advised the family to hover near. Three weeks later, Merrill left the hospital and soon returned to the fence line.

With such models around me, I wanted my chance. By the time I entered fourth grade, I had started cutting deals with God. Each night before I went to sleep, I would pray, "Please, God, let me break my leg tomorrow." I dreamed of the kids at school scribbling their names on my cast, but more than that, I wanted the badge of plaster, the proof that the horses I rode were as tough as those of the men, that I wasn't afraid, that I could "take it."

But I didn't break my leg. So I upped the ante. "Please, God. If you'll break my leg tomorrow, I'll be nice to my brother for a *whole year.*" And then, when my limbs remained discouragingly sound, "Please, God, break my leg tomorrow or I won't believe in you anymore." And finally, "Okay, okay, I'll settle for a broken arm. Are you up there, God? Are you listening?"

I THOUGHT MY PEOPLE WERE IMMORTAL. Deep down, I had always understood that ranch accidents could be tragic. I knew that Biddy Bonham's father had been killed when his horse tripped in a gopher hole, and that old Mr. Shaffer died when he fell off a haystack. But these deaths were so distant form me they hardly seemed real. Then, when tragedy struck close to home, it had nothing to do with the roughness of our work. "The danger," my mother used to say, "is never where you think it is." Which was her way of saying "Look behind."

The night my mother died of an aneurysm at the University Hospital in Denver, my father, brother, and I returned to the Brown Palace Hotel. It was ten o'clock at night, maybe midnight, and we called room service. I ordered vichyssoise, my favorite Brown Palace dish since childhood, and when it came, I took the silver covering off the china bowl. I sprinkled the soup with lime, as I always did, and I remember gazing at the perfect little drops of juice, floating on the surface like tiny shimmering planets. I couldn't get any further and my father, too, pushed his dinner away.

" 'If you can make one heap of all your winnings,' " he said at last, quoting Kipling who always seemed to come to him in crisis,

And risk it on one turn of pitch and toss
And lose and start again at your beginnings
And never breathe a word about your loss . . .

And then he put his face in his hands and broke down. I remember the hugeness of him hunched in his chair. I remember a single tear breaking through the dam of his fingers, winding its way down his broad weathered cheek to catch in his quivering mustache.

WHEN YOU WORK WITH a young colt, there comes a day when you take him up to the bones. In the wide-open spaces of ranch country, animal remains are common. A colt will spook at them, even when the bones are decades old. Unless you work to overcome that fear, he will always shy away. There will be places in the world the colt can't walk. But if you take time, urge the colt closer and closer, not denying its fear but not turning away from it either, the horse will eventually approach what scares him. He will see that bones are just bones. He will move in the world more freely.

Ranchers walk up to most bones. They look physical danger right in the eye and don't blink. But there are other bones that scare them. For my family, the pile we shied away from was grief. Everything in my background prepared me to deal with physical pain. Nothing prepared me for emotional loss.

When my father worked his repetitions with the leg weight, he let the tears flow freely because he knew, when the session was over, he could turn to us with a wry smile. But he never again shared his grief with us after we left that hotel room. We went through the automatic motions of a funeral, returned to the ranch, and sorted through my mother's belongings. Within days, we had discarded almost everything that might remind us of her.

Long before the pain had started to abate, we declared it over. "It's time," my father said, "to rejoin the human race." I returned to college. My father met and soon married a woman who looked exactly like my mother. The marriage was painful for both partners and ended in divorce. And for years I spent so much energy denying my own longing for the dead that I hardly had energy for the living.

If any of us had broken a leg, we would have taken all the time the leg required. If the bone didn't knit in six months, we would have given it twelve. And if it still wasn't sound, we would have strapped on a brace. We might have asked each other, "How's that leg?" But we didn't ask, "How's that loneliness?" We tried to put our grief behind us, but we had only shied away from it. We started walking before we had healed. For years we hardly mentioned my mother's name. And we soon found there were places we didn't dare walk.

I REMEMBER NOTHING of my mother's funeral, absolutely nothing, until the end when we were leaving the cemetery. A neighbor, Sandy Hirsig, Glenna and Buddy's daughter, came up to me. She was a few years my junior, but I had always felt a particular connection with her—she, too, was close to her mother. She approached me just as I was about to get into the limousine, and she hugged me. I had this curious sense of looking down on the two of us as if from above and thinking: She is the only one who could possibly understand.

And then, when just a few years later Sandy was killed in a brutal accident on the Iron Mountain road, I couldn't sleep for nights. She and her mother had been driving to the ranch, and I could almost hear the intense conversation before they came around a corner and slammed into a snowplow; my mother and I always had our very best conversations on that fifty-mile stretch of road. I wrote the Hirsigs the polite, formal letter of sympathy I had been trained to write, and I never told even the man I was living with about the accident, though he was a sensitive man. I was too afraid that, in the telling, I wouldn't take it well—I would break down.

A few months later, I returned to Wyoming and visited the Hirsigs. I wanted to tell them what I hadn't been able to mention in the letter—how Sandy came up to me at my mother's funeral and gave me the single moment of true solace that penetrated that horrible affair. But I couldn't tell them. We talked for an hour and I never mentioned Sandy's name. Buddy Hirsig had ridden all day with a broken ankle at our branding, but I was afraid to tell either him or Glenna how much their daughter touched me. I was too afraid of making them sad, of challenging their ability to take it, of challenging mine.

And losses piled upon losses. Other members of my family passed away, I lost friends to accidents and cancer. I kept reinforcing the dam with each new addition. I left my lover and since I had no place to put my sadness, I started watching movies. I saw *The Black Stallion* eleven times. A boy and a stallion are the sole survivors of a shipwreck and they make it to a desert island. The first half of the film is done almost entirely without dialogue. Halfway through, the boy and the horse are discovered and returned to civilization and then the story becomes just another film. But the first half: something about such deep and wordless communication in total isolation touched me. Eleven times I bought a ticket. Eleven times I sat alone in the dark and wept from the moment the horse first appeared on the screen until the midway point. And then I'd dry my eyes, pick up my bag, and leave.

At some point, I sought out a therapist. I don't remember the year, I don't remember the particulars of despair. There is so much about those years I don't remember. It was the hardest decision I had ever made, an admission, if only to myself, that I couldn't take it. In the first session, I started to cry. I couldn't stop. I remember the terror—my God, I will never stop. I wept in session and I wept out of session. I hid myself away so friends wouldn't know. They didn't miss me; I had already been absent for a long time.

Tears, like rain, can't last forever. In time the flood receded, and I had a sense of emerging into a world that seemed just born: the air crisp, the rustle of leaves surprising and new.

WHEN YOU TAKE A COLT near the bones, every muscle in his body is posed in opposition. He may, at your urging, nudge forward, but his energy is entirely consumed by the posture of escape. If fear overcomes him, he will bolt blindly, crashing into a fence or stumbling over a bank. But if he inches up to the bones, bit by bit and soft assurance by assurance, he will smell them, his ears will twitch a time or two and then fall back in bored relaxation. At that point his whole body will relax, visibly and at once, and in a moment he will be focused on the outside world again, anxious to get on with the rest of the journey.

IN EIGHTEEN YEARS of intermittent ranch work, I never had a serious injury: no major plaster. Recently, though, I had a physical and I was asked to fill out a health questionnaire. When I met with the doctor, she looked over the chart and then started asking about my relationships with men. I answered the first couple of questions perfunctorily, but after the third, I asked her why she cared. "Seven brain concussions," she read off my list of injuries. "A broken cheekbone, a broken rib, bruised kidneys . . ."

How often, I thought later, she must read physical scars for the emotional ruin they hide. How often her questions must probe the deepest shame. But as I explained my own history, I recognized a hint of pride in my voice. I had paid my dues in the world of work. I could "take it." Sometimes, now, physical endurance seems the easy part, but it holds lessons for me if I will only listen.

ALMOST EVERY RANCH-STEAD is littered with bones. The skull of a bull, a deer, or an antelope tacked up over a gate or barn door, a pile of elk antlers by the shed, a cow pelvis in the garden. When you find a bone—a buffalo skull, a bobcat jaw, the precise, tiny foot of a badger—you bring it home. The larger piles you leave alone. Skeletons mark the method of dying, at least until time and coyotes rearrange the evidence. A small pelvis hung up in a larger one: breech birth. Backbone downhill, head flung upward gasping for one last breath: poison weed.

Even to my house in the city, I drag home bones: a deer head for the hearth, a bull skull for the entryway. There's a stark beauty to bones, bleached white by the sun. Bones are as hard as rock and as fragile as rock. They crack, fissure, shatter, and as they wear to dust, they take us with them, both column and conduit of our own evolution. In the bloodline drawn by landscape, all bones are ancestral. Our homage is sincere and yet irreverent, a wry celebration of the fact that we still wrap our own bones with skin.

Maxine Hong Kingston

aₓine Hong Kingston was born October 27, 1940, in Stockton, California, where her family ran a laundry. She was educated at Berkeley and married an actor, Earll Kingston, the same year (1962) she received her A.B. For two years she taught high school English and mathematics in Hayward, next English as a second language in Honolulu, and then college, first at the University of Hawaii and later at Berkeley. The National Book Critics Circle selected her first book, The Woman Warrior, as the best work of nonfiction published in 1976. After the publication of China Men in 1980, on the basis of sheer literary talent, comprehensiveness of vision, and originality of style, the critics hailed her as a major American writer, perhaps the most formidable Asian-American writer in the nation's history. Her most recent book, a novel, Tripmaster Monkey, appeared in 1989. All of her books are wildly inventive and highly poetic cultural epics that illuminate Western American social patterns, particularly cultural misogyny and institutional racism. For Kingston, the American West is not only full of ghost towns but also highly populated with ghosts. (Are our parents and friends, for instance, any less real to us because they are dead?) In this excerpt from The Woman Warrior, Kingston confronts several visions: the stuttering girl, the woman about whom little or nothing is known, the girl whose mother cut her tongue like a mag-

pie's, whose throat hurts, the one who quacks like a mallard duck, the one who talks so much people consider her mad.

"A Song for a Barbarian Reed Pipe"

from *The Woman Warrior*

LONG AGO IN CHINA, KNOT-MAKERS TIED STRING into buttons and frogs, and rope into bell pulls. There was one knot so complicated that it blinded the knot-maker. Finally an emperor outlawed this cruel knot, and the nobles could not order it anymore. If I had lived in China, I would have been an outlaw knot-maker.

Maybe that's why my mother cut my tongue. She pushed my tongue up and sliced the frenum. Or maybe she snipped it with a pair of nail scissors. I don't remember her doing it, only her telling me about it, but all during childhood I felt sorry for the baby whose mother waited with scissors or knife in hand for it to cry—and then, when its mouth was wide open like a baby bird's, cut. The Chinese say "a ready tongue is an evil."

I used to curl up my tongue in front of the mirror and tauten my frenum into a white line, itself as thin as a razor blade. I saw no scars in my mouth. I thought perhaps I had had two frena, and she had cut one. I made other children open their mouths so I could compare theirs to mine. I saw perfect pink membranes stretching into precise edges that looked easy enough to cut. Sometimes I felt very proud that my mother committed such a powerful act upon me. At other times I was terrified—the first thing my mother did when she saw me was to cut my tongue.

"Why did you do that to me, Mother?"

"I told you."

"Tell me again."

"I cut it so that you would not be tongue-tied. Your tongue would be able to move in any language. You'll be able to speak languages that are completely different from one another. You'll be able to pronounce anything. Your frenum looked too tight to do those things, so I cut it."

"But isn't 'a ready tongue an evil'?"

"Things are different in this ghost country."

"Did it hurt me? Did I cry and bleed?"

"I don't remember. Probably."

She didn't cut the other children's. When I asked cousins and other Chinese children whether their mothers had cut their tongues loose, they said, "What?"

"Why didn't you cut my brothers' and sisters' tongues?"

"They didn't need it."

"Why not? Were theirs longer than mine?"

"Why don't you quit blabbering and get to work?"

If my mother was not lying she should have cut more, scraped away the rest of the frenum skin, because I have a terrible time talking. Or she should not have cut at all, tampering with my speech. When I went to kindergarten and had to speak English for the first time, I became silent. A dumbness—a shame—still cracks my voice in two, even when I want to say "hello" casually, or ask an easy question in front of the check-out counter, or ask directions of a bus driver. I stand frozen, or I hold up the line with the complete, grammatical sentence that comes squeaking out at impossible length. "What did you say?" says the cab driver, or "Speak up," so I have to perform again, only weaker the second time. A telephone call makes my throat bleed and takes up that day's courage. It spoils my day with self-disgust when I hear my broken voice come skittering out into the open. It makes people wince to hear it. I'm getting better, though. Recently I asked the postman for special-issue stamps; I've waited since childhood for postmen to give me some of their own accord. I am making progress, a little every day.

My silence was thickest—total—during the three years that I covered my school paintings with black paint. I painted layers of black over houses and flowers and suns, and when I drew on the blackboard, I put a layer of chalk on top. I was making a stage curtain, and it was the moment before the curtain parted or rose. The teachers called my parents to school, and I saw they had been saving my pictures, curling and cracking, all alike and black. The teachers pointed to the pictures and looked serious, talked seriously too, but my parents did not understand English. ("The parents and teachers of criminals were executed," said my father.) My parents took the pictures home. I spread them out (so black and full of possibilities) and pretended the curtains were swinging open, flying up, one after another, sunlight underneath, mighty operas.

During the first silent year I spoke to no one at school, did not ask before going to the lavatory, and flunked kindergarten. My sister also said nothing for three years, silent in the playground and silent at lunch. There were other quiet Chinese girls not of our family, but most of them got over it sooner than we did. I enjoyed the silence. At first it did not occur to me I was supposed to talk or to pass kindergarten. I talked at home and to one or two of the Chinese kids in class. I made motions and even made some jokes. I drank out of a toy saucer when the water spilled out of the cup, and everybody laughed, pointing at me, so I did it some more. I didn't know that Americans don't drink out of saucers.

I liked the Negro students (Black Ghosts) best because they laughed the loudest and talked to me as if I were a daring talker too. One of the Negro girls had her mother coil braids over her ears Shanghai-style like mine; we were Shanghai twins except that she was covered with black like my paintings. Two Negro kids enrolled in Chinese school, and the teachers gave them Chinese names. Some Negro kids walked me to school and home, protecting me from the Japanese kids, who hit me and chased me and stuck gum in my ears.

The Japanese kids were noisy and tough. They appeared one day in kindergarten, released from concentration camp, which was a tic-tac-toe mark, like barbed wire, on the map.

It was when I found out I had to talk that school became a misery, that the silence became a misery. I did not speak and felt bad each time that I did not speak. I read aloud in first grade, though, and heard the barest whisper with little squeaks come out of my throat. "Louder," said the teacher, who scared the voice away again. The other Chinese girls did not talk either, so I knew the silence had to do with being a Chinese girl.

Reading out loud was easier than speaking because we did not have to make up what to say, but I stopped often, and the teacher would think I'd gone quiet again. I could not understand "I." The Chinese "I" has seven strokes, intricacies. How could the American "I," assuredly wearing a hat like the Chinese, have only three strokes, the middle so straight? Was it out of politeness that this writer left off strokes the way a Chinese has to write her own name small and crooked? No, it was not politeness; "I" is a capital and "you" is lower-case. I stared at that middle line and waited so long for its black center to resolve into tight strokes and dots that I forgot to pronounce it. The other troublesome word was "here," no strong consonant to hang on to, and so flat, when "here" is two mountainous ideographs. The teacher, who had already told me every day how to read "I" and "here," put me in the low corner under the stairs again, where the noisy boys usually sat.

When my second grade class did a play, the whole class went to the auditorium except the Chinese girls. The teacher, lovely and Hawaiian, should have understood about us, but instead left us behind in the classroom. Our voices were too soft or nonexistent, and our parents never signed the permission slips anyway. They never signed anything unnecessary. We opened the door a crack and peeked out, but closed it again quickly. One of us (not me) won every spelling bee, though.

I remember telling the Hawaiian teacher, "We Chinese can't sing 'land where our fathers died.' " She argued with me about politics, while I meant because of curses. But how can I have that memory when I couldn't talk? My mother says that we, like the ghosts, have no memories.

After American school, we picked up our cigar boxes, in which we had arranged books, brushes, and an inkbox neatly, and went to Chinese school, from 5:00 to 7:30 P.M. There we chanted together, voices rising and falling, loud and soft, some boys shouting, everybody reading together, reciting together and not alone with one voice. When we had a memorization test, the teacher let each of us come to his desk and say the lesson to him privately, while the rest of the class practiced copying or tracing. Most of the teachers were men. The boys who were so well behaved in the American school played tricks on them and talked back to them. The girls were not mute. They screamed and yelled during recess, when there were no rules; they had fistfights. Nobody was afraid of children hurting themselves or of children hurting school property. The glass doors to the red and green balconies with the gold joy symbols were left wide open so that we could run out and climb the fire escapes. We played capture-the-flag in the auditorium, where Sun Yat-sen and Chiang Kai-shek's pictures hung at the back of the stage, the Chinese flag on their left and the American flag on their right. We climbed the teak ceremonial chairs and made flying leaps off the stage. One flag headquarters was behind the glass door and the other on stage right. Our feet drummed on the hollow stage. During recess the teachers locked themselves up in their office with the shelves of books, copybooks, inks from China. They drank tea and warmed their hands at a stove. There was no play supervision. At recess we had the school to ourselves, and also we could roam as far as we could go—downtown, Chinatown stores, home—as long as we returned before the bell rang.

At exactly 7:30 the teacher again picked up the brass bell that sat on his desk and swung it over our heads, while we charged down the stairs, our cheering magnified in the stairwell. Nobody had to line up.

Not all of the children who were silent at American school found voice at Chinese school. One new teacher said each of us had to get up and recite in front of the class, who was to listen. My sister and I had memorized the lesson perfectly. We said it to each other at home, one chanting, one listening. The teacher called on my sister to recite first. It was the first time a teacher had called on the second-born to go first. My sister was scared. She glanced at me and looked away; I looked down at my desk. I hoped that she could do it because if she could, then I would have to. She opened her mouth and a voice came out that wasn't a whisper, but it wasn't a proper voice either. I hoped that she would not cry, fear breaking up her voice like twigs underfoot. She sounded as if she were trying to sing though weeping and strangling. She did not pause or stop to end the embarrassment. She kept going until she said the last word, and then she sat down. When it was my turn, the same voice came out, a crippled animal running on broken legs. You could hear splinters in my voice, bones rubbing jagged against one another. I was loud, though. I was glad I didn't whisper. There was one little girl who whispered.

You can't entrust your voice to the Chinese, either; they want to capture your voice for their own use. They want to fix up your tongue to speak for them. "How much less can you sell it for?" we have to say. Talk the Sales Ghosts down. Make them take a loss.

We were working at the laundry when a delivery boy came from the Rexall drugstore around the corner. He had a pale blue box of pills, but nobody was sick. Reading the label we saw that it belonged to another Chinese family, Crazy Mary's family. "Not ours," said my father. He pointed out the name to the Delivery Ghost, who took the pills back. My mother muttered for an hour, and then her anger boiled over. "That ghost! That dead ghost! How dare he come to the wrong house?" She could not concentrate on her marking and pressing. "A mistake! Huh!" I was getting angry myself. She fumed. She made her press crash and hiss. "Revenge. We've got to avenge this wrong on our future, on our health, and on our lives. Nobody's going to sicken my children and get away with it." We brothers and sisters did not look at one another. She would do something awful, something embarrassing. She'd already been hinting that during the next eclipse we slam pot lids together to scare the frog from swallowing the moon. (The word for "eclipse" is *frog-swallowing-the-moon*.) When we had not banged lids at the last eclipse and the shadow kept receding anyway, she'd said, "The villagers must be banging and clanging very loudly back home in China."

("On the other side of the world, they aren't having an eclipse, Mama. That's just a shadow the earth makes when it comes between the moon and the sun."

"You're always believing what those Ghost Teachers tell you. Look at the size of the jaws!")

"Aha!" she yelled. "You! The biggest." She was pointing at me. "You go to the drugstore."

"What do you want me to buy, Mother?" I said.

"Buy nothing. Don't bring one cent. Go and make them stop the curse."

"I don't want to go. I don't know how to do that. There are no such things as curses. They'll think I'm crazy."

"If you don't go, I'm holding you responsible for bringing a plague on this family."

"What am I supposed to do when I get there?" I said, sullen, trapped. "Do I say, 'Your delivery boy made a wrong delivery'?"

"They know he made a wrong delivery. I want you to make them rectify their crime."

I felt sick already. She'd make me swing stinky censers around the counter, at the druggist, at the customers. Throw dog blood on the druggist. I couldn't stand her plans.

"You get reparation candy," she said. "You say, 'You have tainted my house with sick medicine and must remove the curse with sweetness.' He'll understand."

"He didn't do it on purpose. And no, he won't, Mother. They don't understand stuff like that. I won't be able to say it right. He'll call us beggars."

"You just translate." She searched me to make sure I wasn't hiding any money. I was sneaky and bad enough to buy the candy and come back pretending it was a free gift.

"Mymotherseztagimmesomecandy," I said to the druggist. Be cute and small. No one hurts the cute and small.

"What? Speak up. Speak English," he said, big in his white druggist coat.

"Tatatagimme somecandy."

The druggist leaned way over the counter and frowned. "Some free candy," I said. "Sample candy."

"We don't give sample candy, young lady," he said.

"My mother said you have to give us candy. She said that is the way the Chinese do it."

"What?"

"That is the way the Chinese do it."

"Do what?"

"Do things." I felt the weight and immensity of things impossible to explain to the druggist.

"Can I give you some money?" he asked.

"No, we want candy."

He reached into a jar and gave me a handful of lollipops. He gave us candy all year round, year after year, every time we went into the drugstore. When different druggists or clerks waited on us, they also gave us candy. They had talked us over. They gave us

Halloween candy in December, Christmas candy around Valentine's day, candy hearts at Easter, and Easter eggs at Halloween. "See?" said our mother. "They understand. You kids just aren't very brave." But I knew they did not understand. They thought we were beggars without a home who lived in back of the laundry. They felt sorry for us. I did not eat their candy. I did not go inside the drugstore or walk past it unless my parents forced me to. Whenever we had a prescription filled, the druggist put candy in the medicine bag. This is what Chinese druggists normally do, except they give raisins. My mother thought she taught the Druggist Ghosts a lesson in good manners (which is the same word as "traditions").

My mouth went permanently crooked with effort, turned down on the left side and straight on the right. How strange that the emigrant villagers are shouters, hollering face to face. My father asks, "Why is it I can hear Chinese from blocks away? Is it that I understand the language? Or is it they talk loud?" They turn the radio up full blast to hear the operas, which do not seem to hurt their ears. And they yell over the singers that wail over the drums, everybody talking at once, big arm gestures, spit flying. You can see the disgust on American faces looking at women like that. It isn't just the loudness. It is the way Chinese sounds, chingchong ugly, to American ears, not beautiful like Japanese sayonara words with the consonants and vowels as regular as Italian. We make guttural peasant noise and have Ton Duc Thang names you can't remember. And the Chinese can't hear Americans at all; the language is too soft and western music unhearable. I've watched a Chinese audience laugh, visit, talk-story, and holler during a piano recital, as if the musician could not hear them. A Chinese-American, somebody's son, was playing Chopin, which has no punctuation, no cymbals, no gongs. Chinese piano music is five black keys. Normal Chinese women's voices are strong and bossy. We American-Chinese girls had to whisper to make ourselves American-feminine. Apparently we whispered even more softly than the Americans. Once a year the teachers referred my sister and me to speech therapy, but our voices would straighten out, unpredictably normal, for the therapists. Some of us gave up, shook our heads, and said nothing, not one word. Some of us could not even shake our heads. At times shaking my head no is more self-assertion than I can manage. Most of us eventually found some voice, however faltering. We invented an American-feminine speaking personality, except for that one girl who could not speak up even in Chinese school.

She was a year older than I and was in my class for twelve years. During all those years she read aloud but would not talk. Her older sister was usually beside her; their parents kept the older daughter back to protect the younger one. They were six and seven years old when they began school. Although I had flunked kindergarten, I was the same age as most other students in our class; my parents had probably lied about my age, so I had had a head start and came out even. My younger sister was in the class below me; we were normal ages and normally separated. The parents of the quiet girl, on the other hand, protected both daughters. When it sprinkled, they kept them home from school. The girls did not work for a living the way we did. But in other ways we were the same.

We were similar in sports. We held the bat on our shoulders until we walked to first base. (You got a strike only when you actually struck at the ball.) Sometimes the pitcher wouldn't bother to throw to us. "Automatic walk," the other children would call, sending us on our way. By fourth or fifth grade, though, some of us would try to hit the ball. "Easy out," the other kids would say. I hit the ball a couple of times. Baseball was nice in that there was a definite spot to run to after hitting the ball. Basketball confused me because when I caught the ball I didn't know whom to throw it to. "Me. Me," the kids would be yelling. "Over here." Suddenly it would occur to me I hadn't memorized which ghosts were on my team and which were on the other. When the kids said, "Automatic walk," the girl who was quieter than I kneeled with one end of the bat in each hand and placed it carefully on the plate. Then she dusted her hands as she walked to first base, where she rubbed her hands softly, fingers spread. She always got tagged out before second base. She would whisper-read but not talk. Her whisper was as soft as if she had no muscles. She seemed to be breathing from a distance. I heard no anger or tension.

I joined in at lunchtime when the other students, the Chinese too, talked about whether or not she was mute, although obviously she was not if she could read aloud. People told how *they* had tried *their* best to be friendly. *They* said hello, but if she refused to answer, well, they didn't see why they had to say hello anymore. She had no friends of her own but followed her sister everywhere, although people and she herself probably thought I was her friend. I also followed her sister about, who was fairly normal. She was almost two years older and read more than anyone else.

I hated the younger sister, the quiet one. I hated her when she was the last chosen for her team and I, the last chosen for my team. I hated her for her China doll hair cut. I hated her at music time for the wheezes that came out of her plastic flute.

One afternoon in the sixth grade (that year I was arrogant with talk, not knowing there were going to be high school dances and college seminars to set me back), I and my little sister and the quiet girl and her big sister stayed late after school for some reason. The cement was cooling, and the tetherball poles made shadows across the gravel. The hooks at the rope ends were clinking against the poles. We shouldn't have been so late; there was laundry work to do and Chinese school to get to by 5:00. The last time we had stayed late, my mother had phoned the police and told them we had been kidnapped by bandits. The radio stations broadcast our descriptions. I had to get home before she did that again. But sometimes if you loitered long enough in the schoolyard, the other children would have gone home and you could play with the equipment before the office took it away. We were chasing one another through the playground and in and out of the basement, where the playroom and lavatory were. During air raid drills (it was during the Korean War, which you knew about because every day the front page of the newspaper printed a map of Korea with the top part red and going up and down like a window shade), we curled up in this basement. Now everyone was gone. The playroom was army green and had nothing in it but a long trough with drinking spigots in rows. Pipes across the ceiling led to the drinking fountains and to the toilets in the next room. When someone flushed you could hear the water and other matter, which the children named, running inside the big pipe above the drinking spigots. There was one playroom for girls next to the girls' lavatory and one playroom for boys next to the boys' lavatory. The stalls were open and the toilets had no lids, by which we knew that ghosts have no sense of shame or privacy.

Inside the playroom the lightbulbs in cages had already been turned off. Daylight came in x-patterns through the caging at the windows. I looked out and, seeing no one in the schoolyard, ran outside to climb the fire escape upside down, hanging on to the metal stairs with fingers and toes.

I did a flip off the fire escape and ran across the schoolyard. The day was a great eye, and it was not paying much attention to me now. I could disappear with the sun; I could turn quickly sideways and slip into a different world. It seemed I could run faster at this time, and by evening I would be able to fly. As the afternoon wore on we could run into the forbidden places—the boys' big yard, the boys' playroom. We could go into the boys' lavatory and look at the urinals. The only time during school hours I had crossed the boys' yard was when a flatbed truck with a giant thing covered with canvas and tied down with ropes had parked across the street. The children had told one another that it was a gorilla in captivity; we couldn't decide whether the sign said "Trail of the Gorilla" or "Trial of the Gorilla." The thing was as big as a house. The teachers couldn't stop us from hysterically rushing to the fence and clinging to the wire mesh. Now I ran across the boys' yard clear to the Cyclone fence and thought about the hair that I had seen sticking out of the canvas. It was going to be summer soon, so you could feel that freedom coming on too.

I ran back into the girls' yard, and there was the quiet sister all by herself. I ran past her, and she followed me into the girls' lavatory. My footsteps rang hard against cement and tile because of the taps I had nailed into my shoes. Her footsteps were soft, padding after me. There was no one in the lavatory but the two of us. I ran all around the rows of twenty-five open stalls to make sure of that. No sisters. I think we must have been playing hide-and-go-seek. She was not good at hiding by herself and usually followed her sister; they'd hide in the same place. They must have gotten separated. In this growing twilight, a child could hide and never be found.

I stopped abruptly in front of the sinks, and she came running toward me before she could stop herself, so that she almost collided with me. I walked closer. She backed away, puzzlement, then alarm in her eyes.

"You're going to talk," I said, my voice steady and normal, as it is when talking to the familiar, the weak, and the small. "I am going to make you talk, you sissy-girl." She stopped backing away and stood fixed.

I looked into her face so I could hate it close up. She wore black bangs, and her cheeks were pink and white. She was baby soft. I thought that I could put my thumb on her nose and push it bonelessly in, indent her face. I could poke dimples into her cheeks. I could work her face around like dough. She stood still, and I did not want to look at her face anymore; I hated fragility. I walked around her, looked her up and down the way the Mexican and Negro girls did when they fought, so tough. I hated her weak neck, the way it did not support her head but let it droop; her head would fall backward. I stared at the curve of her nape. I wished I was able to see what my own neck looked like from the back and sides. I hoped it did not look like hers; I wanted a stout neck. I grew my hair long to hide it in case it was a flower-stem neck. I walked around to the front of her to hate her face some more.

I reached up and took the fatty part of her cheek, not dough, but meat, between my thumb and finger. This close, and I saw no pores. "Talk," I said. "Are you going to talk?" Her skin was fleshy, like squid out of which the glassy blades of bones had been pulled. I wanted tough skin, hard brown skin. I had callused my hands; I had scratched dirt to blacken the nails, which I cut straight across to make stubby fingers. I gave her face a squeeze. "Talk." When I let go, the pink rushed back into my white thumbprint on her skin. I walked around to her side. "Talk!" I shouted into the side of her head. Her straight hair hung, the same all these years, no ringlets or braids or permanents. I squeezed her other cheek. "Are you? Huh? Are you going to talk?" She tried to shake her head, but I had hold of her face. She had no muscles to jerk away. Her skin seemed to stretch. I let go in horror. What if it came away in my hand? "No, huh?" I said, rubbing the touch of her off my fingers. "Say 'No,' then," I said. I gave her another pinch and a twist. "Say 'No.' " She shook her head, her straight hair turning with her head, not swinging side to side like the pretty girls'. She was so neat. Her neatness bothered me. I hated the way she folded the wax paper from her lunch; she did not wad her brown paper bag and her school papers. I hated her clothes—the blue pastel cardigan, the white blouse with the collar that lay flat over the cardigan, the homemade flat, cotton skirt she wore when everybody else was wearing flared skirts. I hated pastels; I would wear black always. I squeezed again, harder, even though her cheek had a weak rubbery feeling I did not like. I squeezed one cheek, then the other, back and forth until the tears ran out of her eyes as if I had pulled them out. "Stop crying," I said, but although she habitually followed me around, she did not obey. Her eyes dripped; her nose dripped. She wiped her eyes with her papery fingers. The skin on her hands and arms seemed powdery-dry, like tracing paper, onion skin. I hated her fingers. I could snap them like breadsticks. I pushed her hands down. "Say 'Hi,' " I said. " 'Hi.' Like that. Say your name. Go ahead. Say it. Or are you stupid? You're so stupid, you don't know your own name, is that it? When I say, 'What's your name?' you just blurt it out, o.k.? What's your name?" Last year the whole class had laughed at a boy who couldn't fill out a form because he didn't know his father's name. The teacher sighed, exasperated, and was very sarcastic, "Don't you notice things? What does your mother call him?" she said. The class laughed at how dumb he was not to notice things. "She calls him father of me," he said. Even we laughed, although we knew that his mother did not call his father by name, and a son does not know his father's name. We laughed and were relieved that our parents had had the foresight to tell us some names we could give the teachers. "If you're not stupid," I said to the quiet girl, "what's your name?" She shook her head, and some hair caught in the tears; wet black hair stuck to the side of the pink and white face. I reached up (she was taller than I) and took a strand of hair. I pulled it. "Well, then, let's honk your hair," I said. "Honk. Honk." Then I pulled the other side—"ho-o-n-nk"—a long pull; "ho-o-n-n-nk"—a longer pull. I could see her little white ears, like white cutworms curled underneath the hair. "Talk!" I yelled into each cutworm.

I looked right at her. "I know you talk," I said. "I've heard you." Her eyebrows flew up. Something in those black eyes was startled, and I pursued it. "I was walking past your house when you didn't know I was there. I heard you yell in English and in Chinese. You weren't just talking. You were shouting. I heard you shout. You were saying, 'Where are you?' Say that again. Go ahead, just the way you did at home." I yanked harder on the hair, but steadily, not jerking. I did not want to pull it out. "Go ahead. Say, 'Where are you?' Say it loud enough for your sister to come. Call her. Make her come help you. Call her name. I'll stop if she comes. So call. Go ahead."

She shook her head, her mouth curved down, crying. I could see her tiny white teeth, baby teeth. I wanted to grow big strong yellow teeth. "You do have a tongue," I said. "So use it." I pulled the hair at her temples, pulled the tears out of her eyes. "Say, 'Ow,' " I said. "Just 'Ow.' Say, 'Let go.' Go ahead. Say it. I'll honk you again if you don't say, 'Let me alone.' Say, 'Leave me alone,' and I'll let you go. I will. I'll let go if you say it. You can stop this anytime you want to, you know. All you have to do is tell me to stop. Just say, 'Stop.' You're just asking for it, aren't you? You're just asking for another honk. Well then, I'll have to give you another honk. Say, 'Stop.' " But she didn't. I had to pull again and again.

Sounds did come out of her mouth, sobs, chokes, noises that were almost words. Snot ran out of her nose. She tried to wipe it on her hands, but there was too much of it. She used her sleeve. "You're disgusting," I told her. "Look at you, snot streaming down your nose, and you won't say a word to stop it. You're such a nothing." I moved behind her and pulled the hair growing out of her weak neck. I let go. I stood silent for a long time. Then I screamed, "Talk!" I would scare the words out of her. If she had had little bound feet, the toes twisted under the balls, I would have jumped up and landed on them—crunch!—stomped on them with my iron shoes. She cried hard, sobbing aloud. "Cry, 'Mama,' " I said. "Come on. Cry, 'Mama.' Say, 'Stop it.' "

I put my finger on her pointed chin. "I don't like you. I don't like the weak little toots you make on your flute. Wheeze. Wheeze. I don't like the way you don't swing at the ball. I don't like the way you're the last one chosen. I don't like the way you can't make a fist for tetherball. Why don't you make a fist? Come on. Get tough. Come on. Throw fists." I pushed at her long hands; they swung limply at her sides. Her fingers were so long, I thought maybe they had an extra joint. They couldn't possibly make fists like other peo-ple's. "Make a fist," I said. "Come on. Just fold those fingers up; fin-gers on the inside, thumbs on the outside. Say something. Honk me back. You're so tall, and you let me pick on you.

"Would you like a hanky? I can't get you one with embroidery on it or crocheting along the edges, but I'll get you some toilet paper if you tell me to. Go ahead. Ask me. I'll get it for you if you ask." She did not stop crying. "Why don't you scream, 'Help'?" I suggested. "Say, 'Help.' Go ahead." She cried on. "O.K. O.K. Don't talk. Just scream, and I'll let you go. Won't that feel good? Go ahead. Like this." I screamed, not too loudly. My voice hit the tile and rang it as if I had thrown a rock at it. The stalls opened wider and the toilets wide and darker. Shadows leaned at angles I had not seen before. It was very late. Maybe a janitor had locked me in with this girl for the night. Her black eyes blinked and stared, blinked and stared. I felt dizzy from hunger. We had been in this lavatory together forever. My mother would call the police again if I didn't bring my sister home soon. "I'll let you go if you say just one word," I said. "You can even say, 'a' or 'the,' and I'll let you go. Come on. Please." She didn't shake her head anymore, only cried steadily, so much water coming out of her. I could see the two duct holes where the tears welled out. Quarts of tears but no words. I grabbed her by the shoulder. I could feel bones. The light was coming in queerly through the frosted glass with the chicken wire embedded in it. Her crying was like an animal's—a seal's—and it echoed around the basement. "Do you want to stay here all night?" I asked. "Your mother is wondering what happened to her baby. You wouldn't want to have her mad at you. You'd better say something." I shook her shoulder. I pulled her hair again. I squeezed her face. "Come on! Talk! Talk! Talk!" She didn't seem to feel it anymore when I pulled her hair. "There's nobody here but you and me. This isn't a class-room or a playground or a crowd. I'm just one person. You can talk in front of one person. Don't make me pull harder and harder until you talk." But her hair seemed to stretch; she did not say a word. "I'm going to pull harder. Don't make me pull anymore, or your hair will come out and you're going to be bald. Do you want to be bald? You don't want to be bald, do you?"

Far away, coming from the edge of town, I heard whistles blow. The cannery was changing shifts, letting out the afternoon people, and still we were here at school. It was a sad sound—work done. The air was lonelier after the sound died.

"Why won't you talk?" I started to cry. What if I couldn't stop, and everyone would want to know what happened? "Now look what you've done," I scolded. "You're going to pay for this. I want to know why. And you're going to tell me why. You don't see I'm trying to help you out, do you? Do you want to be like this, dumb (do you know what dumb means?), your whole life? Don't you ever want to be a cheerleader? Or a pompom girl? What are you going to do for a living? Yeah, you're going to have to work because you can't be a housewife. Somebody has to marry you before you can be a housewife. And you, you are a plant. Do you know that? That's all you are if you don't talk. If you don't talk, you can't have a personality. You'll have no personality and no hair. You've got to let people know you have a personality and a brain. You think somebody is going to take care of you all your stupid life? You think you'll always have your big sister? You think somebody's going to marry you, is that it? Well, you're not the type that gets dates, let alone gets married. Nobody's going to notice you. And you have to talk for interviews, speak right up in front of the boss. Don't you know that? You're so dumb. Why do I waste my time on you?" Sniffling and snorting, I couldn't stop crying and talking at the same time. I kept wiping my nose on my arm, my sweater lost somewhere (probably not worn because my mother said to wear a sweater). It seemed as if I had spent my life in that basement, doing the worst thing I had yet done to another person. "I'm doing this for your own good," I said. "Don't you dare tell anyone I've been bad to you. Talk. Please talk."

I was getting dizzy from the air I was gulping. Her sobs and my sobs were bouncing wildly off the tile, sometimes together, sometimes alternating. "I don't understand why you won't say just one word," I cried, clenching my teeth. My knees were shaking, and I hung on to her hair to stand up. Another time I'd stayed too late, I had had to walk around two Negro kids who were bonking each other's head on the concrete. I went back later to see if the concrete had cracks in it. "Look. I'll give you something if you talk. I'll give you my pencil box. I'll buy you some candy. O.K.? What do you want? Tell me. Just say it, and I'll give it to you. Just say, 'yes,' or, 'O.K.,' or, 'Baby Ruth.' " But she didn't want anything.

I had stopped pinching her cheek because I did not like the feel of her skin. I would go crazy if it came away in my hands. "I skinned her," I would have to confess.

Suddenly I heard footsteps hurrying through the basement, and her sister ran into the lavatory calling her name. "Oh, there you are," I said. "We've been waiting for you. I was only trying to teach her to talk. She wouldn't cooperate, though." Her sister went into one of the stalls and got handfuls of toilet paper and wiped her off. Then we found my sister, and we walked home together. "Your family really ought to force her to speak," I advised all the way home. "You mustn't pamper her."

The world is sometimes just, and I spent the next eighteen months sick in bed with a mysterious illness. There was no pain and no symptoms, though the middle line in my left palm broke in two. Instead of starting junior high school, I lived like the Victorian recluses I read about. I had a rented hospital bed in the living room, where I watched soap operas on t.v., and my family cranked me up and down. I saw no one but my family, who took good care of me. I could have no visitors, no other relatives, no villagers. My bed was against the west window, and I watched the seasons change the peach tree. I had a bell to ring for help. I used a bedpan. It was the best year and a half of my life. Nothing happened.

But one day my mother, the doctor, said, "You're ready to get up today. It's time to get up and go to school." I walked about outside to get my legs working, leaning on a staff I cut from the peach tree. The sky and trees, the sun were immense—no longer framed by a window, no longer grayed with a fly screen. I sat down on the sidewalk in amazement—the night, the stars. But at school I had to figure out again how to talk. I met again the poor girl I had tormented. She had not changed. She wore the same clothes, hair cut, and manner as when we were in elementary school, no make-up on the pink and white face, while the other Asian girls were starting to tape their eyelids. She continued to be able to read aloud. But there was hardly any reading aloud anymore, less and less as we got into high school.

I was wrong about nobody taking care of her. Her sister became a clerk-typist and stayed unmarried. They lived with their mother and father. She did not have to leave the house except to go to the movies. She was supported. She was protected by her family, as they would normally have done in China if they could have afforded it, not sent off to school with strangers, ghosts, boys.

Page Lambert

P age Lambert grew up in Littleton, Colorado, a suburban kid who yearned for the country. She married a fifth-generation rancher, also from Colorado, and they committed to raising their children with a connection to the land. When the family ranch was sold, they decided to look for property removed from the intense development pressure that was overtaking Colorado. They moved first to South Dakota and then onto a small ranch in the Black Hills near Sundance, Wyoming. There they raise cattle and sheep with help from their two children. Sarah, age eight, and Matt, age eleven.

Like many small ranchers, the Lamberts need outside income to make ends meet. Mark works part time for the Forest Service; Page writes at home and handles many of the daily chores of the ranch. This essay is from her work in progress, "In Search of Kinship."

Porcupine Dusk

KIDS CAN BE KIDS, MATT AND SARAH ARE NO DIF-ferent. And dogs are dogs, including Hondo and our new puppy, Freckles—a red-and-white border collie whose presence a few weeks ago Hondo accepted gracefully. Still, I am surprised to hear the four of them down in the draw poking a stick at the dead porcupine.

Last summer we watched a mother and almost-weaned baby move their ponderous bodies slowly across the lawn. In brazen proximity to us, they nibbled and nosed their way along. The youngster gravitated towards his mother, pushing his face into her soft underbelly. She reared up on her hind feet, trying to push him away. He persisted, unwilling to give up her sweet milk. They stayed upright for several minutes and she parried with him gently, allowing this dance of weaning to continue. Finally the youngster gave up and returned to the grass. From that day on, they appeared each evening at dusk, their noses to the ground, chewing on new undergrowth. A pile of broken tree limbs, saved for kindling, served as their den.

Now, the mother lies dead in the draw, a bullet in her head, and the kids and the dogs gather around. Matt's and Sarah's irreverent voices filter in my open window and Freckles barks incessantly, last week's mouthful of quills still a vivid memory. They are having too much fun. I head outside.

"Hi, Mom. See where Dad shot the eye out? He shot it in the mouth too—and once in the stomach. It was right here under this tree. Sarah and I dragged it out."

The porcupine is over two and a half feet long, head to tail, and big around as a basketball. She looked like the female who nested in the kindling wood last summer.

"Matt says it's a boy, Mom."

The porcupine is lying belly-up.

"No, Sarah, she's a girl, a fat one, too—getting ready for winter. Pet her, here, if you want to. See, she's a girl."

"Is that where the babies nurse, Mommy? There's no quills on her tummy."

"That's right Sarah," I say, remembering how much Matt and Sarah had loved watching the porcupines in the yard.

"Get back," I scold Freckles. "We'd better move her out of the draw and get her away from the house. Think you can help me carry her, Matt? Here, grab the feet like this while I get ahold of her on the other side."

We lug her up the steep side of the draw, past the stackyard holding this year's hay crop, and over to the barbed-wire fence which separates the big pasture from the small pastures close to the house. I stop several times to regrip and pull an occasional quill out of my jeans.

Quills. One of the many problems. As the porcupines became accustomed to us, they no longer even waited for dusk. Some of them nested up high, on the broad limbs of the oak trees. Each evening they lowered themselves down slowly, inch by inch, using their tails as a third hind leg. They browsed in the new growth at the foot of the tree before wandering out into the yard.

My husband, Mark, and I had hoped they would migrate away from the house, up into the hundreds of acres which surround us. But they did not. Instead, they became more numerous, less cautious. Five or six usually waddled from the oak trees to the garden, to the salt-lick at the barn, or to the short grass beneath the swing-set.

The horses got quills in their legs. The heifers got quills in their noses. Sarah and Matt got quills in their jeans. Freckles tangled with them several times and after six mouthfuls of quills and an abdominal operation which removed five inches of quill-infected muscle, she still did not learn. Hondo, older and wiser, stayed clear.

Sarah is dawdling behind and finally stops altogether as Matt and I slide the porcupine under the fence.

"What's the matter, honey?" I ask. "What's wrong?"

"She's making me sad."

"Who?"

"Her." Sarah points to the porcupine.

I am glad she no longer wants to poke the dead animal with a stick. Matt, too, grows quiet.

"It's okay to be sad, Sarah. It's a sad thing Daddy had to do."

We continue our trek across the pasture, heading toward a grove of tall scrub oak. I tire often from bending over and carrying the weight sideways. Hondo and Freckles trot behind, leaving to trail fresh scents, then returning.

Hundreds of acres and thousands of trees surround the house and barn. Gnawed scars half-circle an occasional pine, marking porcupine territory. Surely, the woods could handle a few more. But a conversation with the game warden several weeks ago was disheartening.

"Anywhere to take porcupines if you use a live trap?" we asked.

"No, there sure isn't. It's open season on porcupines. They're considered predaceous animals—you can shoot them anytime. But I don't know about releasing them. They're overpopulated as it is—aren't enough natural predators around anymore to keep them under control. They sure create havoc with the trees, though."

I knew they did. They had. During the springtime they gorged themselves on tender grass shoots. During the summer, they sampled our garden fare and nibbled on my flowers. Fall brought a covering of acorns which they crunched beneath strong jaws. None of this caused problems, but winter's food was scarce. The porcupines rarely moved from the oak trees which held them cradled above the ground. We watched as the bark from the old oaks was slowly stripped away. Last winter the upper branches on three of the trees which separate us from the country road were slowly devoured. These trees provide homes for squirrels like Sassy (the fox squirrel who resides in the old bur oak by the house), and blue jays, robins, and chickadees. They shelter the does and fawns.

"Have you noticed those trees?" Mark had asked me a few days ago.

"Yeah," I said, hating to admit it. "Think they'll die?"

"Hard to tell. Guess we'll have to wait and see. But I think we're going to have to do something."

Matt, Sarah, and I, with porcupine in tow, reach the grove. "Let's put her down by that dead tree over there. That one, Matt, where the two logs are."

"Will the coyotes come and eat her?"

"I hope so. At least here they will be able to smell her. Help me pull that other log closer to her, Matt. I don't want the heifers messing with her."

"Should we turn her over, Mom?"

"No, Sarah, she's fine."

"Mom?"

"What, Matt?"

"Could we maybe say a prayer or something for her?"

So Matt's perspective has changed a little too, since helping to carry her up the hill and across the pasture.

The porcupine lies on her back between the two logs, paws reaching toward the sky. Her dark brown claws are long and curved, the pads of her feet tough and smooth.

"If she had babies inside her now, would they be dead yet?"

"Yes, they'd be dead now too."

"Oh."

The three of us sit next to the dead porcupine. The dogs settle into the comforting shade. It is quiet, the time of evening when the shadows stretch across the field as the sun recedes behind the hills. I am glad we decided to move her, glad for this chance to absorb her death.

"Let's hold hands, Mommy, when we say a prayer."

"Okay, Sarah. You want to say the Lord's Prayer?" Together, sitting beneath the scrub oak, we begin.

"Our Father, who art in heaven . . ."

I am surprised when the tears come. Busy watching Matt and

Sarah, my own feelings sneak up on me. I regain my composure as we finish the prayer.

Sarah, too, is crying. Small tears turn into great sobs and a heaving chest. I hug her.

Then Matt says, "I'm sad too, Mom, only I'm not crying."

"I'm glad you're sad, Matt. We should be sad."

Less than an hour ago it was laughter I had heard, and Freckles' frenzied barking. They had been curious and excited about this dead porcupine, staring at the shot-out eye and poking at the long, sharp spines. What a shift has taken place, how different they are now, sitting on this log holding hands. I pull them closer, drying Sarah's tears with the end of my T-shirt. I think of Mark, and the roles we each play in life's unrelenting duties.

The breath of the meadow reaches us, rustling the soft fur on the belly of the porcupine. Her paws, still stretching toward the sky, cast long shadows in the grass.

Patricia Nelson Limerick

P atricia Nelson Limerick is the most well known of the new Western historians who question the traditional view of Western history as a triumphant conquest that "brought civilization to a savage wilderness." Limerick and her colleagues stress that the story of the West looks different through the eyes of each of its many participants: what whites from the Eastern seaboard saw as virgin land, free for the taking, Native Americans saw as home; the building of the transcontinental railroads looked different to Chinese immigrants than it did to Eastern investors; women of all cultures and ethnicities viewed the Western experience differently than did their spouses.

"This reappraisal," writes Limerick, "is not meant to make white Americans 'look bad': the intention is, on the contrary, simply to make it clear that in Western American history, heroism and villainy, virtue and vice, nobility and shoddiness appear in roughly the same proportions as they appear in any other subject of human judgment. . . . This is only disillusioning to those who have come to depend on illusions."

As a writer, Limerick has insisted on clarity and energy. She once quipped that the tangled phrases of standard academic prose are the literary equivalent of barbed wire. A natural storyteller, her humor and candor have won her a large audience. Her books include

The Legacy of Conquest: The Unbroken Past of the American West *(1987)*; Desert Passage: Encounters with American Deserts *(1989)*; *and* Something in the Soil, *a collection of essays (forthcoming in 1997 from W. W. Norton).*

Banning Writ Large

TWENTY YEARS AGO, I WAS BRIEFLY FAMOUS FOR my good works. As a college student in Santa Cruz, I took up the mandate of the times and launched into "community activism." For years, Santa Cruz had been a quiet resort and retirement town. Then, in 1965, to the horror of many of the elderly residents, a new University of California campus opened, and young people with long hair and alarming habits soon arrived. In my case, community action came to mean trying to mediate between these hostile camps of young and old. My peculiar passion for visiting old folks eventually got me written up by the Associated Press, portrayed as a kind of "good teenager," sitting sweetly in nursing homes, while bad college students neglected personal grooming and raised questions about Richard Nixon's conduct of the Vietnam War.

This good-teenager business, appearing on front pages of newspapers across the nation, was not easy to take. Surely the most bothersome part of the whole operation was an unpleasant letter I got from an old person in Boston, who thought that I was condescending to the elderly. Having assaulted my character in every other way she could think of, this unpleasant soul turned to picking on my birthplace and hometown, Banning, California, briefly referred to in the article. The writer knew nothing about Banning, but she nonetheless wrote a damning line, a sentence that seems to deepen in the memory with the passage of two decades. "Banning," she said, "sounds like something in the soil."

Something in the soil?

What town isn't? Didn't Manhattan, or even Boston, once stand in some relationship to some soil?

What my critic meant by "something in the soil," I never figured out. But this woman created a monster—first by giving me the notion that I might someday avenge this attack, and second by making me realize that my hometown and I were not going to escape each other, that anyone who thought that Banning was something in the soil would most likely think that I was something pretty close to the soil myself. This appeared more and more like one of those "one for all and all for one" situations, with solidarity forced on Banning and me, even though solidarity was not exactly the emotion I felt when I lived there.

In the 1980s, I wrote a book called *The Legacy of Conquest*, an effort to get the field of Western American history out of the straitjacket into which it had been strapped by the old frontier school of historians. In 1989, my Alaskan friend John Whitehead, who had heard more than his share of my Banning stories, remarked that my version of Western American history was, in essence, Banning Writ Large. I had, he felt, taken my hometown to be the part that stands for the whole. This claim at first made me wonder, "Could that be true?" The only honest answer, further investigation proved, was "Yes."

Writers of Western American history who were born and raised in the West have, in fact, followed one of two traditions: taking one's hometown seriously; or trying to forget that one has a hometown. For decades the field of Western American history was under the dominance of the historian Frederick Jackson Turner. Turner was certainly the precedent-setter in the "take your hometown seriously" school of Western historiography. This was not entirely good news for the region west of the Mississippi and west of the hundredth meridian, since Turner's hometown was Portage, Wisconsin.

Thanks to Turner, Westerners got stuck with a historical model designed to fit the upper Midwest. Eighty or ninety years later, we were still trying to fit places like Banning, California, or my current hometown, Boulder, Colorado, into a model designed for Wisconsin. For many Western historians, taking Frederick Jackson Turner's hometown as a model meant dismissing the lessons of their own places of origin.

There were two things I knew from growing up in Banning: that the West is arid or semi-arid, quite a world apart from the green lands of Wisconsin, and that the West has, and has had for a long time, a great diversity in its population, with many different Indian tribes, Hispanic people (long-term residents as well as more recent immigrants), Asian people, and every variety of European immigrant, and none of these people had disappeared under a wave of white settlers with proper northern European origins.

I knew this, but for too many years I paid no attention to what I knew. Giving my allegiance to theories derived from Portage, Wisconsin, while ignoring direct lessons taught by Banning, I was replicating the odd behavior of Western historians through the twentieth century. Many of them were natives of the West, or at least long-term residents of the West, and yet they chose theory over lived experience. The custom of Western historians, for much of the twentieth century, was to reject what they knew firsthand, in favor of texts they had read in graduate school.

Despite this tradition, Western historians who have lived in the West have had many opportunities to wake up and say to themselves, "What is all this stuff about the West as a floating frontier zone on the edge of Anglo-American colonization? Why are we thinking of the West as an exotic and shifting place 'out there'? The West is a real place, with a serious, sometimes even tragic history, a history that was not divided into two pieces by a so-called end of the frontier. The West isn't an *abstraction*. It is here; it is, dare I say it, *something in the soil."*

I turn now to that acknowledged, if sometimes scorned, item in the soil, the town of Banning. Banning is eighty miles from Los Angeles, in the San Gorgonio Pass. There are forests on the neighboring mountains, but there is little that is green, and little to hold the soil in place, on the floor of the pass or in the desert to the east. Equalizing the air pressure between the desert and the coast, the winds blow heartily through the San Gorgonio Pass. I might have read more as a child, I sometimes think, or collected more stories of local lore, or perhaps even written a precocious memoir, if so much of my waking time had not gone into coming inside and trying to untangle my hair. There is a considerable amount of dirt under Banning, but on days when the wind is in full power, there is nearly as much dirt on top of Banning. One encounters the earth with all one's senses. For reasons closer to luck than knowledge or intelligence, my correspondent from Boston, with her phrase "something in the soil," had done a fair job of capturing the place.

Like many Western places, Banning is as well supplied with anecdotes as it is with wind. When I was first intoxicated with Garrison Keillor and his Lake Wobegon, I thought that I was scooped, beaten to the draw, that Banning was Lake Wobegon and Lake Wobegon was Banning, and I had no stories left to tell. Then I sobered up, and realized that Lake Wobegon suffers from one illness that Banning never had, and that illness is a plague of cuteness and sweetness. Banning is neither cute nor sweet, and that is its considerable advantage over Lake Wobegon.

My mother's employer, the main attorney in town, would never have met the "quaintness" standard for admission to Lake Wobegon. Mr. Wing came from impeccable Banning lineage, with his mother and father both long-term residents. He was divorced, but he took up from time to time with various ladies, and that was a source of interest and amazement in Banning. My favorite of the candidates was a vamp-like individual, who came to dinner with him at our house. Soon after arrival, declaring that she felt faint, she lay on the sofa with Mr. Wing kneeling beside her, while we all fluttered witlessly around.

People did not swoon, as a rule, in Banning.

Mr. Wing flew a private plane, and he sometimes flew to Las Vegas for the weekend. Once one of his lady friends, on a jaunt to Las Vegas, persuaded him that Grecian Formula was in order. He came back from Las Vegas transformed, with his gray hair suddenly jet black. Banning was not forgiving in these matters.

Mr. Wing hunted in Alaska. He had two giant bear heads and rugs on his floor. He bought a motorcycle, and, standing by the motorcycle with his helmet and his rather thin physique, he himself said that he resembled a toothpick with an olive on top.

As this comparison might suggest, Mr. Wing drank heartily. One afternoon, when I was about fourteen, I rode my bicycle up hill to his house, stopped to say hello, and was pleased, if also surprised, when he asked if I would like to join him in a drink. And so I did, and an hour or two later, as I rode my bicycle home, I sang aloud, and comforted myself with the thought that the chance of injuring anyone else in an incident of drunken bicycle riding was remote.

Up to this point, this is a Lake-Wobegon-like story. It has eccentricity, but it is fundamentally heartwarming, and except for the Alaskan bears on the floor, nonviolent.

Mr. Wing had a number of health problems, and he bounced back from all of them—until he was in his seventies, had cancer, and endured several operations. Then he decided he did not want any more operations.

I saw him in November of 1985. He said I had come to visit because my parents had insisted on it. I said what was true: I had come because, twenty years before, he was the first person to mistake me for an adult.

About a month later, Mr. Wing got up before sunrise, took one of his many guns, and killed himself.

With that bullet, Lake Wobegon and Banning part ways, and, more consequentially, the old Western history and the new Western history part ways. The old Western history was "happy face," "have a nice day" history. White pioneers came to the Western wilderness, and while they may have struggled against hardship, they won, and civilization came to the wilderness, and progress was achieved.

That picture did not allow much room for the story of Mr. Wing.

I am not claiming that the West has a unique hold on tragedy. I am saying that it has its full share, and maybe even a little more than its full share, with the high hopes and expectations that are part of the region's emotional baggage, high hopes and expectations that make frustration, and aging, and frailty hit very hard.

Let us leave tragedy aside, and move to the more lighthearted topic of town government. For years, my father engaged in a long contest with a man I will call Johnson, who built a lumberyard next door in violation of the zoning code.

Johnson had more friends on the city council and on the zoning board. That fact made the outcome predictable.

What we did not predict was the religious response. My older sister was going through a phase of rebellion, and she knew what we all knew: that you could drive my father, a very lapsed Mormon originally from Brigham City, Utah, crazier by flirting with organized religion than by flirting with Banning's wildest hot-rodder with slicked-back hair. So Carole had taken the obvious choice and was sneaking out to the First Baptist Church, where my father's zoning-code-opponent Johnson was a member.

At one Wednesday night prayer meeting, my sister Carole was surprised, with head bowed, to find that the minister was leading the congregation in prayer—in support of Johnson's side of the zoning battle.

Between this and a number of other comparable incidents, one had to assume that if a Turnerian struggle with the wilderness had once created a thriving pioneer democracy in Banning, that pioneer heritage had become a bit frayed, worn down, and weathered, and no treatment, comparable to Mr. Wing's bout with Grecian Formula, could make it look young and fresh again.

Look at Western territorial, state, county, or town governments, in the nineteenth century as well as the twentieth, and you find, in fact, Banning Writ Large. You find a lot in the way of competition for government favors, fights over zoning, horsetrading, even pious invocations of the deity's backing of economic development. You find a lot more of business-as-usual than you find of noble pioneer equality and democracy. And in Banning, as in the rest of the nation, if you wanted to see the ideals of democracy and equality strained to snapping, you turned to the matter of racial and ethnic diversity.

When I was sixteen, I hired on at the Riverside *Press-Enterprise*, mostly as an obituary writer. The first few days on the job, I did my best to keep a proper level of seriousness. But then, after a few calls, as the morticians and I moved to a comfortable, first-name basis, it proved to be extremely difficult to keep a proper level of solemnity. "Hi, this is Patty, got anything for me?" did not seem to convey a proper respect for human life. When, finally, on one day alone, drawing on both Banning and the neighboring town of Beaumont, I had the occasion to exclaim, "Wow! Thirteen in one day!" then I seemed to have lost moral fiber entirely, and to have become Banning's equivalent to Walter Cronkite, dispensing body counts with a diminished sense of reality.

Obituaries are finally not a challenging literary form, and one day in the *Press-Enterprise* office, left alone on a Saturday, I was desperate enough for entertainment to compose my own obituary. "Patricia Nelson died in the *Press-Enterprise*'s Banning office, following a lengthy period of boredom . . ." And then came a terrible round of narrowly resisted temptation: to put the obituary in the courier's envelope, and to see if I could sucker some weekend editor in Riverside into printing it.

But I did not, and I kept my good standing, long enough to have an occasion to write a real story. After Martin Luther King's assassination, I got permission to write a story on the reaction of black teenagers in Banning. In my article, the black teenagers expressed their bitterness about life in a white-dominated town, and one of the kids said, "Banning is no different from Selma, Alabama."

This article led to two follow-up incidents, both of them of considerable instructional value for a future Western historian. In the first one, the Banning Human Relations Commission concluded that they would like to meet with these angry black teenagers. We set up a meeting, at 7 P.M. at the Banning Teen Post on a Monday night. At 7 P.M. the Human Relations Commission and I assembled and began to await the arrival of angry black teenagers, a number of whom had promised me they would come.

But they did not come.

This was a deeply embarrassing experience. Nonetheless, it was remarkably redeemed by going home and receiving a phone call from Sherman Stringer. He had called four or five other Nelsons in the book until he found me, to explain that he and his friends had been cruising Ramsey Street and trying to get geared up to see a bunch of mostly white, middle-aged people at the Teen Post, and they had finally decided they could not do it. Getting the phone call made me feel, and still makes me feel, a lot better.

But look what the angry black teenagers had done for me. My first exercise in community-organizing, in activism, in fostering dialogue, had come up a complete zero. Over the years this memory has been a great comfort. Having begun with a bedrock failure, everything that I have attempted thereafter has been a great success.

The second outgrowth of my article was a bigger, follow-up article by George Ringwald, a Pulitzer Prize–winning reporter for the *Press-Enterprise* who filed his stories in our office. I introduced him to some of my "sources," and he then did a story, Sunday edition, front page of the Desert and Pass section, headlined "Three Angry Young Black Men Tell It Like It Is in Banning." On Monday outraged white citizens of Banning began calling in their subscription cancellations. Within another day, two of the three angry black men had been arrested for some odd charge of trespassing. Rumor had it that the picture of them from the Sunday newspaper could be seen on the dartboard at the Banning police department.

According to the traditional models of Western American history, this story should not have happened in Banning. It should have happened in a northeastern factory town, or a southern town, or in Chicago, or in Washington, D.C. Not in Banning. Not in the West.

Despite myths of a West that had a long exemption from the problems and tensions of the eastern United States, the West imported all those tensions and conflicts *and* added a whole set of its own, with the diversity of Indian tribes, the presence of long-settled Hispanic people as well as later immigrants, and the first arrivals of Asian people. Altogether, the West makes the Northeast and the South look simple in their race relations, even though the old frontier models of Western history never would have let anyone know that.

Here is one of the grand paradoxes of Western history, and a paradox writ large in Banning: we have, historically, the nation's most cosmopolitan region, and yet we also have, historically, some of the nation's most provincial attitudes. Consider, for instance, what Banning offered in the way of an understanding of Judaism.

I, like my sister, took my opportunity to drive my father crazy and trekked off to the First Baptist Church. In sixth grade, in Sunday School, our teacher had an awful moment. One of the kids finally asked a question that had puzzled a number of us. "Just what," the curious student asked the teacher, "is a Jew? We keep reading the word in the Bible, and we don't know what it means."

The teacher looked shaken, but trapped. Suddenly she saw her route out of the trap. "You all know Jeff," she said, pointing to a boy recently arrived in town.

We looked at Jeff.

"Jeff used to be a Jew," she said, "but now he's a Baptist."

Or take the experience I had in 1966, goaded into action by an enterprising high school teacher. Michael Rose persuaded me that it was my mission to undertake an employment survey of Banning, to find out how many minority people were employed in various businesses. So on hot summer days I walked down Ramsey Street, stopping at each business or office, and asking, "How many blacks, Mexican-Americans, Indians, or Asian-Americans do you employ?"

"Not very many," was the general answer, unless, as in the case of the bank, the institution had a substantial need for janitors. But the most memorable encounter came at a county office, where I asked my question, "How many blacks, Mexican-Americans, Indians, or Asian-Americans," and the lady said, "None, we're all Americans here."

We are, are we?

The most cosmopolitan region has some of the most provincial attitudes. And yet we are, in the West, quite genuinely each other's creatures, shaped by this swirl of encounters between people of improbable origins. To make this point, I have long relied on a story about my mother, who had stepped in for a tour of duty as a substitute teacher in the Banning schools when another teacher had a prolonged illness. My mother started working closely with an Indian boy from the Morongo Reservation, who had received little teacherly attention to that point. He stayed after class and worked with her on special exercises, and gradually things started to pick up. But then Mother left, and no one like her took her place, and this fellow did not prosper. Several years later, Mother worked as a legal secretary in an office at the main intersection in town, not far from where her former student now stood, oftentimes with a bottle in a brown paper bag. From time to time, when my mother walked by on her way to work, her ex-student would say, "There's Mrs. Nelson; she made me everything I am today."

This is not supposed to be a joke about Indian drinking problems; it is not supposed to be a joke at all. It is supposed to be an historical fact: that this hodgepodge of people—Indian, Anglo-American, Hispanic, black, Asian, Jew, First Baptist—have accumulated such a history in this region, such a network of ties and connections and friction and dependence, that they have indeed made each other everything they are today.

For much of my time in Banning, I lived with the conviction that a cruel fate had dropped me into a very dull place. Poor, poor me; a couple of teachers had told me I had some talent as a writer, but how was I ever to make anything of that talent if I only had the thin and dreary stories of Banning to tell?

On the east, Banning was framed by an eye-catching sign. Announcing the location of a company specializing in herbal remedies, the sign said, in large letters, "INNERCLEAN HERBAL LAXATIVE." Banning was bounded, on the other side, by a dinosaur. A brontosaurus, later joined by a tyrannosaurus, had been built by a man who simply had a passion to build dinosaurs in the desert, with gift shops in their thoraxes.

And I found Banning dull.

It took a trip to graduate school in New Haven to make Banning blossom with meanings and significance. Though it never occurred to me when I lived there (and certainly no teacher ever asked us to think of it in these terms), Banning was a representative arid-land town, a Western town with some proximity to the Pacific and to the Mexican border, with a cattle ranch to the north and an Indian reservation just between Banning and the dinosaurs, and an aqueduct carrying water from the Colorado River to Los Angeles passing through the nearest mountain.

Was this town really Western? I have mostly managed to stay calm when people have said, "You're not really from the West. You're from California."

Sometimes, in areas like the Rocky Mountains, this remark carries more acknowledged hostility: "You're not from the West; you're from that parasitical vampire of a place that drains the *real* West of its water."

At the University of Colorado, my partner in Western American studies, the legal scholar Charles Wilkinson, and I agree on most things, but on this one we divide. Not only do we divide, we have been known to shout at each other.

Charles says that California is not in the West. When pressed by obvious facts (California has lots of public land, much of northern and interior California is rural), he says that parts of California are in the West, but Los Angeles is not.

Then the script calls for me to shout that he is just making an aesthetic judgment. He wants *his* West to maintain a certain level of attractiveness, and he is simply excluding Los Angeles because it falls below that level. This has been, I guess, a reliable principle for selecting high school cheerleaders, but it really cannot be recommended as a process for drawing the boundaries of a region.

Beyond the aesthetic, what are the arguments for treating California as an alien state? Its mega-cities cannot be the disqualifying factor; the West, as a whole, is the region with the greatest percentage of its residents living in cities. California had, for a while, the poor taste to be prosperous when the rest of the region was depressed; the state seemed to have escaped from the cycle of the extractive economy before other Western states could. But the bust that descended on California in the late 1980s and early 1990s has diminished that difference dramatically. Moreover, to my mind, even during the boom years, the kinship was unbroken. While it is deeply irritating to have one prosperous cousin in a family that is otherwise having hard times, that disparity does not dissolve the fact of common ancestry.

When pressed, some of the advocates for the exclusion of California from the West will admit that this is a chronological exclusion. They will acknowledge that California *was* part of the West; they will agree no overland traveler in the nineteenth century ever crossed the border of Nevada or Arizona and observed, "I do not know exactly where I am, but I am certain that I am no longer in the West." California was part of the West, the exclusionists will say, until World War II, and then, under the stimulus of massive defense spending, it apparently headed out to sea, resolved to become an island again. But here, again, kinship is overpowering. The decades of common experience—Indian travel to and from the interior, Hispanic colonization, fur trade exploration, Anglo-American conquest, struggles with aridity, the common experience of being closer to the Pacific than to the Atlantic—had tied California into the West long before it could either be ousted or try to secede.

And even more to the point, what exactly is this unit called California? Back in graduate school, when I started looking for a topic for a dissertation, I had some idea of writing on Euro-American reactions to California's natural environment. But then I ran afoul of the obvious question: *which* natural environment? There are eight or nine basic California natural environments, and most of them do not respect state borders.

In other words, *something in the soil* suggests that California might actually be part of the West in a way that no aesthetic judgment or economic rivalry can change. The West gets a much better deal from a version of Western history that is based on Banning, California, than the region could ever get from a version based on Portage, Wisconsin.

Banning is significant not only for its past, but as a signifier for the Western future. Banning has grown a lot since I left. My mother continues to send me clippings about utterly improbable plans to add thousands of new homes to Banning. But Banning is dry country. Where is the water for thousands of new homes, thousands of new residents?

This is a crossroads, a chance for one community to weigh the question: Does limitless growth make sense in a region with limited water? One answer is, of course, "Sure it makes sense; Los Angeles has done it for years; why can't we?" In the early twentieth century, the Filipino immigrant Carlos Bulosan got poetic—and practical—advice from another immigrant: "All roads go to California," Bulosan's guide told him, "and all travelers wind up in Los Angeles."

Well, so far, many of them have.

But this is not fate, not predestination.

On the eastern end of Banning was a motel with a pool where we used to go swimming. That motel had a prophetic and resonant name, a name whose meaning was completely lost on the people swimming in the pool. The Desert Edge Motel: a useful name to remember, a reminder that that is indeed the edge we live on, in Denver as much as Los Angeles, in Boulder as much as Banning.

In water use, in conflicts over natural resources, and in race relations, the West faces dilemmas that may have no solutions. The possibility of everyone getting together, talking through these problems, and reaching a consensus is not a prospect on which one would wager much money. The best that I can offer as an antidote to despair is the story of my dinner with Thelma Wood.

I have two older sisters, who were well-adjusted and popular, songleaders and class presidents. Thelma Wood, who taught English for a thousand years at Banning High, knew what my sisters were like. I was a different case. In my sophomore year, Mrs. Wood undertook to make me more like my sisters, keeping me after class and forcibly counseling me, telling me that she remembered how I used to come to the high school with my sisters for open house, when I was such a pleasant, sunshiny child.

Well, I was not pleasant and sunshiny anymore, and Mrs. Wood's efforts brought the clouds in even lower, and darker.

I do not think that many intercultural conflicts in the West today can match the level of my bitterness toward this woman. I hated Mrs. Wood. Preoccupied with my resentment, I was able to keep from feeling any sympathy for her visibly cruel arthritis, able to keep from recognizing that Mrs. Wood had done a lot to make many people's sentences clearer, able to keep from thinking of her as a *person.*

Even after graduation, I continued to hate Mrs. Wood, and to feel no particular fondness for Mr. Smithpeter, Mrs. Wood's contemporary who taught math, or for his wife, Mrs. Smithpeter, who worked at the public library and who once permitted me an orgy of adolescent superiority feelings by responding to a request for the plays of Henrik Ibsen by looking up a fellow named Gibson, Henry.

A couple of years after I had started college, home for a visit, I was riding my bicycle along Williams Street, past the Smithpeters' house. The Smithpeters and Mrs. Wood happened to drive up as I came by, and they said hello. I said hello. When enemies or strangers encounter each other in Banning on summer afternoons, the cause of social cohesion and community carries one great advantage. As they look at each other with blank and panicked minds, even the most hostile people have something they can say to each other. "Good lord," one of them can say, "it's hot this afternoon. Do you think this will go on forever?" Since there is always a place to start, conversation can end up traveling to unexpected destinations.

And so the Smithpeters and Mrs. Wood and I began to chat. Then they said, "Why don't you come in and join us for dinner?"

Well, I thought, why not? The only tough part came when I undertook to call my mother to tell her I'd be late.

When I said to her, "I am having dinner at the Smithpeters with Mrs. Wood," she said, "Sure you are."

When I said Mrs. Smithpeter was coming to the phone to say hello, my mother said, "Look, Patty, I know you are at Barbara Dodge's," mentioning the name of a high school friend who was a talented actress and mimic. "When this voice that you are calling Mrs. Smithpeter comes on, it will actually be Barbara Dodge."

Happily, Mother experienced a moment of doubt when Mrs. Smithpeter said hello, and did not immediately begin denouncing scoundrels who try to trick their parents. At dinner, the Smithpeters and Mrs. Wood told me stories of tornados ripping the fronts off buildings in the Midwest, and other tales from what I still saw as the exotic East. It was quite an agreeable, and deeply disorienting, evening.

Mrs. Wood *was* a tyrant and a bully when she had fifteen-year-olds under her control. Sometimes she bullied them in ways that benefited them, and sometimes she bullied them in ways that were not only futile, but cruel. And yet, for a tyrant and a bully, she was also a rather likable soul. I conclude with this story because I know that Western American history has left us with a legacy of human relations which is sometimes nearly as bitter as the dislike I felt for Mrs. Wood. It is a comfort to know this: if Thelma Wood and I could have dinner together, then anything is possible for the people of the American West.

Nancy Mairs

Although born by accident of war in Long Beach, California, on July 23, 1943, Nancy Mairs grew up in New England. She came west to Tucson in August 1972, the same year she and her physicians first suspected she might have multiple sclerosis—a chronic, incurable, degenerative disease of the central nervous system that affects 350,000 people in the United States—and her diagnosis was confirmed in 1974. In Tucson, where she has lived for the past twenty-two years, Mairs earned both her M.F.A. and her Ph.D. at the University of Arizona. She received an honorary doctorate from her alma mater, Wheaton College, in 1994. Although her first book, In All the Rooms of the Yellow House, won a Western States Book Award for poetry in 1984, it wasn't until she published a collection of autobiographical essays, Plaintext (1986), that she began to establish herself as one of the nation's leading feminist writers. Four more books have followed in quick succession: a memoir, Remembering the Bone House (1989); a second collection of essays, Carnal Acts (1990); a spiritual autobiography, Ordinary Time: Cycles in Marriage, Faith, and Renewal (1993); and a third collection of essays, Voice Lessons: On Becoming a (Woman) Writer (1994). "In my writing," Mairs says, "I aim to speak to the 'unspeakable,' in defiance of polite discourse, so as to expose ways in which my personal experiences inscribe cultural values dangerous to *women and other creatures worth preserving." As this essay from her new work in progress attests, like her writing, Mairs's life is itself a triumph of classic Western American virtues like rugged individualism, self-reliance, and cooperation, not to mention of style, candor, thought, and even form. Her determination to mine her opportunities for rich and varied experiences even as multiple sclerosis visits its terrible debilitation upon her body has taken her on a wide range of travels. Shortly after the adventure in New Mexico with her husband and daughter that she chronicles here and much against the advice of her travel agent, she traveled to Zaire, where her daughter was serving as a Peace Corps volunteer.*

Waist-high in the West

"NO, NOT THAT STORY," THE EDITORS SAY WHEN I send them an essay reflecting on the difficulties I have encountered, as a transplant from the East with multiple sclerosis, in claiming an identity as a chronicler of the West. "That's not at all what we have in mind." To clarify, they give me examples of what they do have in mind, pieces built around backwoodspersons and long reflective walks by the verges of isolated lakes, about the uses of firearms and childhood encounters with Indians; and I can tell that they want me to write a story essentially like other women's stories with the trifling but possibly intriguing difference that I happen to experience whatever befalls me at the height of those women's waists.

But that's not the way disability works. It does not leave one precisely the same woman one would have been without it, only (in my case) shorter. It does not merely alter a few, or even a great many, details in a life story that otherwise conforms to basic narrative conventions: the adventure, the romance, the quest. Instead, it transforms the tale utterly, though often subtly, and these shifts in narrative tone and type arouse resistance in both the "author" and the "reader" of the outlandish plot.

My crippled life began when I moved from Boston to Tucson. This pure coincidence split my history: there was once a whole youthful Nancy, who grew up in a gentle geography though a severe climate; then there was an aging Nancy, who limped and later stumbled and finally stopped walking altogether, in a milder climate but a formidable geography. Although never an athlete, I was an ambler who moved through New England's variegated terrain—bridle path, beach, brook—in all weathers with authentic, though largely sentimental, affection for the natural world, which seemed to me compassable and therefore hospitable. I have lived now for more than twenty years in a landscape too large for me, and getting larger as my physical condition deteriorates. Thus, my relationship to the setting as well as the plot of my life has been skewed, since the conventional West—land, lots of land, 'neath the starry skies above—and the conventional responses to it—exploration, exploitation—demand a physical vigor I've never enjoyed here.

These disparities have had their consequences, for me and for those who have shared my misshapen life, many of which were encapsulated several years ago when my husband, my daughter, and I made a pass through this overlarge landscape in what we have recalled ever after, with no fondness whatsoever, as the Camper from Hell. Anne was soon to join the Peace Corps and spend a couple of years in Zaire, and she wanted to travel in the Southwest before leaving it, perhaps for good. On expeditions in earlier years, we had wandered from campground to campground with an increasingly shabby but serviceable Eureka Space 10 tent, sleeping bags, and air mattresses; but although I was still able to walk short distances, and getting down on the ground was all too easy for me, getting me up again was a group production none of us looked forward to; and so we rented, as cheaply as possible, a camper with a kitchenette, beds, and a toilet.

In hindsight, "as cheaply as possible" turned out to be the falsest of economies. We didn't have any money—we've never had any money—but if we had it to do over again, George and I would probably take a second mortgage on the house rather than search out that dubious director of a rundown nursery school and rent his infernal camper for a week's tour of New Mexico. We should have been wary when the camper wasn't ready as promised; but, as Anne would no doubt be glad to attest, George and I have always been deficient in the wariness department. We loaded hastily and left just a little behind schedule, which would turn out to be our condition throughout the trip, arriving at our first stop, a KOA in Alamogordo, well after dark. There we discovered that the water in the camper's tanks stank sulfurously and the mechanism for converting the dining benches into one of the beds was so broken that the bed could be created only with great wrenchings and swearings. These I could not participate in, of course, but the least I could do was to sleep on the outcome, a mound of lumpen upholstery whose metal frame poked my back and hips no matter which way I twisted. Since I wasn't doing any driving, I didn't think George or Anne ought to spend their nights tossing about à la the Princess and the Pea.

At Carlsbad the next night, the pump for the sulfurous water, which had been working only sporadically, quit entirely. In the morning we found someone to replace the water pump, but we couldn't start out for Santa Fe until after lunch, too long a trip, it turned out, so that we had trouble locating our campground north of the city in the dark. In the mountains miles to the north of Taos the next night, George hit a tree in the dark and banged up the camper, though he refrained from trashing it entirely. In the morning it retaliated by refusing to start altogether, and George had to call the owner, who seemed eerily familiar with the problem and issued elaborate instructions involving many hands and feet and bits of paper.

All along, our primary object had been a return to a place Anne had loved ten years or more before, Chaco Canyon, which didn't look too far from Taos on the map. But of course maps don't show you ways of getting lost on the hills across which Los Alamos is scattered or roads so steep that the wheezing camper won't chug over ten miles an hour. The scenery was breathtaking, especially a huge empty green valley enclosed on every side by mountains up to ten thousand feet high. But it was already getting dark when we reached Cuba, a town so derelict as to seem a parody of the rural West rather than a habitable community. Here Anne suddenly burst out that she was having a terrible time and hadn't enjoyed a single thing—not the dunes at White Sands where she and her father had romped, or the ribbon of bats silvery in the dusk above Carlsbad Caverns, or even the fry bread heaped with beans, meat, lettuce, tomatoes, cheese, and salsa, very tasty and messy, eaten before an audience of four hungry but mannerly dogs on a log in a plaza at Pueblo de Taos—and wanted to head straight home without bothering with Chaco Canyon at all.

She'd been moody all along, and with more reason than even the Camper from Hell provided. She wasn't feeling well, and she was still very upset about the loss, during a burglary of our house a few days before we set out, of an irreplaceable heirloom ring her great-grandmother had just given her for college graduation. Moreover, she'd be leaving home and friends in another month to begin training for her service in Africa, a daunting leap into what might prove to be (though it did not) the fabled heart of darkness. And then there was the bitter though unacknowledged reality that the camper was not the only dilapidated and malfunctioning entity on this trip, no moment of which could be truly carefree.

Traveling with me provides endless exercises in problem-solving and sheer brute force: hunting for accessible parking spaces, toilets, walkways; hauling me and then the wheelchair out of the vehicle and later stowing us both again; and in between incessant pushing, tilting, swerving, pushing, pushing, pushing, pushing. No one can forget for more than an instant that I am a cripple. Of course, I can be parked and left, but then the leaver must deal with feelings of guilt or loneliness or dread of return and so is still not wholly free of me. Whatever we manage to do—and thanks to modifications of terrain or architecture, we can often do a lot—is tinged with the kind of regret I'd felt a few days earlier at Carlsbad Caverns, wishing we could have hiked in instead of plunging 750 feet straight down in an elevator. Still, most of the inside trail was wheelchair accessible, so I'd gotten to see a good bit, though in considerable discomfort, since Anne whipped the wheelchair along at breakneck speed. This is one of the means she's used to punish me for my illness and dependency, though I don't think she's ever known it. Sometimes George too, intentionally though unconsciously, hurts me when he's "helping" me, but not so frequently. I try not to complain at such times, not because I'm a martyr but because I think they need this sort of outlet for their anger, which I share.

That's how the Camper from Hell was functioning too, of course. Anne's fury at my disease (which is not quite the same as fury at me, though the fact that I bear the disease in my flesh renders this distinction problematic) defied direct expression, but it could safely be projected upon our rattling, stinking, hiccoughing conveyance, along with the other griefs and terrors currently plaguing her. I sympathized. But I was also getting sick of tiptoeing every minute to avoid a new attack of ill temper, and I surprised myself by insisting that we stop for something to eat and talk our situation over before planning our next move. Confrontation has never been my style.

So we found a cafe. (Not that we had to do a whole lot of looking. Not that there were a whole lot of places to look.) Anne ordered cauliflower soup, which had the consistency and color (and perhaps flavor—I didn't ask) of library paste, and a glob of cottage cheese floating in the middle of a plate of canned fruit cocktail. George and I had chef's salads, iceberg lettuce with gristly bits of beef and ham and some slices of pasteurized processed cheese food. Over this dismal repast we talked and wept and finally resolved to spend the night in a motel, get the engine checked in the morning, then go to Chaco as planned and from there home. Dinner ended with a soggy three-way hug in the middle of the cafe, which no doubt turned some Cuban heads. So for just over a quarter of the hundred dollars we'd saved by leasing the Camper from Hell instead of a new one at a dealership, we rented a shabby but clean enough room in the Cuba Lodge Motel, run by some Pakistanis, watched a rerun of "Upstairs, Downstairs" and the news, and got some sleep.

I wish I could say that after this imbroglio, no further disasters marred our progress toward home. We would reach Tucson, it turned out, in one piece and more or less speaking to each other. But first there were the miles and miles of washboard road into and then out of Chaco, over which the camper jittered and bucked, raising billows of choking dust, until we were dizzy and bruised. There was the primitive campground in Navajo, arrived at late of course, where George accidently stuck the electrical cord into an unmarked 220 outlet (which shouldn't have been there) and melted the plug, so that our final stop was suitably benighted. We were limp with more than relief by the time we wound through the Salt River Canyon, rounded the Catalinas, and dropped into the Santa Cruz Valley we'd left—could it have been?—only seven days before.

At the time, I half wished that we had stayed there and seen to our responsibilities rather than traipsing off to squander a lot of money and our spirits as well. But I also knew that nothing is ever entirely a waste: visions of dunes carved against searing blue, of glassy cave pools, of a mother pronghorn with her twins behind her, of the little earthen plaza at Tesuque Pueblo, of the gash in the

earth's skin carved by the Rio Grande outside Taos, of low mountains striated with rose and lavender and sage, of a precipitous rock
stairway hacked a thousand years ago into a canyon wall would stay
vivid and cherishable forever. The camper we could hurriedly return to its smarmy owner, pushing its memory back, down, behind
these lovelier images.

Its bodily analogue could not be similarly banished, however,
and so this trip has remained colored, as all my stories are now, by
rage and disappointment. Why then don't I find the master plot a
sad one? And I don't. The recollection of Anne and Nancy, blond
head and brown head bowed, boohooing aloud while their tears
splash onto picked-over fruit cocktail and lettuce, and even George
swiping at his eyes with a crumpled paper napkin, strikes me as poi-
gnant but comic. The story of my life is certainly spoiled, in the
sense sociologist Erving Goffman had in mind in subtitling his
study *Stigma: Notes on the Management of Spoiled Identity*, but it is far
from ruined. It is merely radically unconventional.

The tale of westward migration has always been premised on
possibility: gold hidden in the next black hill, endlessly fertile soil
for wheat and grapes and artichokes, vast tracts of rangeland for
sleek white-faced cattle, and eighteen holes of golf every day of the
sun-drenched year. I moved into a West of impossibility. The East
would be just as forbidding today, of course, but that doesn't matter,
since the East I have in mind is the land of childhood and perfectly
inaccessible anyway. I moved into an adulthood that I, like other
dreamers of the conventional West, could never have conceived: the
strangest of lands. Nevertheless, though instead of loping on Old
Paint across the lone prairie, I may be heading my Quickie P100 on
down the alley and out to Bentley's for an iced cappuccino, it's an
honest-to-God Western adventure I'm having here. Trust me.

Joanne Mulcahy

J oanne Mulcahy *works as a folklorist, an anthropologist, and a writer. Born in Gary, Indiana, on December 20, 1954, she grew up just outside Philadelphia. She earned her B.A. in comparative literature from the University of Pennsylvania, her M.A. in cultural anthropology from the University of Wisconsin–Madison, and her Ph.D. in folklore from the University of Pennsylvania. While working in a rural Alaskan village she met Mary Peterson, a traditional Alutiiq midwife and healer. Mary's life reverberated with meaning for Mulcahy, who has now worked with the women of Kodiak Island, as part of an extensive oral history project, for fifteen years. The essay below is taken from a work in progress about her Alaska experiences that Mulcahy describes as "part memoir, part cultural history." She is at work on two other books: a collection of essays about women and community, and a life history of a Mexican artist and healer, Eva Castellanoz. Mulcahy teaches at Lewis & Clark College in Portland, Oregon, where she is affiliated with the Northwest Writing Institute and the Gender Studies Program. She has also held residencies at the Island Institute (Sitka, Alaska) and cottages at Hedge Brook (Whidbey Island, Washington).*

Through Dreams and Shadows

I LOOKED OUT FROM MY KITCHEN WINDOW AS THE steel hulls of crab boats glided like floating pyramids back into the Kodiak boat harbor. Eleven P.M. and still daylight. Longfellow's "The Children's Hour" played in my mind. "Between the dark and the daylight, when the night is beginning to lower . . ." But no time felt "between" here. There was light. Or deep darkness.

Hand on the telephone, I waited. One of the other crisis line workers from the Kodiak Women's Resource Center had called as I started my shift. "Be ready for a call from a Native woman from one of the villages," she said. "We didn't get her name, but she's in town, and she's in danger. She called from a trailer park—didn't say which one. By the time she got through, she was whispering. Then, nothing. The phone line was cut." A chill went through me.

I watched the crab boats unload their haul, knew the bars would soon be full. An hour passed. Unusually quiet for a summer night. I grew restless. A recurrent thought: Could the woman in danger be Mary Peterson on her way back to the village of Akhiok? I saw the face of the Native woman I'd met only weeks before. She had given me hope in her resolve to leave a violent home and start again in Anchorage. Now, she might be going back.

I got into my battered pickup and drove out Baranof Drive towards the edge of town. I remembered one hard and fast rule we held to at the resource center: never go to the scene of violence. I knew what I was doing was dangerous, but I couldn't stop. I parked a half-mile from the trailer park I guessed the call had come from. Heart pounding, I slipped through the shadows between the narrow rows of trailers. But for the low, constant din of the television sets, silence. I moved towards one trailer, pressing my ear against cold metal. No screams, no violence, no trouble. Sweating, I ran back and collapsed on the front seat of the truck. Something was wrong.

"You're right. Something's wrong—you're crazy," my co-worker Molly said the next day when I told her the story. We waited tables on the early-morning shift in a waterfront restaurant together. She looked up from making coffee. "You're crazy to go out alone at night with all the drunks in this town. People die out there. I know you want to help those women, but it's their violence, their problems, their lives. What does it have to do with you?"

What did it have to do with me—a newcomer to Alaska, a stranger to Native cultures? Why was I driven to bear witness to the violence I saw permeate life on Kodiak Island, resolved to find a way towards healing? Scenes of violence and stories of their aftermath played out in the restaurant where I worked. Stories of abuse from women of all backgrounds filled the crisis line I answered once a week as program coordinator for the Kodiak Women's Resource Center. And from Native women like Mary Peterson, I heard conflicting stories: narratives of a past where women were powerful traditional healers filtered through the shadows of a present filled with violence and pain.

These stories triggered something dark in me. I felt connected to these women but I didn't know why. Years later, when I found the core of my own story, I found the reason. Healing and stories forge connection—our selves to our past, members of a community to one another, women to other women across the chasms of cultural difference.

IN NOVEMBER OF 1979, I moved to Kodiak Island. I knew little about Alaska, but longshoremen who frequented the bar where I worked in San Francisco told stories about Kodiak. The town was rough, the weather worse. One bearded regular used to point outside on gray, drenched days and say, "See this? This is a nice day on Kodiak." Though I hated the cold and dreaded the dark, I ignored his warnings. I packed my bags and moved to a land of endless winter. My friends judged me crazy. But I was restless, troubled, unable to settle down. I'd fallen in love with a fisherman at a wedding two years before. Now, I went north to live with him.

Traces of red still clung to a smattering of deciduous trees when I arrived on Kodiak. The island, a mountainous bear refuge 250 miles southwest of Anchorage in the Gulf of Alaska, was otherwise cloaked in white. By 4 P.M., the long slices of light turned blue and gold, then disappeared for nearly twenty hours. I got a job as a cocktail waitress at a restaurant on the waterfront. I thought I would love moving through the dark hours accompanied by fishermen, cannery workers, and varied transients. I knew I would welcome the nights without dreams. Before I moved to Alaska, a dream that would recur for years had already invaded my nights. *Columns of women line long corridors. They wait for some unknown, unseen force, dreading its inevitable arrival. I watch them, unable to breathe. I wake gasping for air.* Over time, the dream had become more vivid until I could almost see the women's faces. It would be years before they emerged from shadow, before I could name the mine fields embedded in my body, before I could embrace the dark. But during my first night shifts on Kodiak, I simply, unconsciously, embraced wakefulness until dawn.

The bar was ground-level, but so dark that it seemed subterranean. I had been a waitress since age fifteen, served liquor in bars all over the country. Here, each morning until 5 A.M., was a different world of drinking. The smoke was thicker, the booze more abundant, and the customers scruffier and louder than I was used to. On my second shift, a short man in lumberjack shirt and baseball cap staggered up to the register. He looked down. Perplexed, I thought he had dropped his money. Then someone yelled, "This ain't the head!" The drunk leaned against the wall, unzipped his fly, and urinated all over the register. I knew that my bar career would be short.

I learned something else about the long nights during that first week. One night, early in the evening, a bearded man came in and waited restlessly for the music to begin. As I talked with a customer, my back to the bar, I stood paralyzed by the scene I watched in the mirror. The fisherman unwound his long legs from the bar stool, and all at once, I saw the gleam of black metal against the small of a woman's back. As my body shook with a combination of rage and panic, the bartender and the regulars pinned him to the floor, grabbed the gun, and broke up the scene. No shots were fired that night, but I had heard about the blood that still stained the walls of the bar across the parking lot.

That was my last bar shift. Walking home that night, I detoured up the hill towards the light reflected from a blue onion dome. A Russian Orthodox church and seminary sit at the edge of the Kodiak boat harbor, an ongoing legacy of the Russian colonization in the late eighteenth century. There, after the bars had closed and dawn broke through a light snow, I watched a bent figure with a white beard dressed in long black robes walk ahead of me. The light radiated around him as he moved towards the dome of the church, away from the long, bleak night.

MONTHS LATER, I woke for my morning shift to a transformed Kodiak. I shook open my light jacket as I walked from my home overlooking the boat harbor down a hill blanketed with green. Five A.M. and light already. I wanted to soak in the summer warmth like a battery, reserve enough to make it through the next winter. I'd switched to the morning shift in the restaurant right after my first few shifts in the bar. We opened as the bars closed; I found comfort in undoing the night's damage with coffee.

Molly looked up as I entered. "You look exhausted," she said, examining the circles under my eyes. "You must have been up all night partying now that you're a 'crab widow.'" Prices for fish were high, and my partner was gone nearly full-time fishing. But my nights were filled by neither parties nor peaceful solitude. I sat by the phone, waiting for crisis calls. The violence I'd seen during my first week in Kodiak hit somewhere deep. I soon discovered that transience, alcohol, an unstable economy, and extreme weather conspired to give Kodiak extremely high rates of sexual violence. I had cut my waitress job to part-time to work with the Women's Resource Center.

"No parties," I said. "I was on a crisis call." "You never give up," she sighed as she filled small bowls with packets of chemicals posing as powdered cream. I started to respond, then stopped myself. Molly was kind, easygoing, full of life. She held some secret strength which left her unaffected by the darkness around her. I didn't. I thought it was that simple.

I had been up late. The outreach coordinator from the Kodiak Area Native Association called to tell me a Native woman named Mary Peterson was being flown in from Akhiok, the smallest and most remote village on the island. She described Mary's life. A respected elder, she worked as a community health aide, and taught the Alutiiq language. Married as a young girl to an older man chosen by her parents, she had quickly remarried when her first husband drowned. From the two unions, she had given birth to eighteen children, suffered the loss of seven. The second marriage seemed happy at first, but village life began to change. As "booze runs" on bush flights grew more frequent, calls to the crisis line increased. By now, Mary spent nights sleeping under the house to escape the wrath of an otherwise good husband, a man transformed by alcohol. I had never been to Akhiok, but I imagined a treeless expanse, the usual village HUD houses close enough together so that other villagers could know their neighbors' hardships. *Could* know them, but might choose not to, for the alcohol that had seeped into village life breeds a toxic isolation that defies proximity. From the coordinator's description, I pictured Mary: a Native woman strong from hauling water and fishnets, strong from giving birth to eighteen children, strong from learning to survive.

I arrived at the airport just as the bush pilot finished unloading the late plane from Akhiok. A small woman in her early fifties, about five feet two inches and still quite slim, stood waiting. Her gray hair cascaded into long curls that framed a soft, barely lined face. This could not be the woman who had borne eighteen children. Surely she had not survived the life I had heard described. She approached me tentatively. "You're from that center?" she asked, tugging her short Orlon sweater against the fierce winds. This was Mary Peterson. She talked little about what had happened to her but I remembered these words, "I went through so much, sometimes I wonder if it's true when I think about it, you know, and I can't believe what I went through."

I placed her in the home of a religious family, a quiet place to rest until, I assumed, she would return to the village. I went home and tried to sleep. No more calls, but insomnia gripped me. I had spent barely an hour with Mary, yet I was riveted by the schism between her calm presence and what I imagined of her life. How had she survive? The next day, I went back to talk with her, but Mary was gone. She had flown out on the first plane to a shelter in Anchorage to begin her life again.

In the weeks before I met Mary Peterson, I began to dread the coming of night. I feared the calls for help, knowing how many women went back to violent homes. When my partner went fishing, I often sat up late and wondered what happened to these women. But here, finally, was a success story, or at least the potential for one: a woman had left a violent home to reclaim her life. Why, then, did this meeting further darken my spirit? The paradox to the cycles of hope and despair is this: we backslide not when life is darkest, but on the edge of recovery. During the weeks after I met Mary, as the days lengthened and the land renewed itself, my dream returned. *In the dream, it is always night. Long corridors are lined on both*

sides with women. They wait, knowing that their legs are to be broken. I
wake drenched in sweat, fumbling frantically for the light. Horror fills me
but I cannot find its source.

I SEATED MYSELF QUIETLY in a back pew of the brightly lit
Russian Orthodox church. A blond girl and her raven-haired
brother played in the aisle as their parents looked on and smiled. I'd
come to recognize pieces of Alutiiq culture: this ease with children,
a deep religious faith, the unique combination of Native, Russian,
and Swedish or Norwegian descent. The elderly priest I'd seen that
late night as I walked home from the restaurant stood in the vesti-
bule. The priests' silk robes, the hangings which covered the vesti-
bule, the Greek icons on every wall—all seemed familiar and exotic
at once. I breathed in the incense which filled the room, and with it
memories of the Latin masses of my Roman Catholic childhood.

The world of Russian Orthodoxy had become a part of my life.
After my first few weeks in Kodiak, I'd gone to the church out of
curiosity. A priest and teacher at the seminary, Father Kreta, gave
me a tour. He showed me pictures of churches in the six Native villages that ringed the outer edges of Kodiak. Their blue onion domes
beckoned to me. I looked closely at the photo of Akhiok where the
small church stood alone on a hill overlooking the water. "What is
that village like?" I asked. "Oh, they have their troubles, but it's a
wonderful place. You'll get there sometime. But for now," he invited, "please come to church in town and meet the local people."

Now, after mass, we moved downstairs, and I found myself
with a cup of *chai*, the local drink of Tang and instant tea. "Here is
an elder you must meet," Father Kreta said. "She's the town ma-
triarch, a living history archive." A stooped, round figure, Katherine
Chichenoff stepped forward and introduced herself as "Kaba," a di-
minutive for "Babushka," the Russian word for grandmother. "No,
we can't talk here," she said. "There's too much to tell. Come to my
house."

Katherine lived in the nondescript brown prefab housing on the edge of town overlooking the boat harbor, less than one block from the Russian church where she walked each morning for services. Icons, a ubiquitous presence in Russian Orthodox homes, completely dominated one corner of her small apartment. We sat beneath a row of icons which hung adjacent to photographs of her ten children and their numerous offspring. Katherine grew up in the Russian mission that educated many Native children prior to the 1917 revolution. "You know, my father was a sea otter hunter. After my mother died, he couldn't take care of me. That's why I was here in the mission until 1919. Russia had to close it, you know. But I got married before the time came because I didn't want to go back to my father." When I asked why, she answered evasively. "You know, before the mission, he gave me to an old lady to take care of me. She was very mean. When I was at their place, I laid just like a little dog, on a mat. The church found out how they were treating me. The priest came, and they put me in the mission."

Unprepared for stories of child abuse, I stayed silent, witness to a history I had not expected. Disconcerted, I probed a new direction. "How was your experience with your own children?" Katherine brushed back strands of white hair. The lines in her face deepened with her smile. "Oh, the midwives! Before, they were so good. They took such good care of you. We were really spoiled then. All my ten children were delivered by midwives. We never went to doctors. The midwives were so good, so clean. I don't know how they knew what to do. They just knew."

MOVED BY KATHERINE'S STORIES, I combed the local library for background on women's lives and roles as healers. My search turned up little. I found a few references to women and general descriptions of shamans in the journals of early Russian fur traders and monks. One explorer recorded this custom among Kodiak Natives as a frequent cause of stillbirths: pummeling the pregnant woman's abdomen to hasten delivery. Hardly the exalted descriptions of the midwives' recent work that I heard from Katherine. Frustrated by the rift between women's stories and the written record, I turned to other Native women. Some I met through the restaurant and the crisis line, others I sought out at the senior citizens' center. By summer, I had compiled over a dozen taped interviews with Native women. Each echoed Katherine's words of respect, even reverence, for the traditional midwives.

With summer, life on Kodiak blossomed. The long days, the lush vegetation, and the oral history work renewed me. I began to relax into island life. When a friend decided to marry, we waited for the chocolate lilies and wild iris to bloom to pick the wedding bouquets. The light seemed endless that day. This is how life should pass, I thought, timed by wildflowers.

But the number of calls to the crisis line and drunks who spilled into the restaurant also grew with summer. I still joked with customers and pumped them with "black death," the affectionate term for coffee. But now I knew something else about the dark side of their revelry. One morning, a man boasted of leaving "a nice piece" in "pretty bad shape." I went to the bathroom, held my head in my hands, and fought back an emotional explosion. I heard Mary Peterson's voice: "I went through so much, sometimes I wonder if it's true when I think about it, you know, and I can't believe what I went through." I went back out and poured more coffee for a table of fishermen. One old man smiled, turning a weather-beaten face towards me to ask a question. I couldn't hear his voice, deafened by an echo from somewhere deep within.

The privilege of entering other lives, of hearing stories on the crisis line, of recording oral histories, steeping myself in the rich brew of others' words—this process held tremendous power for me. I began to hear women's voices as I moved through my daily tasks at the women's center and at home. My disorientation expanded from the troubled time after dusk into the daylight hours. I no longer knew which thoughts were dreams, which stories were mine, what was shared, what marked me as different from women I met. In search of a tool, a method, some means of sense-making, I decided to leave Kodiak to study anthropology. Before my departure, I tried to find out what had happened to Mary Peterson. She had left the shelter in Anchorage, but no one could tell me where she had gone.

THE SUMMER AFTER MY SECOND YEAR in graduate school, I returned to Kodiak. With a small grant to continue the oral histories with women, I planned to get to all the villages. During my first week back, the clear, bright weather promised smooth flying. As I prepared for my first bush flight, I watched the pilot refuel the Cessna that would take me to Akhiok, Mary Peterson's village. The horror stories I'd heard about flying there made me wary. The village, originally established as a sea otter settlement by the Russians, sits on the southern tip of Kodiak at the edge of Alitak Bay. This end of the island still bears the mark of the Pleistocene glaciers which erased plant life centuries before. Vegetation is sparse, the winds fierce, and travel conditions unpredictable. Even in good weather, there is no certain access. The pilot watched my agitation grow, and he joked, "You can't back out now. You'll wait a long time for skies like this again." But the uneasiness stayed with me as I climbed into the front seat to depart.

On an average flight, a stranger arriving in a village can expect to be greeted by at least one screeching three-wheeler, children and dogs running behind. These noisy, clumsy, oversized bikes are the scourge and savior of bush communities. They manufacture clouds of dust in summer, but ease the walk to mail planes in winter. But as our plane landed in Akhiok that cold July, no one greeted the plane. I looked inquiringly at the pilot, a gregarious man who had regaled me with bear hunting stories all the way over. All at once silent, he shrugged and wished me luck. I walked slowly between the strips of aluminum-sided houses towards the blue onion dome in the distance. Stray dogs roamed between houses; a barefoot boy wandered down the path alone. I heard laughter from a house down by the water, and walked towards it. Inside, a bingo game in full swing. I knocked on the window, but no one looked up. An old man in the next house stood at the door, a young girl behind him. He smiled, began to speak. But by then, alienated, alone, I panicked. I found my way to the clinic, hoping to call for a charter flight out. I lifted the receiver. Nothing. The phone lines were down. I glimpsed the despair that Mary must have felt when she left.

Only later did I learn that almost the entire village was drunk. In time, one elder would recount, "I hate to say it, but even the children were drinking. That alcohol could have wiped us out." But on that first trip, I stayed hidden in the elementary school library, waiting for a plane to get in. Alcohol nurtures isolation—the villagers from one another, them from me. I pushed the isolation further, seeking refuge from my own memories. The school was a citadel of light at this edge of the world: by nightfall, I was terrified. Afraid to turn out the lights, afraid to dream, I sat up all night and read the children's Golden Book encyclopedias. Finally, the weather broke. I flew out to town the next day, then back East. I thought that I would never return.

BY THE FALL OF 1985, I still hadn't finished graduate school, but longing for Alaska drove me north. I returned to Anchorage, then drove north to Fairbanks to watch the last of the birch trees shed their leaves. I stopped at the university to visit friends; in a narrow hallway, I saw a figure in a long black robe. A priest I'd known on Kodiak startled me back to the world of Russian Orthodoxy. "You teach here now?" I asked, surprised. "Yes," he said. "And you? Are you still on the midwives project?" I should be writing, I thought, no more interviews. But instead I responded offhandedly, "Oh, I'm always open to more stories." "Then," he said, "you should look for an Alutiiq woman from Kodiak now living in Anchorage. She knows all about traditional healing."

A week later, I tracked this woman to a mustard-colored boardinghouse near prostitutes' strip. The door to the boarding-house opened slowly. There stood Mary Peterson: the small, grace-ful figure, the same youthful face framed by long, curly hair. She invited me in, graciously, but her reaction didn't mirror my shock. "Do you remember me, Mary?" I asked, barely recovered. "Oh, sure," she said pleasantly. I couldn't tell if this was Native polite-ness, or if she really did. But clearly, Mary Peterson had started over. She agreed to let me interview her. In the ensuing hours, she described bearing eighteen children, losing seven, the life she had left in the village. She detailed her early years as a midwife and her work as a community health aide. "Ever since I can remember, I was taking care of old people, helping them," she said when I asked how she had learned to be a midwife. "I always wanted to be around them because they used to tell stories." When I asked about having her own children, she replied, "My mom helped me. She delivered almost all of them except a few that were born here in the hospital. I never trusted the others in the hospital. I trusted my mom only be-cause I know she knows what she's doing." And then, she echoed the words I had heard from other women on Kodiak. "I don't know how, but she just knew."

What did it mean, the midwives' "knowing"? I heard its fugue-like overtones resonate through the stories of every woman I inter-viewed. When I asked Mary about "knowing," she told the story of the first birth she assisted. One sister of her original seventeen sib-lings went into labor alone. "My sister was worried," she said, "but those other people in the village weren't in condition to help, so I did the best I could. Only after the baby was born, after I got every-thing done, took care of the afterbirth and the baby . . . then I started shaking and sweating all over! When I think about it, it seems like I just came out of a trance or something. It seems like it wasn't me. I always think God was using my hands to help this lady."

Traces of village life filled Mary's home: small plastic bags of dried herbs and flowers on a shelf, stacks of grass for weaving baskets drying under the couch. How could she bear to be separated from her home? Mary moved towards a photograph of her son, Bobby, now an emerging village leader in Akhiok. She continued, "You know, some of my kids are in the village. It's hard." She spoke of the life she had left—not only family, but her work as a teacher's aide, and a community health aide. "I hated to leave that! Because I love to work with the kids and being the health aide, helping people. But my job is not gonna help my health. No matter how much money I have, it won't bring my life back together. I went through so much, sometimes I wonder if it's true when I think about it, you know, and I can't believe what I went through. Ever since I could remember, that's what it was like. Hiding, running out the house in nightgown, no shoes. Oh, when I think about it, I wonder if it was true! Staying outside the house at night, I don't want to go into people's houses, because I was afraid he would go pounding on their doors. But when he's sober, you wouldn't even know he's around." When Mary finally called the Women's Resource Center, she says that "I just didn't know that people in town could help. The older I was getting, the more scared I was. I couldn't stand the constant drinking. I knew it was now or never. I decided."

On the bus going home, I heard Mary's words again: "Sometimes I wonder if it's true when I think about it, you know, and I can't believe what I went through." And I remembered the light in her face when she described the process of "knowing" how to be a midwife, the same radiance I'd seen in the faces of other Native women. To say the midwives "knew" was an assertion of belief. Belief in Russian Orthodoxy. Belief in the realm of traditional healing. Belief in Native identity and in traditional village life. Exact words from each story fit together, braided into a strand of resistance, refined and steeled in the telling and retelling. A wave of energy shot through me.

Later that night, the dream returned. *A line of Native women stand in columns. Light surrounds them. The danger remains, but their faces are radiant. Only one figure remains cloaked in shadows. Even in the darkness, I see myself.*

I dreaded returning to urban life and graduate school, but I went back. In Philadelphia, a gang rape on the campus catalyzed growing awareness of violence against women. At a rally, I stood mesmerized as one professor described a childhood experience that taught her early about violence and self-protection. On a basketball court, a group of boys had picked her up and tried to use her as a ball. In the ensuing days, I couldn't sleep. Then I dreamed that I was back in Akhiok, in a small house by the sea. *It is dark, the phone lines are down, I cannot leave the village. An old man has given me shelter, but he keeps young Native girls as slaves. He makes them pile up our wood, clean, and haul water. At night, we hear wailing, and scraping beneath the house. Restless spirits, angry, vengeful. The voices of women.* I wake and want to know: Why does this pain feel so familiar?

THE LANDSCAPES OF THE WEST stayed with me as I passed endless days writing my dissertation about the Kodiak midwives. First in Philadelphia, then in Washington, D.C., I lived in my imagination. Mentally, I returned to the Kodiak Russian graveyards and Sitka spruce. Good friends, school, then a job at the Smithsonian kept me East for four years, but nothing matched the vise-like grip of my memories of the West. I craved water. I longed for the wildflowers to mark time. Unlike Mary, I could end my exile. When I finished my dissertation, I decided to go West again. My car packed with all that I owned, I headed through the Southwest and up the back side of the Sierras.

My western homecoming was bittersweet. After an afternoon of reading in my favorite Portland bookstore, I returned to find my car emptied of my belongings. I laughed it off, joked about how it would ease my unpacking. But within days, I grew restless and uneasy. I abandoned Portland and headed north to Seattle. I found a waitress job and a roommate. I dismissed the robbery as I set up my new life. After a week in town, my roommate left for a conference in Montana. On my first night alone, I awoke in a cold sweat. The shadowed figure of a man, his back to me, sorted through my closet, fingering my scarves and clothing. I panicked. Hadn't these items been stolen just the week before? Paralyzed by fear, I sat motionless, barely breathing. When I finally could move, I crept across the floor in the dark, forcing a knee forward, then a hand. My energy focused on the figure in the closet. I almost felt his touch as I fumbled with the phone to dial 911. "Get the lights on!" The emergency operator's voice was clear and strong. "He's not there? Was he there?" One hand on the phone, the other clasped my throat. The feel of my own flesh on my neck unleashed a wave of memory. *Clammy hands on my body and neck.* Phone still in hand, I laid on the floor. My body shook. *I feel them now, seventeen years later. Hands, like octopus tentacles from the bodies of so many men. I feel the waist-length hair I wore at age seventeen, cling to the pieces of a blouse that remain clutched in my hand, to the one moccasin on my left foot. Smells overwhelm me, my own sweat merged with the muggy blackness. If darkness has a scent, it is dank, like wet earth.* "Hello?" The operator yanked me back to the present. "Are you sure he was there? Are you hallucinating?" Was I? Did seven men really drag me to the ground in the blackness of an unknown woods more than sixteen years before? The operator asked if I'd ever been through any trauma. *I see the kindly stranger in a house near the dark woods. A thundering silence and the look of horror on his face. He offers his phone, some clean clothes. Why doesn't he ask me what happened? Why can't I tell him? I have no words.* It was only later when I told one friend my story that I had a name for what had happened: gang rape. Its echo reverberated through my dreams for sixteen years.

"Sometimes I wonder if it's true when I think about it, you know, and I can't believe what I went through." I thought of Mary's words. I took the list of numbers the operator gave me, but it wasn't until the following summer that I went to the first group support meeting of the Seattle Rape Crisis Center. Through three months of sessions with other women, I listened to stories. Rapes in parking lots, in laundromats, in homes, by fathers, and strangers, and lovers. I battled insomnia first, then intensified nightmares. The fear I had kept at bay came back with full force. But the process cleansed my spirit and brought me back to Mary and the women from Kodiak. I knew then how their stories of the "knowing" women and heroic midwives countered these narratives: childhood abuse, creeping alcoholism and violence, women driven from their homes, families rent apart. The stories of traditional life, of women's connection through healing, forged ties and re-created bonds. Through two centuries of battering by human hands and governmental bodies, their stories persevered. I glimpsed a truth that I had previously known only as shadow: telling about pain creates us anew. Through shared stories, we heal.

FLYING INTO KODIAK, one sees only water until the plane descends a few hundred feet short of the runway. I arrived for Kodiak's first Alutiiq Cultural Heritage Conference on a brilliant February morning in 1988, dizzy from the sense of flying into the sea. For years, scholars as well as local people had ignored or misunderstood the ethnic identity of Kodiak Natives. Now, people from all over Alaska as well as Europe and the Soviet Union gathered to discuss the revitalization of Alutiiq culture. Settled in Seattle by then, I flew to Kodiak for the conference, eager to see Mary, who was staying with her daughter in town. I hoped to do further interviews, and finally to delve into difficult issues about violence in her life. After months in a support group, I thought that I could ask the questions I had avoided before. I hoped to write Mary's life story.

As I wandered downtown, I felt the almost palpable local pride. Kodiak's ambivalence about its isolation is proclaimed on a tourist T-shirt: "It's not the end of the world, but you can see it from here." Now others had sought out this cultural and geographical edge, an otherwise unmarked point on the map. I stopped at the restaurant where I had passed so many dark winter mornings, to look out at the boat harbor, to remember. In the booth behind me, a group of Native people talked about the tragedy in Akhiok. Another suicide. That young village leader, Bobby Simeonoff, had shot himself. Mary's youngest son, he had showed so much promise. I saw the glimmer of light before despair.

Bobby Simeonoff joined the casualties of a statewide epidemic chronicled in a Pulitzer Prize–winning series run by the *Anchorage Daily News* in 1988, "A People in Peril." For two weeks, stories publicized an epidemic of suicide and alcoholic destruction in village Alaska. Young men aged twenty to twenty-four were committing suicide at four times the national average. Akhiok now contributed to the statistics.

"Bobby was the one who used to get me firewood," Mary said later. "I knew that I could count on him." I had found her at her daughter's home in Kodiak, sitting on the couch watching television. She balanced a cup of tea long ago turned cold, the powdered milk congealed. I feared speaking of the death; I feared not speaking of it. She didn't cry as she took my hand, and said, "It's so hard, Joanne." Hard compared to what? Harder than years of abuse? Harder than crawling under your own house to sleep to escape your terror? Harder than losing the other six of your eighteen children, and six siblings of the eighteen your own mother bore? The questions I had brought for her seemed trivial, my own bad dreams unreal. If suffering has a hierarchy, I had lost all sense of measure.

SOME ANTHROPOLOGISTS SEE themselves as "cultural translators." After the death of Mary's son, I wondered if I could

ever comprehend her life. Was it ethical or even possible to translate it? I continued to write to her, sending tea and little soaps, gifts
she said "spoiled" her. But it was several years before we could do
interviews again, and it wasn't until 1992 that the possibility of
telling her story opened. That year capped changes in the village of
Akhiok so profound that Mary, after years of living in exile in
Anchorage, could return there. When I went back to see her, I
found a woman and a village transformed.

On a rare, brilliantly sunny day in April, I flew back to Alaska.
I lived by then in Oregon, and worked as a folklorist and a teacher. I
went to Akhiok to do oral history workshops in the schools; finally,
after years of taking stories out of this community, I could return
something. I planned intentionally; I wanted to be back for Russian
Orthodox Easter. I also hoped to see the transformation which had
brought the village to the attention of the *Anchorage Daily News*, the
Tundra Times, and other state papers as a model of the village sobri-
ety movement among Alaska Natives. After the plane landed, I pi-
voted between yelping dogs to knock on Mary's door. She didn't
recognize me at first. Then she smiled broadly, "Oh, I wondered if
that could be you!" She motioned towards the kitchen. "Are you
married yet?" she asked as we entered. When I said no, she turned
back to knead dough for *kulich*, an Easter bread often frosted with
bright flowers and the Russian Orthodox double cross. She smiled
again. "Sometimes it's good to be alone." Did "alone" mean the
same thing to us, I wondered? Did anything translate?

Carefully, I asked her how things had changed after her son's
death. "After he died, they're telling each other what alcohol is
doing and there were several suicide attempts after. They're afraid
what might happen to the kids if they keep on drinking, you know,
and that kind of woke them up. They all try to help each other now,
with AA meetings and talking to each other. They talk about how
good they feel to be doing something else instead of just craving for
alcohol." When villagers finally stopped drinking, the violence sub-

sided, and Mary returned. I watched the light enter her face as she described her homecoming. "It feels so good to be back. The village is so different now that people aren't drinking. The people in the village just did it themselves, which I'm really proud of."

I walked back to the school, heartened by the changes in the village. Children played again on the dusty paths. The community center, long dormant, bustled with activity as Akhiok prepared for Easter. I returned to the children's room of the Akhiok school library where I had passed such a fitful and troubled night so many years before. I leafed through the Golden Book encyclopedias almost nostalgically, then laid down in the corner on my sleeping bag to rest before midnight mass. Sleepiness reminded me that my insomnia and nightmares had diminished, almost disappeared. Then, at 11:30 P.M., I panicked. I realized that I had no flashlight. My momentary confidence vanished. How could I make it over half a mile down the dark path and up the hill to find a seat for the service? I thought of Mary's face as she kneaded *kulich* and described what it meant to be here for the celebration. I couldn't miss this ceremony. I had to be in church for Easter.

I looked out from the school window at the blackness. For most of my adult life, I had feared even the relative darkness of my urban existence. But we don't know darkness in its complete sense in cities; its meaning is something archaic that we can only imagine as metaphor. Here darkness demands complete surrender. I had waited for over a decade to be in Akhiok for Easter, to sit in the church which had first gripped my heart in a photograph. Yet now I sat, unable to move. It seemed ludicrous, even shameful, for an adult to sit imprisoned by the dark. But when I pushed open the metal door of the school and ventured out, a clammy sensation rose from the bottom of my spine. Two forces waged war within me: the terror born in the darkness of that distant woods so long ago and the centripetal pull to the church, to Easter, to hope. Resurrection. I backed up to the school wall, glued to this fortress of light. Then I

remembered Mary's words: "I knew it was now or never. I decided."
I padded my knees with extra socks, drew my collar up around my
neck for protection. I slammed the heavy metal door to lock behind
me. Then, on my hands and knees, I began to crawl. Fingers dug
into roots and plants, I dragged myself in the direction of the path. I
held a hand in front of my face. Nothing. Each time I stopped, I
heard the frantic beating of my heart. Finally, nearing a cleared
area, I looked up at the faint glimmer of a flashlight. An elder late
for church chuckled as she helped me to my feet, "The last stranger
who wandered in the dark landed in the cesspool." I felt like a child
as she took my hand.

We hurried to the church, where I found my way to the
women's side, several rows behind Mary, as the reader began to
sing in Church Slavonic. Hanging icons, pink and yellow paper
flowers prepared by village women weeks ago, and rows of elabo-
rately frosted *kulich* filled the church with color. I stood hypnotized
as the others lit candles, their chants rising into the dome of the
church. Some deep terror in me melted into the heat, the candle
glow, the spoken music. I remembered the fugue of "knowing." I
started to inch my way towards Mary. I wanted to tell her what she
had taught me, how I knew all at once why I had returned each time
to Alaska, to this village, to her stories. But a child in a faded rayon
dress and dirty ski jacket stepped between us. Tears streamed down
my face as she handed me a candle. I held it to hers for light as we
moved outside to circle the church three times, the initiation of the
ceremony. I looked out at the radiant beam from a fishing boat
which broke the cover of blackness. The light seemed to fill the sky.
For the first time in many years, I felt safe.

Kathleen Norris

T he infamous insularity, cultural vacancy, and divisiveness of small Western towns get plenty of play in the literature, as Kathleen Norris notes in her first book of nonfiction (Dakota: A Spiritual Geography, 1993). Her essay "Gatsby on the Plains" opens with a remark addressed to her in 1984 by a woman in her thirties: "You don't understand this town because you're an outsider. You don't know what it was like here twenty years ago. But that's what we want; that's what we have to get back to." In fact, Norris had moved back to the house her grandparents built in Lemmon, an isolated town on the border between North and South Dakota, in the early 1970s and so had already survived a prodigal's return by nearly ten years. "In forsaking the ability to change," Norris argues, we usually diminish our "capacity for hope." "Disconnecting from change," she concludes, "does not recapture the past. It loses the future."

Less publicized is what Norris presents for us here in another essay from the same book. "Getting to Hope" focuses on some quiet and modest virtues of village life: spirituality, a strong sense of place and connection to the outside world, cooperation and creative problem solving, a tradition that acts as a bridge between the past and the present and the future. In Hope, an award-winning poet with two books (Falling Off, 1971, and The Middle of the World, 1981) *can become the lay pastor to a congregation of farmers and ranchers who daily "touch the earth, the real earth," not only to produce food but to restore their souls.*

"Getting to Hope"

from *Dakota*

TO GET TO HOPE, TURN SOUTH OFF U.S. HIGHWAY 12 at Keldron, South Dakota. It's easy to miss, as the town is not much more than a gas station and general store with a well-kept house behind it, and a sign announcing that Cammy Varland of Keldron was Miss Teen South Dakota of 1987.

Turn onto the gravel section-line road and look for a wooden map on your right. Built by the Busy Beavers 4-H Club, it has the mysterious yet utilitarian air of the seashell, twine, and bamboo maps that South Sea islanders once made for navigational purposes. The Keldron map consists of wooden slats painted with names and numerical inscriptions. Peterson 8 S 4 E 1 N indicates that you would drive eight miles south, four miles east, and one mile north to find the Peterson ranch.

The small metal sign for Hope (13 S) may or may not be up. The wind pulls it down and it can be a while before someone notices and reattaches it. But you don't need directions; just follow the road south and turn when it turns 90 degrees west, then another 90 degrees south, and then it's just another mile or so.

Ten and a half miles along the road, at the crest of the second hill, you'll be able to see where you're going, a tiny ark in a sea of land that unfolds before you for nearly fifty miles. At night you can see the lights of Isabel, South Dakota, some forty-five miles south, and Bison, about the same distance to the southwest.

The breaks of the Grand River are visible, land crumpled like brown paper. The river itself lies at the base of the steep cliffs it has carved into the prairie, sandstone glinting in the morning sun. *Paha Sunkawakan Sapa*, or Black Horse Butte, is a brooding presence on the horizon south of the river.

You will pass a few modest homes and farm buildings along the way, some in use, others in disrepair. The most recently abandoned, a classic two-story farmhouse, has boarded-up windows and an extensive but weed-choked corral. A house abandoned years ago is open to the elements, all its windows and most of its shingles gone. A large shelterbelt, planted in the 1930s, is now a thicket of dead trees. Once the trees are gone the house will lean with the wind until it collapses; but that will be a while.

Like the others who have business in Hope, I know who left; I know why. Every time I pass the abandoned houses I am reminded of them. "Hope Presbyterian Church is located by itself on the South Dakota prairie," is what the church history says. But that doesn't begin to tell it. Hope Church, which fifteen years ago had a membership of 46, is down to 25 today, scattered on ranches for thirty miles around. The loss is due to older farmers retiring and moving to town, and younger farmers leaving the area.

Hope Church is an unassuming frame building that stands in a pasture at the edge of a coulee where ash trees and berry bushes flourish; chokecherry, snowberry, buffalo berry. The place doesn't look like much, even when most of the membership has arrived on Sunday morning, yet it's one of the most successful churches I know. Along with Center School, the one-room schoolhouse that currently serves nine children from Grand Valley, Riverside, and Rolling Green townships in southwest Corson County, Hope Church gives the people who live around it a sense of identity.

"It doesn't matter what religion they are," says one longtime

member. "The Lutherans and Catholics tell us that Hope is important to them, too, and becoming more so. We're *the church* in the
neighborhood." A former pastor said of Hope Church, "It seemed
that whatever was going on, a farm sale or a funeral or wedding,
Hope was a part of what happened in that community." A measure
of this may be seen at the annual Vacation Bible School for children,
which is attended by both Lutheran and Catholic children.

The current church was built by its members in 1961 on the
cement foundation of an old barn. But its roots go back to 1916,
when people gathered for Sunday worship in the dance halls of the
small settlements at White Deer and Glad Valley. "Church wasn't
awfully regular in the horse and buggy days," says an older member
of Hope, the son of one of the founders. "The ministers at McIntosh
or Thunder Hawk were circuit riders then, and it could take them
half a day to get down to us." Neither congregation ever had a
church building. Until they merged in 1950, one congregation met
in a one-room school, and the other in a hall that served as a community center where baby showers, funeral luncheons, wedding
dances, and anniversary celebrations are also held.

Hope is well cared for. Both the outhouse and the sanctuary are
freshly painted. Two small, attractive stained glass windows depict-
ing a cross in the center of a sunburst and a dove with an olive
branch flying over a landscape that resembles the fields around
Hope Church were recently added to the south wall behind the pulpit, placed on either side of a handmade cross of varnished wood.
The elegantly curved oak pews with carved endpieces are hand-me-
downs from a church in Minnesota. A member of Hope drove his
grain truck more than three hundred miles to get them.

Hope has a noble and well-used upright piano whose sound reminds me of the honky-tonk pianos in Western movies. But when
Carolyn plays her quiet-down music at the beginning of a service,
"Shall We Gather at the River" or "Holy, Holy, Holy," she's as ef-
fective as a Russian Orthodox deacon striding sternly through a

church with censer and bells. We know it's time now to listen, that we will soon take our journey into word and song, and maybe change a little along the way. By the time we're into our first hymn, we know where we are. To paraphrase Isaiah 62, it's a place no longer desolate but delightful.

There is no indoor plumbing at Hope, but the congregation celebrates with food and drink at every opportunity. Once, when I arrived on Sunday, I noticed several popcorn poppers in a back pew. That was for after church, to help everyone get through the annual congregational meeting. Once, Hope gave me a party with homemade cake, coffee and iced tea, and Kool-Aid in big coolers that the men carried into the basement.

In the manner of the other tiny country churches I know (United Tribes in Bismarck and Saint Philip's in Maili, Hawaii) Hope is such a hospitable place that I suspect that no matter who you are or where you come from, you will be made to feel at home. But don't get so comfortable that you underestimate the people around you; don't entertain for a moment the notion that these farmers and ranchers are quaint country folk. Most of them have college degrees, though the figure is down slightly from 85 percent in the mid-1980s, a statistic that startled the pastor, who had last worked in Scranton, Pennsylvania, where 3 percent of her congregation was college educated.

Hope's people read, and they think about what is going on in the world. If you want to know anything about agriculture on a global scale—the cattle market in Argentina or prospects for the wheat crop in Australia—this is the place to ask. As one pastor recently put it, "the thing that makes Hope so vibrant is that the congregation is so alive to the world."

Hope's members take seriously their responsibility as members of the world's diverse and largely poor human race. A few years ago, reasoning that people who raise food (and often have a hard time getting a price for it that covers their expenses) should know more about why so many in the world can't afford to feed themselves, they conducted a study of the politics of hunger. To conclude the study they invited an expert on the subject to come from Chicago to address churchpeople in the area. They also studied the ethical issues of raising animals for food. As ranchers who know the life history and temperament of every cow in their herds, they were dismayed to discover the inroads factory farming had made in American agriculture.

In recent hard times, while Hope's membership declined by nearly half, the amount the church donates for mission has increased every year. It now ranks near the top in per capita giving among Presbyterian churches in the state of South Dakota.

One former pastor said, "It can be astonishing how tiny Hope Church makes you feel so strongly that you're part of a global entity." This is a long tradition at Hope. A rancher whose three daughters spent several years in ecumenical church work in Sydney, Paris, Rome, and Brussels says: "Our girls always knew that the world was bigger than just us. They had cousins who were missionaries in China in the 1950s and 1960s. In those days missionaries got every seventh year off, and they'd stay with us on the ranch. Our children grew up hearing stories about other places."

For this and other reasons pastors find the Hope congregation stimulating to work with. One told me if he could sum them up in one word it would be "appreciative." Another said: "Hope was where I realized how much the members of a rural church actually work as well as worship together. They live supporting each other. We'd spoken of such things at seminary, as an ideal, but this was the first time in twenty years of ministry I'd actually seen it done. It made me realize how vital a small country church can be."

Perhaps it's not surprising that so tiny a rural congregation is not often well served by the larger church of which it is a part. For all their pious talk of "small is beautiful," church bureaucrats, like bureaucrats everywhere, concentrate their attention on places with better demographics; bigger numbers, more power and money. The power of Hope Church and country churches like it is subtle and not easily quantifiable. It's a power derived from smallness and lack of power, a concept the apostle Paul would appreciate, even if modern church bureaucrats lose sight of it.

In the manner of country people everywhere (and poets also for that matter) the people at Hope tend to be conservators of language. Once, when I found myself staggering through a benediction provided by the denomination that, among other things, invited us to "authenticate the past," I stopped and said, "I'm sorry, but that's ridiculous English." Laughter became our benediction that morning.

Like most small churches in the western Dakotas, Hope must be yoked to another, larger church in order to afford a full-time pastor. When Hope's sister church in Lemmon, thirty miles away, received memorial money to purchase a new Presbyterian hymnal that includes many contemporary hymns and more inclusive language, Hope decided to stay with their 1955 model. Not because its members aren't progressive. It's a relatively youthful congregation, in fact, with nary a fundamentalist bone among them. But the old hymnal works well for them, and many of their standards are not included in the new book: "I Need Thee Every Hour" and "I Love to Tell the Story" (which, not surprisingly, has been a favorite of mine since childhood), and "Nearer, My God, to Thee." That last hymn was a revelation to me when I first came back to church. Like many people, I couldn't think of it without picturing the band on the Titanic in *A Night to Remember*. I was pleased to discover that the hymn is an evocative retelling of the story of Jacob's dream.

As one pastor of Hope, a graduate of Princeton seminary, said to me, "Church intellectuals always want to root out the pietistic hymns, but in a rural area like this those hymns of intimacy are necessary for the spiritual welfare of people who are living at such a distance from each other." He added, "City people want hymns that reassure them that God is at work in the world, but people in the western Dakotas take that for granted."

The conflict between urban and rural theologies is an old one in the Christian church. Back in fourth-century Egypt, the Bishop of Alexandria, at the urging of intellectuals smitten with Greek philosophy, announced as church doctrine that when you pray you must not have any picture of God in your mind. One old monk is reported to have wept, saying, "They have taken away my God, and I have none I can hold now, and know not whom to adore or to address myself." Some monks took to their boats and traveled the Nile to Alexandria, where they rioted in front of the bishop's palace until he recanted. Hope's people have been more quiet about letting the greater Church go its way.

I find it ironic that the new inclusiveness of the official church tends to exclude people as rural as those of Hope. But I may have been spoiled by the company I keep on the prairie, the Benedictine monks and country people, some well educated, some not, who know from their experience that prayer is important, that worship serves a purpose, that God is part of everyday life, and that singing "Nearer, My God, to Thee" may be good for a person. It's a rural hymn: it's the rare city person who can imagine sleeping out in the open, a stone for a pillow and a heaven of stars above.

Maybe we're all anachronisms in Dakota, a bunch of hicks, and the fact that the images in many old hymns, images of seed and wheat, planting and reaping, images as old as the human race and as new as the harvest in the fields around Hope Church, really aren't relevant any more. Twenty-five Presbyterian farmers, or a handful of monks for that matter, don't have much to say to the world.

And yet I wonder. I wonder if a church like Hope doesn't teach the world in the way a monastery does, not by loudly voicing its views but by existing quietly in its own place. I wonder if what Columba Stewart, a contemporary Benedictine, has said about such earthy metaphors, that "the significance of field, vineyard and gar-

den metaphors in biblical and post-biblical texts . . . lies beyond
their relevance to the agricultural economy of ancient peoples," really means that our urban civilization surpasses such metaphors at
its peril. As Stewart says, "these images describe the process of
human cultivation," and as such they may be an essential part of
being human, and of being religious in a human way.

Does the city, any city, need Hope Church? Does America need
people on the land? In the last volume of Ole Rolvaag's *Giants in the
Earth* trilogy a country pastor, addressing Norwegian farmers in
Dakota who are losing their "old country" ways, and in fact are
eager to lose them in order to become good Americans, declares
that "a people that has lost its traditions is doomed." He adds:

> If this process of leveling down, of making everybody alike
> . . . is allowed to continue, America is doomed to become the
> most impoverished land spiritually on the face of the earth;
> out of our highly praised melting pot will come a dull . . .
> smug complacency, barren of all creative thought . . . Soon
> we will have reached the perfect democracy of barrenness
> . . . Dead will be the hidden life of the heart which is nour-
> ished by tradition, the idioms of language, and our attitude to
> life. It is out of these elements that character grows.

The process of acculturation to American life has traditionally
been accelerated in cities; it takes more time for rural people to
change. But Rolvaag's pastor is as relevant as the contemporary de-
bate about multiculturalism. "If we're to accomplish anything
worthwhile," he says, "we must do it as Norwegians. Otherwise we
may meet the same fate as corn in too strong a sun."

I wonder if roles are now reversed, and America's urban majority, native born or not, might be seen as immigrants to a world of
asphalt and cement, and what they need more than anything is access to the old ways of being. Access to the spirits of land and of

place. The image of a democracy of barrenness rings true when one turns on the television and finds bland programs designed for the widest possible audience, or when one drives a busy freeway or walks through an airport parking garage, places that are no place, where you can't tell by looking if you are in Tulsa or Tacoma, Minneapolis or Memphis.

The sense of place is unavoidable in western Dakota, and maybe that's our gift to the world. Maybe that's why most Americans choose to ignore us. Upward mobility is a virtue in this society; and if we must keep moving on, leaving any place that doesn't pay off, it's better to pretend that place doesn't matter. But Hope Church, south of Keldron, is a real place, a holy place; you know that when you first see it, one small building in a vast land. You know it when you walk in the door. It can't be moved from where it is on the prairie. Physically, yes, but that's beside the point.

Hope's people are traditional people, country people, and they know that the spirits of a place cannot be transported or replaced. They're second-, third-, and fourth-generation Americans who have lived on the land for many years, apart from the mainstream of American culture, which has become more urban with every passing year. Hope's people have become one with their place: this is not romanticism, but truth. You can hear it in the way people speak, referring to their land in the first person: "I'm so dry I'm starting to blow," or "I'm so wet now I'll be a month to seeding."

A pastor who was raised on a farm in Kansas said he thought what made Hope special was that the members were "all, or nearly all, totally dependent on the land." He didn't seem to mind that church attendance got sparse at haying time and at calving, which is a round-the-clock operation for most ranch families; every three hours or so someone must check the pregnant heifers. The fact that this often coincides with brutal spring blizzards doesn't help; newborns can freeze to death in a matter of minutes.

"I spent some time on trail rides with Hope's ranchers," the pastor said, "and also helped at lambing. But they were a bigger help to me than I was to them. To touch the earth, the real earth, once again, restored my soul."

I once heard Martin Broken Leg, a Rosebud Sioux who is an Episcopal priest, address an audience of Lutheran pastors on the subject of bridging the Native American/white culture gap. "Ghosts don't exist in some cultures," he said, adding dismissively, "They think time exists." There was nervous laughter; we knew he had us. Time is real to us in America, time is money. Ghosts are nothing, and place is nothing. But Hope Church claims by its very existence that place is important, that place has meaning in and of itself. You're still in America in the monastery, and in Hope Church—these absurd and holy places—you're still in the modern world. But these places demand that you give up any notion of dominance or control. In these places you wait, and the places mold you.

Hope is small, dying, and beautifully alive. It's tribal in a way, as most of its members are related. But it does not suffer from tribalism, the deadening and often deadly insularity that can cause groups of people to fear or despise anyone who is not like them. I find in Hope many of the graces of a monastery, with stability of place and a surprisingly wide generosity in its hospitality.

It was hospitality that allowed the people at Hope to welcome me as a lay pastor. It was absurd for me to be giving sermons to them, the only person in the room who hadn't been to church in the past twenty years. I had little experience of the Bible apart from childhood memories; no training in either Scripture studies or homiletics. What could I possibly say to these people about scriptures they had been absorbing all their lives?

I did what I could, and my long apprenticeship as a poet served me well. I didn't preach much, in the traditional sense of the word; instead I stayed close to those texts, talking about the stories I found there and how I thought they might resonate with our own stories. And I got some thoughtful and encouraging response. I followed the lectionary for discipline, but got a laugh one Sunday when I mentioned that I'd chosen to ignore the advice I'd found in a guide for pastors, that one shouldn't try to connect the Old Testament, Gospel, and Epistle texts but concentrate instead on one brief passage. I said that telling a poet not to look for connections is like telling a farmer not to look at the rain gauge after a storm.

Preaching sermons was a new and unnerving experience for me, and having the people at Hope to work with was my salvation. They made it easier for me to do in those sermons what I saw I had to do, that is, disclose myself in ways different from those I was used to, hiding behind the comfortable mask of fiction. The "I" in a poem is never me—how could it be? But the "I" in my sermons came closer to home, and that was risky. "That's why we appreciated you," one Hope member told me.

I got to try out my sermons first at Hope, as the Sunday morning service there is at 9:00 A.M. and the one in town is at 11:00 A.M. More than once I finished at Hope by asking, "Can I get away with saying this in town?" Once a woman replied, "That depends on how much faith you have," which was a good answer, as the Gospel text that day was the story of Jesus hollering at his disciples in the middle of a storm, "Why are you so afraid?" The church in town had been through a stormy period a few years back, and my sermon was an attempt to help put those bad times to rest. I knew that if I had misjudged, I would only stir things up again.

I began to find that Hope Church opened doors for me the way that Benedictine monasteries had, and it offered similar surprises. Every time I read the Scriptures aloud in the Sunday service at Hope I became aware of sparks in those texts that I had missed in preparing my sermon, and that was a wonderful experience for a poet to have, as it said much about the power of words to continually astonish and invigorate us, and even to surpass human understanding.

Monks, with their conscious attempt to do the little things

peaceably and well—daily things like liturgy or chores, or preparing and serving meals—have a lot in common with the farmers and ranchers of Hope. Both have a down-to-earth realism on the subject of death. Benedict, in a section of his *Rule* entitled "Tools for Good Works," asks monks to "Day by day remind yourself that you are going to die," and I would suggest that this is not necessarily a morbid pursuit. Benedict is correct in terming the awareness of death a tool. It can be humbling, when we find ourselves at odds with another person, to remember that both of us will die one day, presumably not at one another's hands. If, as Dr. Johnson said, "the prospect of being hanged in the morning wonderfully concentrates the mind," recalling our mortality can be a healthy realism in an age when we spend so much time, energy, and money denying death.

But maybe denying death is something people need to do. One might even look at a medieval cathedral as an expression of that need. Those buildings, however, were also made for celebrating life with music and art, with the play of light and shadow on stone and colored glass. They are beautiful in ways that modern exercise machines and lifestyles leading to that tofu-in-the-sky are not.

Tofu is still a novelty at Hope; people there obtain their protein from animals they raise on land that is suitable for nothing else. I learned at Hope Church just how profoundly the activities of farming and ranching, working the land and working closely with animals, affect the way people approach matters of life and death. Preaching in both a town and a country church, I found that the hard texts of Advent—texts about waiting, about judgment and last things—were accepted in the country while in town there was already pressure to start celebrating Christmas.

When the great wheel of the lectionary came round to the text in Isaiah that begins, "Comfort ye, comfort ye my people," and reminds us that "all flesh is grass," I preached a sermon at Hope that attempted to address the meaning of Advent in terms of the tangle of pain and joy we feel in preparing for birth and death. The town church had opted for no sermon that day. Instead, we sang Christmas carols and listened to sentimental poems from *Ideals* magazine. That text from Isaiah was read aloud during the service, but its meaning was clouded by cheer. We were busy comforting ourselves and had no wish to be reminded of our mortality.

The difference between the two churches on that Sunday confirmed what I had begun to suspect: the people of Hope Church were less afraid than the people in town to look into the heart of their pain, a pain they share with many monasteries, which also have a diminishing and aging population. When these people ask, "Who will replace us?" the answer is, "who knows, maybe no one," and it's not easy to live with that truth. The temptation is to deny it or to look for scapegoats. The challenge is to go on living graciously and thankfully, cultivating love. Not sentimental love but true charity, which, as Flannery O'Connor said, "is hard and endures."

The people of Hope live far apart from each other on the land: paradoxically, I suspect this is one reason they seem better at creating community than people in town, better at being together while leaving each other alone, as I once heard the monastic ideal defined. How are we to get along with our neighbor in hard times and good? How can we make relationships that last? Those who live in small rural communities, who come to know their neighbors all too well over the years, know the truth of the words of a sixth-century monk, Dorotheus of Gaza: "The root of all disturbance, if one will go to its source, is that no one will blame himself." When I read those words in a sermon at Hope Church, one old farmer forgot himself; he nodded and said aloud, "That's right." He was assenting to a hard truth, one confirmed by a lifetime of experience.

"All flesh is grass" is a hard truth, too, and it has real meaning for people who grow grass, cut it, bale it, and go out every day in winter to feed it to cows. They watch that grass turning into flesh, knowing that they in turn will eat it as beef. They can't pretend not to know that their flesh, too, is grass. And they know that grass dies, not just in the winter, but in summer's dry heat. "All flesh is grass, and its beauty is as the flower of the field." That image comes alive in the West River of Dakota, and also an image from Psalm 90 that speaks of "grass that springs up in the morning" and "by evening withers and fades."

It's hard for me to imagine Hope Church dying, almost impossible to picture it abandoned or falling into ruins, as human constructions inevitably do. Absurdly, I think of its death the way I think of our sun dying. Eventually, long after anyone is around to see it, the sun will grow redder and perhaps more beautiful before it finally burns out. The Grand River will have turned to ice by then, and Black Horse Butte may be stripped of its skin of grass and soil.

It's absurd, too, that I find a Benedictine monastery and a tiny Presbyterian church in the middle of nowhere to be so absolutely and perfectly complementary. I am not showing due respect to religion as I was taught it: as a matter of the fine points of who's in, who's out, who's what as defined by dogmatic and denominational distinctions. But then, I don't have to. This is the Wild West. Out at Hope, in the summer, bellowing cows at a nearby watering tank sometimes join in the call to worship; one year baby rattlesnakes showed up for Vacation Bible School.

One former minister at Hope who had come from the urban East told me that her strongest memory of Hope Church was of an evening service in July. Standing in the pulpit she could see down the length of the church and out the open door to a large round hay bale catching the last rays of sunlight. "It was dark on one side and pure gold on the other," she said, "and I thought, that's a measure of the wealth here, that will help make things come out right this year."

She also told me that she couldn't imagine what was happening at the first funeral service she conducted for a member of Hope Church when, as people gathered for the graveside service, the men, some kneeling, began studying the open grave. It was early November, and someone explained that they were checking the frost and moisture levels in the ground. They were farmers and ranchers worried about a drought. They were mourners giving a good friend back to the earth. They were people of earth, looking for a sign of hope.

Brenda Peterson

renda Peterson's father worked for the U.S. Forest Service; she was born on a Forest Service ranger station in the Sierra Nevadas. "My father, himself part Seminole, French Canadian, and Cherokee Indian . . . knew trees the way some people do finances or racehorses," she wrote in her collection of essays, Living by Water (1990). "He called them by name as if they were simply a tribe of very tall, silent neighbors who had their own ways. What he did not know was babies, and so he and my young, distracted mother raised me like the animals my father knew so well. If I cried, I was a coyote; if I sang, a mockingbird. And when I was the most inconsolable, my father suggested I hold on to a tree . . . The tree took the tears from me, transforming them into sweet-smelling sap I could chew like a child's cud. I hardly knew I was human until I left the forest."

Peterson first gained national attention for her novels, including River of Light (1978), Becoming the Enemy (1988), and Duck and Cover (a New York Times notable book of 1991). Living by Water, followed by Nature and Other Mothers: Reflections on the Feminine in Everyday Life (1992), established her in the first rank of nature writers as well. Her latest nonfiction book, Sister Stories: The Many Mirrors of Sisterhood, was published by Viking Penguin in 1995.

"Growing Up Game"

WHEN I WENT OFF TO COLLEGE MY FATHER GAVE me, as part of my tuition, 50 pounds of moose meat. In 1969, eating moose meat at the University of California was a contradiction in terms. Hippies didn't hunt. I lived in a rambling Victorian house which boasted sweeping circular staircases, built-in lofts, and a landlady who dreamed of opening her own health food restaurant. I told my housemates that my moose meat in its nondescript white butcher paper was from a side of beef my father had bought. The carnivores in the house helped me finish off such suppers as sweet and sour moose meatballs, mooseburgers (garnished with the obligatory avocado and sprouts), and mooseghetti. The same dinner guests who remarked upon the lean sweetness of the meat would have recoiled if I'd told them the not-so-simple truth: that I grew up on game, and the moose they were eating had been brought down, with one shot through his magnificent heart, by my father—a man who had hunted all his life and all of mine.

One of my earliest memories is of crawling across the vast continent of crinkled linoleum in our Forest Service cabin kitchen, down splintered back steps, through wildflowers growing wheat-high. I was eye-level with grasshoppers who scolded me on my first solo trip outside. I made it to the shed, a cool and comfortingly square shelter that held phantasmagoric metal parts; they smelled good, like dirt and grease. I had played a long time in this shed before some maternal shriek made me lift up on my haunches to listen to those urgent, possessive sounds that were my name. Rearing up, my head bumped into something hanging in the dark; gleaming white, it felt sleek and cold against my cheek. Its smell was dense and musty and not unlike the slabs of my grandmother's great arms after her cool, evening sponge baths. In that shed I looked up and saw the flensed body of a doe; it swung gently, slap-ping my face. I felt then as I do even now when eating game: horror and awe and hunger.

Growing up those first years on a forest station high in the Sierra was somewhat like belonging to a white tribe. The men hiked off every day into their forest and the women stayed behind in the circle of official cabins, breeding. So far away from a store, we ate venison and squirrel, rattlesnake and duck. My brother's first rattle, in fact, was from a King Rattler my father killed as we watched, by snatching it up with a stick and winding it, whiplike, around a red-wood sapling. Rattlesnake tastes just like chicken, but has many fragile bones to slither one's way through; we also ate salmon, rab-bit, and geese galore. The game was accompanied by such daily gar-den dainties as fried okra, mustard greens, corn fritters, wilted let-tuce (our favorite because of that rare, blackened bacon), new potatoes and peas, stewed tomatoes, barbecued butter beans.

I was 4 before I ever had a beef hamburger and I remember being disappointed by its fatty, nothing taste and the way it fell apart at the seams whenever my teeth sank into it. Smoked pork shoulder came much later in the South; and I was 21, living in New York City, before I ever tasted leg of lamb. I approached that glazed rack of meat with a certain guilty self-consciousness, as if I unfairly stalked those sweet-tempered white creatures myself. But how would I explain my squeamishness to those urban sophisticates? How explain that I was shy with mutton when I had been bred on wild things?

Part of it, I suspect, had to do with the belief I'd also been bred on—we become the spirit and body of animals we eat. As a child eating venison I liked to think of myself as lean and lovely just like the deer. I would never be caught dead just grazing while some man who wasn't even a skillful hunter crept up and konked me over the head. If someone wanted to hunt me, he must be wily and outwit-ting. He must earn me.

My father had also taught us as children that animals were our brothers and sisters under their skin. They died so that we might live. And of this sacrifice we must be mindful. "God make us grateful for what we are about to receive," took on a new meaning when one knew the animal's struggle pitted against our own appetite. We also used *all* the animal so that an elk became elk steaks, stew, salami, and sausage. His head and horns went on the wall to watch us more earnestly than any babysitter, and every Christmas Eve we had a ceremony of making our own moccasins for the new year out of whatever Father had tanned. "Nothing wasted," my father would always say, or, as we munched on sausage cookies made from moosemeat or venison, "Think about who you're eating." We thought of ourselves as intricately linked to the food chain. We knew, for example, that a forest fire meant, at the end of the line, we'd suffer too. We'd have buck stew instead of venison steak and the meat would be stringy, withered-tasting because in the animal kingdom, as it seemed with humans, only the meanest and leanest and orneriest survived.

Once when I was in my early teens, I went along on a hunting trip as the "main cook and bottle-washer," though I don't remember any bottles; none of these hunters drank alcohol. There was something else coursing through their veins as they rose long before dawn and disappeared, returning to my little camp most often dragging a doe or pheasant or rabbit. We ate innumerable cornmeal-fried catfish, had rabbit stew seasoned only with blood and black pepper.

This hunting trip was the first time I remember eating game as a conscious act. My father and Buddy Earl shot a big doe and she lay with me in the back of the tarp-draped station wagon all the way home. It was not the smell I minded, it was the glazed great, dark eyes and the way that head flopped around crazily on what I knew was once a graceful neck. I found myself petting this doe, murmuring all those graces we'd been taught long ago as children. *Thank you for the sacrifice, thank you for letting us be like you so that we can grow up strong as game.* But there was an uneasiness in me that night as I bounced along in the back of the car with the deer.

What was uneasy is still uneasy—perhaps it always will be. It's not easy when one really starts thinking about all this: the eating game, the food chain, the sacrifice of one for the other. It's never easy when one begins to think about one's most basic actions, like eating. Like becoming what one eats: lean and lovely and mortal.

Why should it be that the purchase of meat at a butcher shop is somehow more righteous than eating something wild? Perhaps it has to do with our collective unconscious that sees the animal bred for slaughter as doomed. But that wild doe or moose might make it without the hunter. Perhaps on this primitive level of archetype and unconscious knowing we even believe that what's wild lives forever.

My father once told this story around a hunting campfire. His own father, who raised cattle during the Depression on a dirt farm in the Ozarks, once fell on such hard times that he had to butcher the pet lamb for supper. My father, bred on game or their own hogs all his life, took one look at the family pet on that meat platter and pushed his plate away from him. His siblings followed suit. To hear my grandfather tell it, it was the funniest thing he'd ever seen. "They just couldn't eat Bo-Peep," Grandfather said. And to hear my father tell it years later around that campfire, it was funny, but I saw for the first time his sadness. And I realized that eating had become a conscious act for him that day at the dinner table when Bo-Peep offered herself up.

Now when someone offers me game I will eat it with all the qualms and memories and reverence with which I grew up eating it. And I think it will always be this feeling of horror and awe and hunger. And something else—full knowledge of what I do, what I become.

Mary Helen Ponce

Mary Helen Ponce grew up in Pacoima, California, about twenty miles northeast of Los Angeles, and came of age just as World War II was ending. Her parents, like most of her neighbors, were Mexican immigrants and the extended familia that nurtured her included her parents, four sisters and three brothers (three older siblings died before she really knew them), uncles and aunts, adopted grandmothers, dozens of cousins, relatives just up from Mexico looking for work, and all sorts of friends and neighbors.

The author of two novels, Taking Control (1987) and The Wedding (1989), Ponce began what would become her autobiography, Hoyt Street (1993), as a research paper on Easter observances for a folklore seminar. "In the process of recollecting specifics about Holy Week," she wrote in the preface to that book, ". . . I began to recall other events—the fun things that took place in our town of Pacoima, California: el circo, last jamaicas, las misiones, las vistas. Each one was a potential cuento. . . . My original plan . . . was to write anecdotes of Mexican-American culture in general, but I found myself writing of family and friends. Of Pacoima. I later realized I was writing a social history of sorts. So be it."

Ponce's stories are so full of detail that her world leaps full-blown off the page. "Hoyt Street is meticulous, precise, and (don't

*let the little girl's voice fool you) full of bite," wrote Sandra Cisneros.
"Thank you, Mary Helen, for placing your house on the map. . . ."
Here, Ponce recalls the anguish and excitement of approaching puberty.*

"Coming of Age"

from *Hoyt Street*

WHEN I WAS ELEVEN I HAD A CRUSH ON A BOY named Santos, or Sandy, as everyone on Hoyt Street called him. He was a grade ahead of me in Pacoima Elementary, highly intelligent, and a regular speaker at school assemblies. He was of medium height, with dark eyes and hair and a row of freckles on his pert nose. He had beautiful white teeth that shone every time he smiled, which was often. I thought him very handsome, except for his hair; it was cut by his father and stuck out where either the bowl or the scissors had slipped.

One reason Sandy was so well liked was because he had lovely manners; Old World manners, Mexican manners. He rose when a teacher entered the classroom, stood at attention during the flag salute, and sang the national anthem in a loud clear voice. He never talked back to his elders as did other boys, nor did he cheat on exams. He respected authority, which is why the teachers and our kind principal, Mrs. Goodsome, all loved him. Even Father Mueller knew he could count on Sandy to be on time for Sunday mass. Everyone smiled when Sandy was around.

Sandy had one sister, Ana Teresa, a pretty girl with a round face, big eyes, and an old-fashioned hair style that set her apart from the rest of us girls, who doted on Shirley Temple curls and French braids. Ana Teresa's hair was pulled back into what resembled my mother's chongo. She insisted on being called by her full Spanish name, although the name "Terry" was then the current rage. (My good friend Teresa López went from "Teresa" to "Tére" to "Terry" in one week!).

During the late 1940s, it seemed that kids in the barrio disliked their Spanish names. Not so Ana Teresa; she liked her name! She and Sandy were born in Mexico; they disdained American names and customs and took pride in everything to do with their native language. I thought of Ana Teresa as a little old lady. She neither joined in our games nor came by to watch, but sat quietly to embroider. Still we tolerated her, mostly because she was related to Sandy, whom everyone liked.

Sandy spoke English with an accent more pronounced than that of other kids whose primary language was Spanish and who were now forced to speak el inglés. At school we were constantly told to speak English; the teachers would chant: "English, English, you're Americans now." This was difficult for Sandy.

Sandy pronounced "comfortable" as "comfort-table," "establish" as "establich," and "ships" as "cheeps." He was good at math and science, though, and was a superb athlete. The teachers forgave his lack of inglés.

He lived in a white clapboard house surrounded by fruit trees. Each morning on the way to school, I saw his mother hosing down the yard and watering geraniums. She was a hard-working woman seldom seen in public. The family kept a pen of chickens and goats en el llano, the open field we crossed to get to school; Sandy was in charge of the goats.

One day on the way to school, I saw Sandy near the goat pen. I stopped to admire the goats—and Sandy. After that I waved at him at school and began to think of him as my boyfriend, mi novio. Often he waited for me near the goat pen. Once school was over I would dash to the girls' bathroom to wash and pinch my cheeks; I scrubbed and pinched until they shone pink, as if I wore rouge! Unlike my sister Trina and her friends, I was not allowed to wear any makeup. Once satisfied that my face had a rosy glow, I dashed off to the goat pen, to Sandy. While the goats bleated and nibbled grass, Sandy and I talked.

"How come you can't play."

"I have to feed the shickens."

He then excused himself to go indoors, change his clothes, and return to change the goats' water and feed the chickens.

He began to come by my house, whether by accident or on his way to the store, I don't remember. Then he joined us at baseball and hide-and-seek. Soon Sandy and I were on the same team! It made me happy to see him at play. He had so little time for fun and rarely could play in the street until dinner, occupied as he was with the countless chores that befell the eldest son. As was the custom, he was expected to help at home and then have fun, unlike the rest of us whose older siblings did our chores while we played in the street.

Sandy never picked a fight. He did, however, have one enemy: Mundo, whom everyone on our street disliked. Mundo was mean, loud, and the street bully. He was jealous of Sandy, too.

Once in sixth grade, Undo asked Sandy to help him cheat on a test.

"*Pssst* Santos. What's the answer to number three?"

"I can't tell you."

"Yeah, you can. Come on, or else . . ."

"I can't help you sheet, Mundo."

"I'll get you for this."

"Shhhhhh. Here comes the teacher."

When school let out, we ran outside in time to see Mundo push Sandy against the fence and pull at his shirt sleeve. He kept hitting

Sandy, who appeared not to want to fight. Mundo's face turned a deep red; he pushed and shoved at the pale-faced Sandy, while we formed a circle. Suddenly Mundo stepped back and with the same ferocity (and meanness) he showed when he played kickball or beat up on stray dogs, Mundo kicked Sandy in the shin. Still Sandy resisted.

"Stupid wetback. Pendejo."

Silence.

"Pendejo chivero."

This time Mundo went too far. Sandy could take an insult, but did not allow anyone to call him a stupid goatherd or demean his goats. Suddenly he turned, raised his right arm, then gave Mundo a swift uppercut, just like Joe Louis! Mundo was sent reeling to the ground; the fight began in earnest. No one took Mundo's side. We rooted for our favorite, for Sandy, especially Virgie, who more than once had been socked by Mundo. We cheered for Sandy to win, as from nearby homes women and children emerged to watch el faite.

"Jesús, María, y José," screeched Doña Juanita from her porch. "Those boys are fighting again!"

"Que vergüenza," lamented Doña Remedios, for whom everything we kids did was a shame.

We ignored the women watching from the safety of their front doors. We knew this was going to be a good fight. We rated fights as we did movies: good or bad.

Sandy and Mundo continued to fight. Sandy was clearly winning, while Mundo, out of breath and bleeding from the nose, kept missing punches. Suddenly Mundo stepped back, put down his hands, and mumbled, "I quit." We stared, our mouths wide open. The street bully was giving up!

"So? Now who's stupeed?" asked Sandy.

"Yo," answered Mundo, grinning broadly, "Me." He brushed the dirt off his pants, wiped his nose, then, still grinning, took off for home. We stood there smiling at Sandy, who now sprouted a black eye, then left, since nothing else was about to happen. After that no one ever dared to use the word *chivero* around Sandy.

Most of us kids liked to ride bikes and to race against our friends on Carl Street, yet few of us had bikes. Sandy didn't. When I borrowed my brother Josey's bike I would loan it to Sandy, then climb onto Concha's handlebars. We would fly up Hoyt Street, turn right toward Carl, then come back around to Hoyt. We rode in the dirt streets, careful to stay clear of the pepper trees, los pirules, that lined the street on the next block.

They were huge. They met high up overhead, obscuring the light, and even in the daytime they gave the street an eerie, haunted look. The street is haunted, it was said. Allí asustan. We avoided that area; rather than walk through the scary trees, we circled the block and ran home.

One summer day Concha suggested to Beto and Sandy, whom we considered our novios, that we go riding. I ran to tell Sandy, who agreed, providing I got the bike; Concha cornered Beto. We made plans to meet on Carl Street, near the church, so as not to arouse suspicion. In those days girls were not supposed to play alone with boys, but only in groups. I ran to get my brother's bike, anxious to get going.

Josey had a Frankenstein bike. It was made from leftover bike parts: tires, handlebars, and rims he had taken from our older brothers. I constantly rode the bike without his permission. After all, I reasoned, I was older—and much bigger. I neither needed nor wanted his permission.

That day Concha and I "borrowed" bikes, then rode off to meet Sandy and Beto, nuestros novios. The boys were first to ride around the quiet streets. They rode like the wind, their backs hunched over the handlebars. They made crazy, daring turns and jumped over bumps. They whizzed by, hands off the handlebars until a car approached, then they quickly grabbed them again. Concha and I were most impressed, but said nothing. We were biding our time until we too could show off.

When it was our turn, Concha and I went wild. We rode around, getting a feel for the bikes, making sure we did not show our calzones. Girls did not wear jeans then, nor were we allowed to borrow our brothers' pantalones. As we pedaled, Concha and I kept our dresses down and our legs close together.

Then we asked the boys to ride us on the handlebars. This was considered daring and somewhat romantic. While Sandy and Beto held the bikes steady, we climbed onto the bars, adjusted our dresses, then hunched our bodies forward while the boys pushed off. Then off we went. We rode down Carl Street, by the church, as kids played tag and hide-and-seek. We rode by . . . and away.

Concha and Beto set the pace. With them in the lead, we rode until early evening, as shadows came and went; lights came on inside warm kitchens. Then, unbeknownst to Sandy and me, Concha (who sometimes appeared timid) asked Beto to ride towards los pirules, or the ghost trees, as I called them. Sandy and I followed, laughing aloud in the early evening light, eager to catch up with them. I was scared but determined not to show it. I hunched forward as we sped down the dark road.

I noticed that Sandy was huffing and puffing; I knew it was because of my weight. I was chubby. Very chubby. I weighed much more than Concha and most of my other friends. I ignored Sandy's gasps for air, but shifted my weight. We rode after Concha and Beto, and had just entered the ghost trees, when suddenly Sandy stopped the bike and jumped off. He said nothing, only stood gasping for air. He took a deep breath, then walked alongside me, pushing the bike as I sat quietly on the handlebars. Concha and Beta were nowhere to be seen. Sandy and I were alone in the middle of los pirules!

My skin began to crawl. I could hear funny noises. I was scared but did not volunteer to jump off the bike. The ride, with Sandy pumping furiously to keep us moving, *had* been romantic! I liked the feel of his strong arms as they brushed against me. I wanted him to *ride*, not push me. And so I sat.

Sandy stood alongside the bike; I sat deathly still. Suddenly from the pepper tree behind us came an eerie wail: "Eeeeeee. Wooooooo." It was a ghost! The monster that lived in the ghost trees! My heart thumped; my hands felt clammy. I knew we were about to die. Sandy said nothing. He stood still, hands tight on the handlebars.

"Eeeeeee. Eeeeee." The sound came closer.

"I'm scaaaaaared."

"Shhhhhhh."

"It's gonna get us!"

"Nehhhhh."

I was scared stiff. The trees seemed to come closer and closer. I was about to scream for my mother, when a cat jumped from behind a tree and scooted across the street. Faint with fear I remained on the handlebars. Sandy tried to push the bike forward. He grabbed the pedals with his hand and pushed with all his might, but they would not budge.

"Your dress is stuck on the chain!"

"Gosh! What are we gonna do?"

"I dunno."

Sandy pulled at the material, but it would not come loose. He turned the pedals back and forth, trying to release my dress, but the chain seemed to eat up the cloth. He grappled with the bike chain as I shivered atop the handlebars, my eyes on the menacing ghost trees.

High above, the tree branches, like long hairy arms, swooped down on us. I was sure they would carry us off; this was the end. The end of carefree rides, of Josey's Frankenstein bike, and of mi novio. Just then Sandy gave my dress a tug; the ruffle came off. Without a word he shoved the torn cloth into my hand, pushed off, jumped onto the bike, and pedaled home. When we neared my house, Sandy jumped off. Then slowly and reluctantly, I got off too. I put the ruffle in my pocket, then turned to bid Sandy goodbye, but he had already disappeared down the dark street.

Early the next morning, I awoke to hear Josey screaming. He had discovered the damaged bike chain and wanted to hit me. My mother, however, intervened. As he went toward the garage, Josey screamed at me: "Fat cow. Fat stupid." I was itching to chase him, but had lately noticed that Josey was almost as tall as I was.

I never went riding with Sandy again. He moved away soon after; rumor had it that his family returned to Mexico. I later heard that Mrs. Goodsome, the school principal, had tried to dissuade them from moving. She feared that Sandy would not complete his education. She admired his leadership qualities and the straight-*A* report cards. But Sandy did not have a choice. As was the custom, his father decided for him. I never got to say goodbye. They left before the new school year started, while our family was away picking walnuts.

Years later, when I no longer feared los pirules and often walked through the ghost trees on my way to the store, I thought of Sandy and the romantic and scary bike ride. The sweeping branches no longer appeared menacing. No longer did I perceive of the trees as a home to monsters, but as a meeting place for novios. Boys who walked a sweetheart home from a party appeared to stray toward the pepper trees, where the low branches shielded them from prying eyes.

I thought of Sandy. Gallant Sandy, who while riding through the scary trees had not panicked nor insisted that I get off the bike. I wondered if at that moment he had vowed never, ever to ride with a girl who weighed more than he did.

THAT SAME YEAR, my best friend was la Nancy. Unlike Concha and Virgie, girls my age who giggled and acted silly, Nancy, at twelve, was quite sophisticated. She walked with a slight swing of her skinny hips and tilted her head to the left when talking to boys. Often she halfway closed her eyes, wanting to look like the movie stars who were supposed to have "bedroom eyes." She licked her lips to make them glisten and plucked her eyebrows into a wide arch.

I yearned to be like Nancy; at home I locked myself in the bathroom to imitate her. I put out the lights to create "an atmosphere" (as in the movies), then stood in front of the mirror to tilt my head and close my eyes halfway. I pushed my hair back, just like Nancy did, then strained to see the effect. When I was unable to see anything in the dark room, I quit doing it. But every chance I had, I studied Nancy.

Nancy was almost as tall as I, with light brown hair, light skin, a pert nose, and eyes already caked with Maybelline. She no longer wore her hair in braids, but piled it atop her head in what was called an "upsweep." She took makeup from her sister, then ran to find me and Concha. We would tear off to sit underneath a pepper tree, as Nancy, her dark eyes glowing with excitement, rubbed our olive cheeks a warm rosy color and slathered us with Evening in Paris perfume.

"Do I look older?"

"Not yet. Here, try the magenta lipstick."

"I like how the powder smells. Did you buy it at . . ."

"Neh, I took it."

As she painted our lips, Nancy told us about her boyfriends and who she planned to marry once we graduated from Pacoima Elementary.

Nancy was the first of my friends to wear a bra. The tiny size 32AA bra that hung over her skinny chest sold for $1.99 and was the smallest one available. It was bought for her by her sister. Nancy, however, didn't mind that the brassiere did not fit correctly; she was concerned only with the lace "cups." She constantly pulled at the straps, making sure we knew she now wore a bra.

She also wore rayon panties bought at the Five & Dime. I thought them ugly and cheap-looking, but Nancy liked them because they came in all colors: lavender, pink, and her favorite, black. I was jealous of her underwear. All I had to wear were cotton underpants and the white undershirts that stretched across my flat chest.

Nancy thought she was "so big" because she had an Anglo name, one associated with blond hair and blue eyes. Her real name, I knew was Natcha, but her older sisters had Anglicized it so that she was now called Nancy.

During summer Nancy hated to attend both catechism and church, saying they were boring and took up too much time. She rarely showed up at the Stella Maris Club, saying she had to help wash the supper dishes. She often missed school, too, saying the teachers were dumb, stupid even, and she knew more than they did. This I believed, for Nancy was the most advanced of my friends. Certainly she knew more about boys and kissing than Concha did.

She also knew how to French-kiss, or so she hinted to Concha, who immediately told me. French kissing was something that we never saw in the movies, but I knew this kind of thing could get a girl in trouble. I once heard Trina and her friends, all older and wiser than me, talk about a girl who had "gotten in trouble."

"Miranda thinks she's P.G."

"How come?"

" 'Cause Bennie gave her a French kiss."

When I repeated this to Nancy, she bent over laughing. When she had regained her composure, she tilted her head to the left and said that it was all a lie, because nobody in France had died from kissing. She tried to teach Concha and me, along with some other girls from Hoyt Street, how to kiss properly.

"We need a boy."

"We can ask Mundo."

"Uggghh."

"How about Sandy?"

"Neh. Tiene miedo. I asked him, but he ran off."

Nancy knew where babies came from, but refused to tell anyone. She alluded to "things" that boys and girls did underneath the pepper trees and in the back row of the San Fernando theatre. When asked for details, Nancy pulled at her bra, swung her skinny hips, and with a wicked grin, stalked home.

Whenever a new boy came to Pacoima Elementary, Nancy was the first to spot him. She then took it upon herself to decide whether or not he was cute. She circled him, her pointy chest sticking way out, then tilted her head to observe him better. We slouched against the chain link fence that bordered the playground, until she joined us. With baited breath we waited to see what pronouncements would spew from Nancy's bright red mouth.

"He's cute, but . . ."

"But what?"

"He smells of sobacos."

Having smelly armpits was one of the worse things that could befall a boy. Stinky feet were acceptable, as was bad breath and greasy hair. But the smell of sobacos was terribly offensive and meant that a kid was poor, backward even, and never took a bath except at Christmas. At school when I was assigned to sit next to someone who reeked of sweaty armpits, I would quickly ask to be moved.

In the seventh grade Nancy, who still read and wrote at the fifth-grade level, claimed to be receiving love letters from a boy in San Fernando named Ramón. He lived in a nice house with a wide sidewalk and a pretty lawn, and "sat" with her at the movies. During school recess one day she called us over.

"I got a love letter from Ramón."

"Another one?"

"No stupid, that was from Jimmy."

Nancy knew how to fight, too, and often beat up on the boys who teased her about her skinny legs. All of them were scared of her except for Mundo, who was meaner than she was; given the chance, he would kick anyone who "asked for it." However, she was loyal to the kids that lived on Hoyt Street, and during an argument could be counted on to take my side. In return I had to treat her to candy at the corner store. It was good to have Nancy as a friend.

During the summer Nancy and I attended all the church bazaars held at Guardian Angel Church. We not only went on Saturday nights but also on Sundays, when the prizes were raffled off. We helped the older girls make boutonnieres of fresh flowers that were sold, usually to men and boys, for a dime each. Nancy and I were considered too young to do the "fun" part: sauntering around the boys at the fiesta with a box of carnations in our hands and an eager smile on our lips. The older girls, all experts at flirting, had this job. They would sidle up to an unsuspecting boy, pin a botón on his chest, then smirk as he fidgeted for change. When a guy was really cute, the girls pinned not one but two carnations on his jacket.

"How are you, Bartolo?"

"Uhh . . ."

"That will be fifty cents, please!"

"Keep the change, girls!"

The boutonnieres were of red and white carnations and crespón, a fragile fern. They were kept in a zinc tub filled with water at the back of the church hall, away from the flow of traffic and bothersome kids.

One Sunday night Nancy and I, being the best of friends and inseparable (for at least those two weeks), were preparing to fix the carnations. Nancy wore a red jumper and a red-and-white polka-dot blouse. She reeked of Evening in Paris. Right before we began, she went into the bathroom to paint her mouth. I gaped at her glowing lips and at her pretty outfit, one I had never seen before. We worked quickly, aware that the girls would be angry if we kept them waiting.

I was busy swishing water off the carnations, taking care not to spot my newly shined shoes. Engrossed in cutting the stems from the flowers, I glanced up after awhile to see Nancy near the door, talking to an older man. I paid little attention; people often entered the fiesta through the church hall, then went out a side door and on to the booths.

Nancy began to trim the flowers, her brown eyes full of excitement. Her face was flushed a deep pink. She tossed her hair back, licked her lips, and kept looking out the door. She then walked over to me, pushed back my thick hair, and whispered:

"I know how we can make twenty-five cents!"

"How?"

"See that man over there? The one . . ."

". . . you were talking to?"

"Yeah. He'll give us some money if . . ."

At that time twenty-five cents was a lot of money. At the jamaica, most things cost either a nickel or a dime. A quarter at the Penny Pitch would go a long way, it might even earn me a prize.

"Yes, I want to earn twenty-five cents."

Nancy took my hand; we went outside. I could smell Evening in Paris. It was dark; the streetlight flickered as if it were about to go out. The street was completely empty. The tall shrubs behind the church hall appeared menacing. Nancy in the lead, we turned the corner, then stopped.

"What are we waitin' for?" I hissed, eager to return to the flowers. In my haste I had walked off with a red carnation; I was afraid it would lose its freshness.

"Wait here." She took a deep breath, looked around for oncoming cars, and said: "If you let him see under your dress, he'll give ya twenty-five cents . . . and if you let him touch *it*, he'll give ya fifty cents!"

What she was saying didn't make sense. I turned to leave, but Nancy pulled me back. In my confusion I didn't see the dark figure emerging from the shadows, until he got close. I gasped in surprise at the familiar figure of el Señor José, a respected church member and friend of my father's. He hesitated then stepped back into the shadows, as Nancy went up to him.

"Aquí estamos," she said, her dark eyes bright. "Here we are."

He glared at Nancy, mumbled something inaudible, then walked off toward Hoyt Street, his heavy tread echoing in the dark night. We lingered near the shrubs as Don José disappeared. I was trying to understand what had happened, when an angry Nancy turned to me.

"You spoiled it," she hissed. "Now he won't give me any more money. I hate you! You're not my best friend anymore." She stomped off, leaving a wake of French perfume behind her. I was left holding the wet carnation. It was some time before I understood that the "friend" Nancy said would give us money had recognized me and bolted. I was so shocked I could barely make the botones after that.

I never told my mother or anyone else about that incident. I thought of telling our new pastor, who was understanding of younger kids, but was too ashamed. After that night I hardly saw Nancy. I did, however, see Don José, but he avoided my glance. I began to fear him. During Sunday mass, when he came by with the collection basket, I cringed when he drew near. Later, when I was allowed to sell the boutonnieres to the men and boys, I never approached him, but avoided him for the rest of my life.

I REMEMBER WELL MY TWELFTH BIRTHDAY, a cold Sunday in January. The icy wind that blew through the pepper trees and bedroom window had kept me awake most of the night. I felt sick; my head ached, my stomach hurt.

The day before, when we were dismissed from el catecismo, Virgie, Concha, and I rushed back to Don Jesús's store, anxious to sample los dulces, the Mexican candy only he sold. Virgie quickly found what she wanted: jelly beans, gumdrops, and cacahuates, peanuts in the shell, sold in tiny bags. Concha bought two pieces of calabasa, sweet pumpkin jelled into squares. I walked around the store, my shoes scraping against the wooden floor, but couldn't decide what it was I wanted. The pan I loved so much appeared dry, unappetizing. I wanted something different from the usual candy that stuck to the roof of my mouth and clung to my teeth, but all I saw were shelves of arroz, leche de bote, and dusty cans of Campbell's soup. I fingered ripe tomatoes and crispy green chiles nestled in crates near the entrance, and was about to pinch grapes from a tray, when I spotted the patas de cochi, pink pigs' feet swimming in a jar. The patas, including the hooves, were kept in a wide jar next to the cash register; their wrinkled skin shimmered in the brine. Pigs' feet, kids on Hoyt Street said, were a favorite of the winos who hung around the alley behind the store. Still they *were* different.

I turned the jar around as the piggy feet slapped against the glass, and pondered. Did I really want a pata? Should I spend my nickels on wino food? Hungry for something and eager to get home to my chores, I asked Virgie for my share of our bottle money, selected the biggest pata, paid, then ran out of the store. We walked back along the dusty path next to Doña Chonita's house. As I gnawed on the gristly skin, I smiled at Virgie, whose mouth was smeared with chocolate.

I pretended that the pig's foot was delicious, determined not to gag on the vinegar. Once at home I changed clothes, then went about my Saturday chores: washing out my underwear and cleaning the dining room chairs, both of which I hated. When I had finished with the loathsome jobs, I pulled back the cotton spread on my bed and lay down in the bedroom I shared with Trina.

I felt sick. My stomach was making funny noises. I could taste the vinegar, la pata. I began to moan and groan as I rubbed my stomach. Trina, busy plucking her eyebrows, became alarmed at my cries and ran to fetch Elizabet. The two of them stood in the hallway, dark heads pressed close, whispering in low, muted voices.

"Her stomach hurts . . ."

"Hmmm, well, she *is* twelve."

Elizabet went into the bathroom, then returned with a purple box, which she silently slid under my bed. She then filled the hot-water bottle from the kitchen faucet and gave it to me to press against my tender middle. She tiptoed out of the room, then softly closed the door. I lay in bed, pale and wan, waiting for It.

It seemed I had been waiting for It for so long! At least since the summer before, when Nancy got It and acted even more superior. Upon hearing Nancy's news, I moped around the house for days, feeling terribly juvenile and left out. Later that year, when Virgie, a smug look on her round face, announced she was now a señorita, I became even more depressed. It just wasn't fair! Morning, noon, and night, I checked my calzones, frantic to see signs of It. I was sorely disappointed not to find even a trace.

I still wore camisetas, undershirts that I couldn't wait to replace with lacy bras. I also hated the cotton slips with the tiny tucks in the front that looked so childish, infantile really. My itching breasts were beginning to push against my dresses. My clothes are all wrong, I grumbled to my mother, refusing to wear the prissy dresses with white collar and cuffs from the previous year. When Trina wasn't looking, I would squeeze into her clothes, feeling terribly grown-up; until the day when I burst the zipper of her favorite skirt. Determined to update my wardrobe, I took my mother's sewing basket and hid in the bathroom to hike up the hem of my favorite skirt. All in preparation for It.

I had a mustache, which I hated. I had hairy legs that I was not allowed to shave. Sometimes I could almost smell my sobacos, a smell I attributed to the scraggly armpit hairs I had recently sprouted. The long black hairs visible on my arms appeared longer each day; at times I wound them around a pencil. And hated it. I resorted to wearing long-sleeved dresses even on hot days. And hated that, too.

My curly, black hair was unmanageable; it surrounded my face like a dark juniper bush. On wet and rainy days it got frizzier and frizzier, so that it resembled Brillo Pads. But I detested the Shirley Temple curls that earlier were my trademark and refused to wear the common trensas that I associated with elementary kids. On school days an amused Elizabet secured my unruly hair with shiny barrettes bought in town, saying I looked fine. But once I was out the door, I yanked them off, stuck them in my pocket, then slipped a handful of bobby pins into place.

One March day while Mundo, Concha, and I were playing kickball, we needed a fourth player.

"Can Virgie come out?"

"No."

"Por qué?"

"Ummm, she's sort of sick . . ."

Virgie, I was told, could not play for at least three days; I immediately knew why. So did Mundo and Concha. Virgie had It! Later in our game I fell and scraped my knee; I stopped the blood with the hem of my dress, then ran home. When my mother saw the stains on my dress, she told me to go wait for her in the bathroom. Her face held a look of respect. Clearly she thought I had It.

When she realized I had only cut my knee, however, she scolded me por andar en la calle and for ruining a good dress. Doña Luisa, never too far from a crisis, cautioned me not to run around too much. "No es good for you," she said, her eyes troubled, "no es good." She then walked me to her house, stoked the wooden stove,

and fed me warm milk and bread. Satiated with cinnamon toast, I
sat back to wait for It.

That evening, when it was my turn to wash the supper dishes, I
began to moan.

"My stomach hurts. Me duele el estógamo."

"Estómago. And do you feel dizzy too?"

"Sí."

I was excused from clearing the table, washing dishes, and
sweeping the kitchen floor. Told to lie down in my bedroom with
the hot-water bottle, I did just that.

Then Concha got It. And Josie too, followed by Terry, who
was only eleven! Only I was left. I, the tallest girl in our class, had
not gotten It! And then it was June, July. Childhood games of hide-
and-seek bored me, as did bike rides down Hoyt Street. I now preferred to spend the afternoon beneath a cool pirul, my favorite pepper tree, to embroider flowers and birds on bleached sacking. I sat
with my legs primly crossed, the skirt of my dress pulled low. Just
in case It creeped up on me.

I began to stuff Kleenex inside my underwear, just in case It
caught me unawares, until one day, while running across el llano, I
dropped a batch.

My mustache grew darker. I sneaked Pancake Number 2 from
Nora, wet a sponge, then smeared it across the offensive black veil,
but it still showed. I then sought out la Nancy, who knew everything.

"I hate my bigote."

"Well bleach it! Como yo."

I ran to the store, bought the necessary supplies, then locked
myself in the bathroom. In a small bowl I mixed peroxide and white
henna, making sure to use a wooden spoon. I slathered the smelly
potion on my upper lip, then (while Josey pounded on the bathroom
door) washed off the dried powder and stared into the mirror. I was

dismayed to see no immediate results. Within days, however, my mustache turned first a brownish-red and then a bright yellow.

Each month my legs got hairier and hairier. I dared not wear summer shorts, but began to borrow Norbert's Levis, making sure not to roll them past my calf. When I could stand it no longer, I waited for Berney to leave, then shaved my legs with his trusty Gillette razor, making sure I had first secured the bathroom door. I then spent hours applying alcohol and adhesive tape to the many cuts that decorated my legs. All the while I longed for It.

More than anything, though, I hated my hair. Nancy now sported un permanente that was the envy of the girls on Hoyt Street. Not to be outdone, Concha had her hair cut in cute bangs. Desperate to be rid of the curl and having read that braiding kinky hair made it straight, I began to braid my hair at night. Each morning I fought to be first in the bathroom. With mounting excitement I would unbraid my thick trensa, but my hair sprang out around my face like a dark bush again.

When school started in September of my twelfth year, I was sent to the nurse for a routine checkup. I was weighed and measured; my eyes, ears and throat checked, and my reflexes measured with a tap on the knee. The nurse then read my chart and asked if I had experienced any changes since school let out. It was disappointing to have nothing to report. Check!

And then a new girl came to our school. Her name was Barbara. I hated her because she had an American name, two dimples, and had already started It! I now hated anyone with dimples, too. I began to sleep with a pinto bean attached with surgical tape to each cheek, confident that in time I, too, would have dimples. When I swallowed a bean in my sleep and nearly gagged, I decided that dimples were not all that important. Certainly not as important as It.

During Christmas I stuffed myself with my mother's sugar tamales. I ate so much masa I got a stomach ache. Once more I was put to bed with the trusty water bottle. And then it was January again. I would soon be all of thirteen. A teenager! A tall teenager who still had not gotten It! I began to cross off each day on a calendar hidden from Trina's prying eyes. I waited until evening to make an X across the date; just in case It arrived during the day.

As my birthday approached, I began to panic. I begged Elizabet to take me to the doctor in San Fernando. "Something is wrong," I wailed, "something's wrong with me!" But Elizabet only smiled and went about her business. In my bedroom I kicked the purple box against the wall. It had not helped me at all!

I dared not miss mass; I was diligent in taking Holy Communion. But I avoided sitting next to viejitas said to be "barren," thinking I might catch their disease. I made sure not to eat meat on Fridays, certain that God in all His glory would reward this sacrifice. I prayed to all the female saints to intercede with the Virgin Mary on my behalf. "Saint Teresa of Avila, please send It. Santa Cecilia, help me get over It. All ye holy saints in Heaven, tell God I can't live without It."

I feared living out my life as an old maid, relegated to dusting church pews and caring for plaster saints. A vestir santos. I could never marry without It, that much was certain. Nor could I have children! Only when a girl had gotten It could she have babies, as everyone on Hoyt Street already knew. And so I waited for God to send me a sign of It.

My thirteenth birthday came and went. I now stood at five feet five inches in my bare feet. I was taller than my sisters and mother; I towered over Doña Luisa and most of my friends. My green winter coat came to above my knees; the waist of my red jumper rode above my midriff. My shoe size jumped from six to seven to eight. This made my older sisters, all of whom wore size five and six shoes, smirk with satisfaction.

And then one day, as if by magic, my arms lost their hairy look. My yellow mustache grew out; the dark veil no longer was visible.

My legs grew long and lean, with less and less hair. I threw out las camisetas and was bought a cotton bra. When my mother wasn't looking, I hiked up my skirt hems, then opened up the slits on each side. I lavished Palmolive soap on my face, then followed with Ponds Cream, for that seven-day complexion wonder. My thick hair fell across my shoulders in a wavy pageboy.

I studied movie magazines in search of my face type: Oval? Square? Heart-shaped? I experimented with tweezers and wound up with two bloody, crooked lines, which I filled in with an eyebrow pencil snitched from Nora. I bought a cheap lipbrush and replaced Tangee Natural with Tangee Fire Red. I bought a red plastic belt (size 22 waist) for $1.99, and inherited, from a reluctant Trina, my first pair of high heels, on which I tottered to church each Sunday.

And then finally I got It! I was on my way to the store, about to climb the fence that led to the alley, when I detected signs of It on my beige culottes. I straddled the fence, not knowing whether to jump over or slide down, in a ladylike manner. My tomboy days were clearly over. I disengaged my legs, smoothed down my pants, and walked home feeling dizzy, elated. At last! At last I was a bona-fide teenager! I itched to blurt out my news to Nancy, Virgie, and Concha, but told only Elizabet, who once more brought out the purple box.

That balmy night as I lay in bed, the hot-water bottle secure against my belly, I flipped through the booklet in the purple box. I think it was entitled "What Every Teenage Girl Should Know." I memorized everything about fallopians, ovaries, and twenty-eight-day cycles. I snuggled under the covers, sipping té de canela, cinnamon tea, said to be good for It. I touched myself down there, just to make sure I still had It, then turned over and went to sleep.

Sharmon Apt Russell

For her nonfiction, Sharmon Apt Russell has received a Henry Joseph Jackson Award, a Pushcart Prize, and a Mountain and Plains Booksellers Award. Her most recent book, Kill the Cowboy: A Battle of Mythology in the New West, *appeared in 1993. She teaches writing at Western New Mexico University and lives in Mimbres, a small agricultural valley in southwestern New Mexico where, after ten years in Montana, she and her husband, Peter, came as newlyweds in 1981 to build their home, brick by adobe brick, on twelve acres of land. (In college she had majored in natural resources.) Russell had grown up in Arizona's exotic Sonoran Desert. Her father, Mel Apt, was an aeronautical engineer and a test pilot. In 1956, when Russell was two, her father tested the experimental X-2 and set a new speed record on his first flight before losing control of the plane. He died in the crash. In the title essay of her first book,* Songs of the Fluteplayer: Seasons of Life in the Southwest *(1991), she writes that the "central fact" of her father's life "remains that what he loved best killed him and that he chose, on some level, to die the way that he did." But the same desire to create and live an intentional life is precisely what has always compelled people like the Russells to choose to live in the remoteness and isolation of the rural West. Likewise, it is the same desire that annually motivates more than one million illegal aliens to cross the border into the United States from Mexico. Russell's reverence for the land, its history, and native inhabitants informs all of her writing, and while the 1988 immigration law now makes it possible to impose penalties on those who hire illegal aliens, in this essay she tells us why she and her husband did. In doing so, she also shows us how two "illegals" turned the "relationship between American and 'wetback' on its head."*

"Illegal Aliens"

from *Songs of the Fluteplayer*

EVERY YEAR, FOR THE PAST MANY YEARS, OVER A million illegal aliens are arrested as they cross the sometimes invisible line that defines and encloses the United States of America. In the El Paso sector—a pastel-colored desert stretching from Van Horn, Texas to the western end of New Mexico—hundreds of thousands of "undocumented men and women" are caught annually by the Border Patrol, with an estimated twice that number passing through undeterred. A small percentage of this traffic will come through the Mexican town of Palomas, which in English means dove and which lies a mile south of Columbus, New Mexico and its desultory border checkpoint. Most Mexicans crossing through Palomas are seasonal workers who expect to return via the same route. Over the years, what has come to pass for industry in Palomas is a strip of adobe storefronts, brothels, and hotels used by such men coming home with their new-won wages shoved deep in pockets or sewn into the hems of clothing. From nearby ranching and mining communities, Anglos have helped build up this trade in sex and recreation. Although Mexicans entering the States are not likely to partake of the town's luxuries, this is not to say they don't plan to on their return.

From Palomas, an even smaller percentage of *mojados* or "wet ones" will choose to walk up through the sparse creosote of the Chihuahuan Desert, past the town of Deming on Interstate 10, past— walking steadily on, in their fifth day by now—the thrust of Cooke's Peak with its barrel cactus and hidden shelves of pictographs. Under the shadow of this mountain, these men will gravitate to the green-lined Mimbres River and follow its cottonwoods up a narrow valley of irrigated fields and apple orchards. Here, sometimes alone, sometimes in groups of two or three, they might begin to look for work. By the time they reach my house, at the northern end of the valley, the memory of Palomas belongs to another life, another country, and they will have walked nearly a hundred miles.

When I first came to the Mimbres, I often saw illegal aliens traveling purposefully at the edge of the road and my peripheral vision. I did not recognize them as such, although in defineable and undefineable ways they seemed out of place on the black-topped highway. As I drove, silver mailboxes flashed by with the inevitable dirt road, adobe home, or trailer attached. Cattle and horses grazed on the brown hills of grama grass. Fields blazed green along the banks of the river. Against this setting, there was something odd about the isolation of these men dressed in polyester pants and carrying a paper sack, small bag, or bundle of clothing. Miles from any town, they did not hitchhike and did not seem to be walking to or from a car. Strangely detached, they kept their gaze directed ahead, on a focus which resolved not on the road but at someone's door. The door opened, and the man or woman inside had something for them to do: adobes to make, walls to lay up, fences to fix, or—less satisfactorily—a garden to weed.

In my late twenties and by all standards an adult, I had never thought of myself as an employer, much less one who hired people who hid when a police car passed. So when the men began to appear at my door with their diffident smiles and gestures, I felt uneasy. I did not know how to respond to their questions, how to supply food or even water. Not speaking Spanish was my excuse. But the truth lay more in the way they looked. They looked different. They looked poor. And they were, after all, men. I imagine that in the 1930s other women shared my feelings when the hobos first began to appear on porch steps. Like these women, I adapted, in surprisingly little time, to the stranger at the door.

As the crow flies, the Mimbres Valley lies over a hundred miles north of the nearest metropolis (El Paso), thirty miles east of the nearest town (population 12,000), and directly south of the Gila National Forest. It is hard to make a living here and we miss the proximity of bookstores and corner cafes. In this rural area, our neighbors divide neatly into those who live here because it is familiar and those who came here because it is not. Most of my friends fall in the latter category, and for us the subject of illegal aliens was new and interesting. One friend, who speaks French and Spanish and who has tried unsuccessfully to serve his workers borscht, described the knock at the door as an "informal cultural exchange program." He wrote down the addresses of men he liked and assumed that one day he would visit and be welcomed. Another friend argued that hiring aliens takes jobs from Americans who would work for less if the welfare system were suitably altered. To this, a third friend responded that Mexicans need to work as much as anyone and that she hires for humanness, not nationality.

Some of us theorized that the flow of unemployed and ambitious out of Mexico gave that country a necessary release valve and prevented turmoil, i.e., revolution. This idea, too, divided into two camps: those who thought it was good to prevent revolution and those who thought it was not. From a different viewpoint, many of us believed the current system—in which "aliens" were illegal but hiring an alien was not—wrong because it permitted too much abuse. We all knew of the rancher who turned his workers into the Immigration Service the day before payday. Other employers withheld pay until the job was completed and, in the meantime, fed their workers poorly. It was easy to see how inequity could flourish when the employed had no avenue of complaint or redress. At the same time, we also all knew scores of perfectly decent people—a Hispanic farmer in Deming or a chili grower in Hatch—whose small business depended on alien labor.

More to the point was the Mexican couple who had dinner with us one winter night, a week before Christmas. She was eight months pregnant. He was desperately seeking work. We told them that with the layoffs at the copper mine, unemployment in our county had reached 40 percent. He replied it was 80 percent where he came from. They had just walked nine days in the cold and rain. We did not suggest they turn around and go back.

Increasingly, it seemed that the problem of undocumented men and women could only be examined one focal length at a time. There was the big picture, and there was a man with a bundle of clothes. As one came into focus, the other blurred.

In any event, for my husband and me, the discussions were academic. We learned to give food. We pointed directions. We sometimes chatted. But when asked about work, we spoke without thinking, without hesitation. *"No trabajo."* No work here.

Then we began to build.

IN SOUTHWESTERN NEW MEXICO, building an adobe home is an intense rite of passage which requires, in its purest form, no previous construction experience. For financial reasons, we started with one large room. After the kind of research that involves a lot of driving and staring at other people's houses, we decided to make a traditional mountain adobe altered by passive-solar, south-facing windows. As teachers, we had the summer to make the bricks, lay up the walls, and put on the sloping hipped tin roof. This was traditional "wetback" work, but we never gave a thought to hiring someone else. We would do it together, alone.

It began well. Although a good adobero can talk at interminable length about R values and thermal efficiency, he or she knows that transformation is the truer miracle. A patch of soil becomes a bedroom. Solid ground is transmogrified into a windowsill. An unsightly hole will be a wall nine feet high. For us, such miracles depended upon a borrowed and ancient cement mixer whose idiosyncrasies were my bane as I shoveled dirt and sprayed water into its maw. The mud was then wheelbarrowed away by my husband and poured into a wooden form for three bricks fourteen-by-ten-by-four inches.

Adobe is a cunning mixture of clay and sand. Too much clay and the brick cracks while drying, too little and it lacks strength. We tested the proportions of our soil by throwing handfuls of dirt into a jar of water, shaking vigorously, and watching the layers settle. Amazingly, our land appeared to be a huge dehydrated adobe mix—add water, stir, and pour. This we did, every day, ten hours a day, for three weeks. It was hard work, but not unpleasant. Transformation! The ground formed into squares that we set on their sides to dry and then gingerly stacked. On one good day, eighty wet-looking bricks lay in soldierly rows before us. On most days, there were only sixty or fifty. We ended up with thirteen hundred adobes: a hundred less than we thought we should have, a hundred more than we would actually need.

While we waited two weeks for the bricks to dry, we began to dig the foundation footings, which had to be large to support the heavy walls. In a matter of days, etched deep in the ground, our room became defined. Into these holes, we inserted stakes of metal to which we fastened, at a ninety-degree angle, the longer slim poles of steel rebar. There was something elegant about these complex layers, running in their rectangle of fifteen-by-twenty feet. I almost hated to cover them with cement. I hated it even more as we began to do it, for cement is nothing at all like adobe. The magic was gone, or rather, reversed. It had become bad magic. At the mixer, I glumly shoveled in heavy gravel and two buckets of cement. Moistened with water, the backbreaking load was then dumped into the wheelbarrow which my husband manfully directed in tottering form to the foundation's edge. The stuff slopped out to disappear into the earth. Again, the process was repeated and another load swallowed. Again, another load, and another, as our muscles strained and our skin split from the alkaline lime.

At this point, things went downhill. There is a Mimbres Valley saying that the couple who builds together divorces together. As our visions of the house altered, diverged, and then collided, as our bodies reminded us that we were only getting older, we moved from bad temper to the kind of free-floating anger rooted in childhood. Through a haze of misunderstandings, we peeled pine logs for *vigas*, built forms for the next step of the foundation, and eternally mixed more cement. At night, we talked about the house rather than sensibly talking about other things. One day, I left for a brief respite in town. On another day, so did my husband.

When the dust settled, we began again.

Down the road, our neighbor has a small trailer where he once housed illegal Mexican workers who came every year and built what seemed to us a dizzying array of fences. That summer, two young men were busy digging holes on his land, erecting posts, and nailing up expensive-looking wire. They began each day at eight and when they stopped at five the afternoon stretched before them, light and long and empty of things to do. One evening, in the cooling hours of midsummer, they wandered over to watch us lay our sixth course of adobe. With finicky slowness we placed each brick flush to the outside string that served as our level. At intervals, we also put wooden blocks where we estimated heavy pictures or cupboards would go. At that time we agreed, quite incorrectly, that it would be easy enough to install the electrical wires later.

My husband, who speaks Spanish, offered our visitors a beer and conversation. He inquired as to what part of Mexico they came from. Chihuahua? A nice city. He had been there. He wanted to know the latest exchange rate for pesos. He asked how many adobes they could make in a day. Four hundred? We looked at each other. He asked the Spanish word for hammer. He told them he was a high school teacher.

At five the next afternoon, they showed up again. This time, they clamored into the room like a crew just hired. One took over my task of lifting up the forty-pound brick; another elbowed my husband aside and demonstrated the proper way of setting the adobe in its mortar of mud. They stayed until the sun tipped over the ridge of our western hills. They had taken pity on us.

Although we offered, neither Manuel nor Gabriel wanted money. They liked the cold slide of our beer at the end of the day. But more, they liked the companionship of working with equals. This was their free time, their gift. For two more weeks, they came uncalled when their own day was through—and we, who also had been working since eight and who would work on until dark, were in their debt. The relationship between American and "wetback" turned on its head, and some tension in us relaxed. That next summer, when we started building again, we understood well that we had plenty of work for a skilled adobero. So we began our career of hiring illegal aliens.

EFFREM AND JESUS sat rather stiffly on the edge of the couch while Shirley Grijalva—rodeo rider and mother of three—spoke swiftly to them in Spanish and then as swiftly to us in English. Shirley knew Effrem well; he was an "old friend" and we were letting her handle the negotiations with our first employees. At that time, in 1983, the going rate was eight dollars a day, plus food and board. (In the next four years, the price would rise to ten or twelve dollars, with strenuous work on a farm or ranch paying fifteen and more. At that time, most wage earners in Mexico were getting the equivalent of three dollars a day.) We offered a dollar above the norm and consulted with Shirley as to what was board. Beans, she said. Beans, meat, tortillas, eggs, potatoes, coffee, and canned food. Effrem, she noted, preferred white bread to tortillas. Employers also had the option of providing cigarettes, beer, and the occasional pair of socks. We would do that, we agreed quickly. We believed in keeping Mexican wages, nine dollars a day, intact for the trip home to Mexico.

I was never to know Effrem or Jesus very well or, for that matter, any of the men who eventually worked for us. Each morning, my husband and they conferred, gathered tools, and went off together making more adobes, stuccoing walls, or digging ditches. I went inside our now completed room to my own projects and, later, child-rearing duties. At lunchtime I cooked a hot meal of beans, eggs, and tortillas which the three men ate outside in the shade of the patio. Then I washed the dishes. In the late afternoon, I prepared a bag of dinner and breakfast food for the workers to take and cook in our neighbor's trailer. My husband and I assumed these segregated roles because we believed that the men would be more comfortable if we did so. Certainly, I felt a need to appear "traditional" and did not, for example, publicly contradict my husband's building ideas (something I did in private) or wear short skirts while hanging up the laundry. My job, as I saw it, was to oil these days, in which we were getting a great deal of work done, with a flow of domesticity.

What I learned, I learned in the evening, second hand. Effrem, my husband told me, had six children and four hundred acres in Chihuahua. Most of his land was scrub desert. The rest was a small but viable apple orchard. Early in the summer, before his harvest, he fell short of cash and came up to the States. In his late forties, his dark hair touched by gray, Effrem proved to be slow, reliable, and meticulous in his work. His gentle manners and soft voice made him seem a very serious man, a family man, sensitive and thoughtful.

Jesus provided a contrast. While Effrem looked broad and solid, Jesus had a tall skinny frame that alternated between nervous energy and an indolent loll. With the dapper moustache and groomed hair appropriate to a twenty-two-year-old, Jesus was full of plans, the owner of a future in which the strokes were broad and the details still vague. Already, he boasted, he had traveled as far south as Nicaragua and as far north as Washington. He was out to see the world, on a young man's lark that required financing along the way. More voluble than Effrem, Jesus came up with a running series of deals. Would we contract to lay the tiles instead of paying a daily wage? Would we sell his cousin in El Paso our old car? Would we hire another worker, a good friend of his, who could do the finish work we so clearly needed? When it came time for Jesus to go, he asked us for a pair of converse tennis shoes. No matter the cost, he said with largesse, he would pay. We shopped around and came up with a better price, not a Converse, but a good shoe. No, Jesus said. The brand name was important.

Effrem and Jesus promised to return the next summer. Effrem did and first went to work for one of our neighbors, whom he didn't much like. After a week he moved on and settled further north as a ranch hand. From another young man who stopped at our house, we were shocked to learn that Jesus had been shot to death in a Palomas bar. The young man added that Jesus had been a *coyote*, a descriptive term for those who take money from aliens—usually refugees fleeing Central America—in exchange for transporting them across the border.

The same grapevine that spread the news of Jesus's death also put us on the circuit as a place to stop for information, food, and a day or two of work. By now, we knew that although we could hire aliens and transport them in a southerly direction, there were serious penalties for driving an alien north: possible fines, imprisonment, and an impounded car. We knew that, on their way home, some men liked to be picked up by the green trucks bearing the Immigration's seal—*la Migra,* as we called them. Depending on where they lived, this could save them a walk and usually meant they wound up in an American cell overnight where their money might be safer than on the road. On the other hand, it could also mean being turned over for a shakedown to the Mexican authorities. For this reason, some workers liked their pay put in a postal order they could send home. Others didn't.

That was the summer Ernesto and his "son Luis" came to help us put on an adobe floor for our second room. Ernesto would continue to help us at various tasks for the next three years. He was a small man, possibly in his sixties, with gray stubble and ropy muscles. Each season he came accompanied by a male relative whom he always referred to as his son Luis. Sometimes it was his son. As likely, it could have been a grandson, cousin, or son-in-law. Once the man's name was actually Luis. For the others, their real names only emerged gradually in conversation. This simplification of relationships and names was, I think, Ernesto's version of making the Anglos comfortable.

Ernesto's forte was stonework, and although we didn't plan on terracing our back yard with dry stone walls, his expertise convinced us. Like Effrem, he worked slowly and steadily. The younger relative played the role of helper, fetching the stones in a wheelbarrow and lounging, bored, while Ernesto made his selections. If necessary, Ernesto would trim the stone with a sharp blow of his hammer before fitting it carefully into its arranged niche. The result was a layered work of art, which Ernesto would always want to cap with cement—a practical touch we always vetoed.

In our longer relationship with Ernesto, we learned more about familial patterns and life in Mexico. We watched the pecking order quickly established between relatives, the respect given Ernesto as a skilled worker, and the way in which he jealously guarded his skills. No hands but his placed the stone, for he did not jeopardize his livelihood by teaching it—at least, not yet. We knew that by extending our house into three rooms, 1,000 square feet, we were doubling the size of Ernesto's home. By the fourth year, too, we had worked twice with the son-in-law whose name was really Luis. A genial but restless man with five children, he was widowed when we first met him and newly married the second summer. His first wife, Ernesto's daughter, had died in childbirth and the son-in-law was still coming to the States to pay off the doctor's bill. "I was a screwball for marrying again," he said in Spanish to my husband, and Ernesto agreed.

Because of our growing sense of familiarity, even friendship, it remained a shock when the morning came that we did not see Ernesto and his relative walking up the hill to our house. By nine o'-clock we knew they were not coming, and we realized that once again they had left suddenly without telling us. We understood now, but did not condone, why some employers paid at the end of the job. It was to ensure that the job get done, that the adobe bricks were not left unfinished in the rain or a wall half-stuccoed or a floor half-laid. Here, at least, unreliability was the alien's trademark and privilege. His abrupt departures illustrated how tenuous the relationship really was and how unbound by social rules. Sometimes the explanation got back to us: a brother had fallen ill or a child was born. Sometimes the men left because they had an argument in the trailer, or because they were tired of working, or because they were homesick. Since Ernesto didn't trust the postal system, he would be carrying all his money in a handkerchief wadded tightly in his pocket. If he had worked as long as two weeks, that would be $120 in savings—equal in Mexico to two months work. If he was lucky, Ernesto would avoid La Migra's green trucks. If he was lucky, he would catch a ride on the highway and spend the night, not on the road, but in a Palomas hotel.

IN JUNE OF 1988 a new immigration law began to impose penalties on the employers of illegal aliens. The law requires any employer to ask for documentation—a birth certificate, passport, or driver's license—before hiring. If the employer does not and hires an illegal alien, he or she is liable to a civil fine ranging from $250 to $2,000. For a second offense, the penalty can rise to $5,000 per worker. A third offense may mean six months in jail. (There are, however, many exceptions and workers in certain crops are exempt.) The law also provided amnesty and American citizenship for aliens who had been living in the country since January 1982. Amnesty, of course, did not affect the men we knew since they did not want American citizenship; they wanted to work here seasonally and return to their own country. How the act did affect them is unclear. In some parts of the country, studies seem to show that the 1988 Immigration Law has not significantly stopped the flow of illegal workers. But here in the Mimbres Valley, Ernesto and his relatives do not come anymore. I rarely see men like them along the edge of the highway. And no one drops by our house to ask for food or work.

In truth, we could not say that we would hire any alien who did come. Now that we too risk being illegal, we would have to think that through all over again. We never really knew what we were doing. We never found an answer, right or wrong, but in the end responded to personal needs, ours and theirs. We let the big picture blur and focused on the small. It seemed to work for a time.

Maxine Scates

M axine Scates was raised in a working-class neighborhood of Los Angeles. Her family celebrated her grandfather's Irishness; her grandmother's Mexican roots were never mentioned. "Because of my father's alcoholism, my family existed in a very closed, very isolated atmosphere. My writing comes, I suppose, from a compelling need to understand my family, to tell its story and understand that story in relation to the culture at large. It comes from a need to be heard. I was a silent kid and a silent young woman. Writing became my means to communicate."

As a child of the city, Scates was eleven or twelve years old before she experienced mountains and trees for the first time. From that moment, she knew she wanted out of Los Angeles. Eventually she headed north to Oregon for graduate school—where she earned an MFA in creative writing from the University of Oregon and an Ed.M. in Adult Education from Oregon State University—and she has been there ever since. "I'm a Westerner, but more than that, I'm a West Coaster. I like living on a rim, living on the edge."

A former poetry editor of Northwest Review, her poems and essays have appeared in The American Poetry Review, The American Voice, and many other publications. She has written two books of poems, Toluca Street (1989), which received the Agnes

*Lynch Starrett Poetry Prize and the Oregon Book Award for Po-
etry, and* Forgiveness *(forthcoming). She has taught throughout
Oregon, most recently as poet-in-residence at Reed College in Portland, Oregon.*

Nana

THE PORCH WAS GREEN, WOOD SPLINTERING BE-
neath my hands or my legs as I sat looking out over the city on
Sunday visits to the house on Toluca Street, in downtown Los Angeles, where my grandmother was born and where my grandparents now lived. It could be any year in the late fifties or early sixties,
but I know it's 1963 because I'm sitting with my brother and sister-
in-law and their daughter, an infant. So I'm thirteen. The pink stone
steps lead down to the street where my mother is walking her
mother across to Evelyn Miney's house. I look downhill, to the left,
for my grandfather on his way home from mass at Saint Viviana's.

On that Sunday in 1963, the scene I recall is a peaceful one, and
I feel protected and surrounded by family. Or should I say, as protected as I ever felt in the presence of my family? Why, after all, is
my mother walking my grandmother across the street? It is because
Nana is afraid to cross the street by herself. In fact, her visit to the
Mineys' is the result of my mother's insistent urging, and during
the visit itself it is not likely that she will offer more than three or
four monosyllabic responses to questions asked her. But I do not
question Nana's silence—it is all I have ever known of her, and this
afternoon in memory does strike me as a particularly peaceful one.
Perhaps it is because all of us are sitting on the steps and no one sits

in the house, with its cracked plaster and sagging couches and dirty kitchen. More often than not the scenes I recall are when I am sitting on the steps alone waiting for someone to come and take me away. No one ever does. Inside all of the adults are talking; no, not all of them—Nana is among them walking or sitting silently, words ebbing around and over her. Outside I look out at the city, hazy and yellow even then. I see the tower of Belmont High School that cracked in the 1933 earthquake, the red brick school itself, the cars that glitter through the haze, glinting with sunlight as they turn corners far away.

Or I'm eleven and I'm walking uphill with my mother—we are always walking uphill. If I were six I would have my hand in hers, but I'm not six, I'm eleven, and we've walked up the hill sidestepping the broken glass on the sidewalk, and now we stop and talk to the Mineys before we cross the street to walk up the steps to the house we refer to by its number, 138. Does my mother tell Evelyn that I'm going to be a writer? Do I only imagine it? Or is it at that moment that I know I will write? What is it, then? Do I associate reaching the hilltop where my silent grandmother lives with the same rising I feel in me when I want to write? Then, I am lifted, I have risen to the top of the hill once again. But the fact is we are only halfway up the hill and at the top the dirty oil wells sit chugging continuously, yet, this, too, is like that rising precisely because it is never finished and though it may be a lifting it is also a dredging, continuous and sometimes dirty. Yes, we are halfway up, standing in front of the postman's shuttered windows on the plum-stained sidewalk where, because no one picks the plums, they fall down into the gutters and rot, and it's right there I begin to know something, or to want to know it.

DADDY. Nana drawls. Her voice is uninflected and monotonous because she's on drugs. Maybe she's on lithium. When I ask my mother and my Aunt Milly about the drugs now, they tell me that when I was a child she may have been drugged. Further questioning reveals that yes, she must have been drugged, though by the fifties they have grown so used to her silent presence among us that they still attribute it to the shock treatments she had in the thirties after her first breakdown. My mother now remembers that in some months and years across time there were whole days where my grandmother simply sat looking at her hands. Grampa called her "Tony" and pointed his hand to the side of his head tracing the slow spiral of a crazy sign and though I'd rather not remember it now, I laughed.

I loved my grandfather. It was more difficult to love Nana, who seemed, after all, to be an absence among us. Yet it is Nana's story, or the lack of it, that I come back to again and again, because it seems to me that Nana's silence was a silence not only linked with the secrecy and shame of what we thought of as her "madness," but also inextricably tangled with the internalized self-hatreds of race and class that coming to understand my family has magnified for me, while also helping me to understand some of my own motivations and actions. Particularly, as I have come more fully to realize the contradictions between the stories my mother told me about her family and what I have found to be true about their lives, I associate the feeling of that rising, that finding one's way towards a truth which forms its own story, with the contradictions of the house on Toluca Street. There, I experienced a truth I didn't yet have the words or authority to say, but because children do *know*, it is the *feeling* of that underlying truth, the desire to find a means to say that truth, which was contradicted by a story constructed out of shame as a response to the perception of "how things are supposed to be," that pulls me back to that house on Toluca. At the center of this story is my grandmother's silence.

NANA, HELEN RUTH BAILEY, was born in 1898 in Los Angeles in the house on Toluca, which had been built by her grandfather, Jonathan Denny Bailey, a carpenter and a member of the Knights of Labor, who had emigrated from Missouri in 1886. Her father was Charles Bailey, a plumber, and her mother was Lila Dolores Orozco, born Maria Dolores Orozco somewhere in the state of Oaxaca, Mexico, in 1878. My great-grandmother, who at some point in her life changed her name from Maria to Lila, was sent north from Mexico City at the age of fourteen to finish her education in a convent. Her education was cut short, however, when she met my great-grandfather, several years her senior, while he was at work on the convent plumbing. She married at fifteen. She was short and her husband was tall; in their wedding photograph, though he sits and she stands, her head barely clears his. She was dark and he was light. She is remembered for her vivacity, and he is remembered for his sternness. Lila had three children; Nana was the second. Her husband, Charles, did not allow her to speak Spanish in the house nor did he allow his children to learn Spanish. Not too surprisingly, the radical impulses of a Knights of Labor upbringing did not extend to the acceptance of racial difference. The story, when it was referred to, had it that Lila's family was *Spanish* rather than Mexican (they were, in fact, Mexican), and of a middle or professional class, as the ability to send her to Los Angeles might confirm. Though the little I know of her suggests that, at times, Lila functioned independently within the Mexican-American community in Boyle Heights, from the beginning the emphasis was on assimilation—though that emphasis may have been of a more genteel nature during Nana's childhood than during her own marriage. Photographs taken of my grandmother, her sister, brother, mother and father, around 1914, the year of my grandmother's marriage, show a taciturn Charles Bailey and his dark-haired family, the women dressed in white and the two men in suits. They are a quite beautiful family.

At sixteen Nana married my grandfather, Michael Joseph Greeley, a Los Angeles Police patrolman one generation removed from Ireland and twelve years my grandmother's senior. In 1906, my grandfather had come from Boston to San Francisco to see the results of the earthquake, though some accounts actually have him living through the earthquake itself. My grandparents began buying the house on Toluca from Nana's parents early in their marriage. My Aunt Milly was born in 1916 and my mother, Lucy, in 1918. Six pregnancies and four children followed, and in 1930, during the birth of her sixth child, Nana had what I have been told was a complete mental and physical breakdown. My mother tells me that Nana's hair turned white overnight. Unaware of the possibility of involuntary sterilization, she also tells me that by the time Nana came home she had experienced early menopause. In that first and longest period of institutionalization, Nana didn't come home for six years.

These times, as much as they still exist, are buried in the consciousness of my Aunt Milly and my mother, the oldest children at the time of the first breakdown. My mother remembers selectively. My Aunt Milly remembers more. After Nana was institutionalized, Milly was forced to leave home and live with her grandparents because she and my grandfather fought constantly. Though he had stopped drinking by the time I came along, he drank heavily as a younger man and by any account, including the box of yellow newspaper articles I read and reread as a child, one of which labeled him "Two-Gun Mike," he was severe. Milly remembers the violent late night arguments preceding Nana's first breakdown. She tells me that my grandfather became convinced that Nana was having an affair with a poet who read his work on the radio and that my grandfather threatened to kill both of them. Apparently Nana did at least know the poet since Milly also remembers a picnic where he and my grandfather argued over my grandfather's treatment of Nana.

My mother remembers that Nana worked all day cooking, cleaning, and taking care of five children. She doesn't ever remember seeing any sign of physical affection between her parents. She says she spent as much time as possible in her room "cutting out paper dolls, reading and dreaming of marriage and babies." She remembers her father, by then a sergeant, resplendent in his uniform as a patrol car dropped him at the curb each night. Both Milly and my mother say that the worry of having yet another child in the midst of the Depression must have contributed greatly to Nana's mental state.

Milly tells me that Lila, Nana's mother, also spent intervals of two or three months at a time institutionalized and that, in fact, Lila and all of her children were intermittently institutionalized during the course of their lives. Most surprisingly, and for me most unimaginably, Milly tells me that in 1933 Lila and Nana were in Norwalk State Hospital at the same time in different wards. Milly remembers, at the age of seventeen, sitting in the offices of a staff psychiatrist with her grandfather, Charles. She remembers the doctor describing her mother as manic-depressive and her grandmother as manic-depressive and schizophrenic. She remembers that the doctor told her that these conditions were hereditary, but "that you would be broken only if you let yourself be broken." My aunt also remembers that at that moment she decided never to have children. She never did.

It was during another visit to Nana that Milly recalls her grandfather being told by the doctor that Nana was ready to come home but that she would not be released to my grandfather. Perhaps this was because, on the few occasions towards the end of that six years when Nana came home for a short visit, her condition worsened immediately, and, as a result, she had to be taken back to the hospital before her allotted time was over. Neither Milly nor my mother can recall my grandfather ever visiting Nana. Late in life my mother remembers the screams from the wards on her own Sunday afternoon visits and when she does I am sorry that I made her. Reluctantly, my mother also remembers that during those years my grandfather spent his free time drinking with his mistress. My mother never fought with her father, and, self-described as his "pet" and the eldest living at home, it was her job to fetch him home from the bars down on Second Street each night.

When the time came for Nana to be discharged, she was released to the guardianship of her parents. However, soon enough my grandfather "made" her parents bring Nana home. Shortly thereafter, he demanded that Milly return home to take care of her mother. Milly obeyed but fought so intensely with her father that she left after only a few weeks and soon after was married.

In the years after Nana came home, her stays and her sanity were intermittent. She had been a beautiful young woman. Yet although she was no more than thirty-eight when she was released from the hospital that first time, photographs of her show a much older woman, her features somehow blunted, her hair white, her face grim and unsmiling. By all accounts, my grandfather's brutality towards her in the years after her release did much to exacerbate and maintain her mental condition. Both my mother and Milly were married shortly after Nana's return and so no longer lived on Toluca, but on one occasion Milly remembers coming into the house and going upstairs to find her mother handcuffed to her bed. Even my mother, whose versions of her family's life when I was a child glorified my grandfather's police exploits while treating Nana's illness as something that had simply happened apart from any life she was living, now admits that my grandfather treated Nana like a "servant." Unlike Milly, she says she cannot remember physical violence, but she does say she remembers her mother's "subservience." She remembers how my grandfather never spoke directly to Nana but to give her orders. She remembers, as I do, how he constantly belittled her and in her presence told everyone that she was "crazy."

Though my mother would later tell me there had been some good years during the forties, by the time of my own childhood, in the fifties and sixties, Nana's silence, as well as my grandfather's mockery of her, had come to be taken for granted—codified by her shuffling walk and her toneless responses. When I was a child, the only glimpse I ever had of who Nana might have been came in my mother's stories of the first twelve years of her own life—the years before her mother's breakdown. Those brief glimpses gave no inkling of what it was that might have led to her breakdown. Nana died in 1986, when I was thirty-six, and she was eighty-eight.

ON THOSE SUNDAY AFTERNOONS of my childhood on Toluca, the scenes I remember now seem to approach the absurd: my mother talking away to her mother as if she could actually rouse her; my grandfather mocking my grandmother and telling jokes, my mother chiding him when his remarks grow too profane or racist, I and whatever other cousins were present perhaps laughing with him, already complicitous with his authority and dominance. Yet my mother did not try to rouse my grandmother out of mockery, but out of love and out of her own memory of her and perhaps even out of a belief that she could bring her back.

My mother knew very little of what had caused her mother's illness, and, of course, she feared for her own children. What I understood of Nana's illness was what my mother understood and what my mother understood was that Nana hadn't talked enough, hadn't told anybody what was wrong. If the diagnosis my Aunt Milly had heard thirty years earlier in the state psychiatrist's office was somewhat more sophisticated, it hadn't offered her any less terror. And though Milly remained childless, my mother had children, and she bore her terror and responsibility for our fates just as she bore her own alcoholic husband. The mystery of Nana's illness, the horror of it, was so great that my mother would not see it. What her voice, her actions, offered instead was her version of normalcy. Thus, my mother spun the story that protected me, though my brother, ten years older, knew and remembered more. And the story? The story was filtered, any fact that she thought would disturb altered or omitted. The conditions of Nana's life, the outright brutality, the mockery and the indifference that had to have contributed to her state of mind were not acknowledged. Nana lived among us, the institution waiting if she got too "high," yet why she was the way she was had no association but fear and shame, no story, and this omission built an even higher wall around her silence. Bellicose and garrulous, my grandfather amused us: He was the story. Nana had none.

SO MUCH BEGINS THERE, in the living room of that old house. Who told any of us that what occurred there was not normal? Who stepped into that living room and noted its absurdity or its brutality? No one. When I think about the pathology of my own racism and the desire to "get over," to identify with the dominant, which I have come to associate with my identification with a white working-class background, I see the origins there where so much was learned amidst the contradictory and conflicting images: There, I learn to love my grandfather and his Irishness, which is, by turn, our Irishness. Though I am vaguely aware that Nana's mother was born in Mexico, Mexicanness is far removed from our cultural identity, an erasure then in its third generation. In the second generation, Milly now remembers becoming aware when she was a junior high school student that her grandmother was born in Mexico. She says that she "started bragging about it in school. I was proud of it." Because there were many Mexican-American students in her class, she saw her own burgeoning sense of identity as a means of identifying with them. A good student, she started to "write about it" until her father forbade her to admit to being, as she now says, "Spanish or Mexican." Later, he wouldn't allow her to take Spanish in high school and though, when she went to live with her grandparents, Lila tried to teach her, Milly says it was too late, she couldn't learn.

Thus, my grandfather had told his children never to claim who they were, and they have passed that denial on to their own children. If the subject comes up, we know only that Lila was born in Mexico; we have the claims of her father's *Spanish ancestry, his blondness*. Beyond that there are no facts. And after all, if Nana is an absence among us, how can her racial identity be a presence—yet, of course, that absence is its own negative presence. The story filters and favors my grandfather; Nana is apart from us, isolated and separate, a removal, an easy "other." He is the best and she is the least of us. The emphasis on our Irishness and the overt racism, the horrible private language of that house, the constant and casual use of racial epithets seem to be directed without, but even as the epithets are directed without, the denial of everything Mexican tells me that they are also directed toward Nana, that carefully removed, omitted, and defiled "other" within. From my family, I am learning the benefits of being white. Though we are not among the privileged, we are claiming our various hatreds because we recognize their relation to privilege.

Now, as an adult, when I look for the richness of tradition that a mixture of Mexican and Irish might suggest, I find only the false bottom of that Irishness, the claims for it a refuge in the racist pride of its overriding whiteness rather than a sense of its own story. I have no relation to the cultural realities of either community that I might claim as familiar. When I look for an identity, the story of who I might be, the identity I find seems based on abnegation—a denial of who we were based on self-hatred. Yet, isn't that, hasn't that become my cultural reality, my American story? A story based less on fact than a denial of fact? A silencing around mental illness and race that consciously or not understands the benefits of identifying with who and what is dominant? A story that aligns itself with a wishful version until it becomes that version? And finally, a story that leaves me obsessed with recapturing some sense of the lives of both Nana and Lila, a feeling for them and of them—perhaps because their lives seem emblematic to me of the lost lives of so many women, but certainly because I am of them.

YET, if I am a pure product of America, to paraphrase William Carlos Williams, it's the purity of that product and the perfection of its indoctrination that demonstrate the difficulties in realizing the truth of these American lives. Given the lack of facts, it's not without a certain irony that on a recent trip to Southern California to visit my mother, I found perhaps the only existing part of the record that Nana, herself, had left. Searching through the family papers and photographs that my mother had in her possession, I felt that I was looking for something, anything that would provide me with answers about Nana's life, and I felt that the time to find those answers was running out—as it already so clearly has when it comes to the life of my great-grandmother, Lila. One evening, after reading through endless records, I finally came to Nana's photographs. They were in a large plastic sack in miscellaneous order. For some reason I turned over the first photograph I picked up and found that it was covered with a maze of writing. I had never seen more than a sentence of Nana's handwriting during her life, and I was so moved that I called my mother over to the table to look. But she already knew. Indeed, my grandmother had apparently written a great deal during the last years of her life, the years after my grandfather had died, when, no longer drugged, she lived with one of my aunts. My mother told me Nana called that writing her "autobiography" but that my aunt had destroyed all of it because she couldn't make sense of it.

Today, I still feel the anger I felt then that what Nana had written was destroyed. As I sat there at that table, my first instinct was to believe not that the writing didn't make sense, but that the story she was telling was unpalatable, unconforming in the way I imagine the true story was. Yet, as I read on, the backs of those photographs revealed nothing particularly unpalatable. My aunt need not have been fearful of them, for the words seemed sometimes to attempt to reconstruct nothing more than the memory the photograph might suggest. They were the jottings of a woman who was trying to remember and make some sense of her life. For instance, of a photograph of a dog standing next to a eucalyptus tree she wrote: "Our Scotch collie Mama had to go to court over. That's the way it looked in the lot next door. I had a big rope swing. My brother had a tree house. It does not show in the picture." Or on a photograph of her on what clearly seems her wedding day, she said, "I can't remember the occasion," and, much to my surprise, on the back of a photograph of my brother's wedding I found myself, long before I had articulated it, identified as "the one who wants to write"—surprised because, in life, I never had any indication that she was even aware of my desire. Occasionally, her words were addressed to an other she might only imagine, as a miscellaneous line strayed from the maze of observations about the photograph itself, as in: "My Ethel Bert Niven you never play at my request." Sometimes she addressed the reader as "you," as in the photograph which showed her in a family group that includes her mother and brother: "Maybe you can pick me out." And since I had looked for, and found, those photographs, my anger gave way to exhilaration as I became more than willing, fated, to be that "you" she addressed. In all the years of our lives, Nana had never spoken to me of her life and now I believed she was. Yet, as I continued looking at those photographs, I also realized, as I heard the voice, the diction of a woman who had never spoken to me in more than short sentences, that in all our years together I had never asked her anything that mattered. And then and now the gap between my grandmother's knowledge of me and my lack of knowledge of her makes me question how complicitous I was in maintaining her silence.

Now, a year later, I wonder what she could have told me. I wonder why I didn't ask her what she knew. I accepted, long into adulthood, the taboos that had been in place in my family for as long as I could remember. And now I begin to understand my failure to ask as part of what perhaps perpetuated her silence as we and she waited her life out.

Often, when I read my poetry, people tell me how moved they are by an elegy for Nana called "We Never Knew You." I usually preface the poem by saying that I write from her silence. But could I have known her? Now, I have to wonder if I allowed her silence to become a symbol precisely because I was as interested in controlling and simplifying the story, in my writerly way, as was the rest of my family—in letting that silence become a symbol that lent itself and conformed more easily to the purposes of my poetry. Didn't my version of Nana keep her a victim, when, had she spoken, had I asked, we both might have broken that silence? Hadn't I, too, constructed a story that deleted the truth of what she might have said because the questions went unasked? I'll never know what Nana might have said, but the questions I have to ask myself now are: Did I call her silent because that silence fit the version of her I had created? Did I call her silent because I was afraid of what she had to say?

IN THE LATE FIFTIES, when I was about nine, the upper floor of the house on Toluca burned. I have always believed that it was Nana who lit the fire, but recently, both Milly and my mother have told me that faulty wiring was the cause. When I consider how I came to my earlier conclusion, I know that as a child I believed that Nana lit that fire because she hated my grandfather, an act I associated not with the drugged and silent Nana but with the other Nana, the dangerous Nana who was "high."

There were two occasions when I saw Nana "break," as my mother called it. The first was a year or so before the fire, when we were visiting an aunt who lived in Camarillo near the state hospital where Nana was often institutionalized during my childhood. Nana had left the hospital on a day pass for my birthday celebration. My grandfather, who had never accompanied us before, had come along that day. I was seven or eight, but I knew that whatever gaiety there was about the day was forced, false, and, in keeping with that falseness, I remember expressing surprise at opening a package whose contents I already knew. The next thing I remember is standing in the living room holding a bullet in the palm of my hand from the gun my grandfather always carried with him. He had unloaded the gun and placed the bullet in my palm. I was terrified; he was laughing. And somewhere at the edge of it all, I was aware of Nana edgy, nervous, and active in a way she never was. Years later, my mother admitted that Nana was in the kitchen waving a knife which my mother and aunt were trying to get away from her. I was in the living room holding a bullet and Nana was in the kitchen waving a knife. My grandfather's presence was acting on both of us that day. Perhaps because of my own fear, for the first time I was aware of Nana's terror, though it is only now that I can claim it as the truth of that room.

The only other occasion I saw Nana break was when she was on the verge of being institutionalized. I will never forget the fury in the eyes of a woman who normally shuffled when she walked and always spoke in the same monosyllabic tone—the eyes of a woman who knew no one wanted to hear what she had to say. In those moments something else broke through—the rage that required containment. I know as little now about her illness as I did when I was a child, but now I will believe there were no means or place to express what she felt, and certainly no one to listen—and I'll certainly believe that this contributed to her state of mind.

When my grandfather died in 1969, I remember Nana saying, "Now I can live in peace." As I think about her life, I remember hearing her say that sentence, but at the time I simply ignored her. I mourned my grandfather and I did not have the means or the words to reconcile what she was saying with my very real grief over his death, with his presence and her absence. And she did live in peace. For the seventeen years of life that remained for her, Nana was not drugged—there was no longer any necessity.

Leslie Marmon Silko

Pueblo Laguna poet and novelist Leslie Marmon Silko is the recipient of a MacArthur Foundation grant and the author of Storyteller *(1981), a collection of prose and poetry; and two* novels, Ceremony *(1977) and* Almanac of the Dead *(1991).* "White ethnologists have reported that the oral tradition among Native American groups has died out," *she wrote in* Storyteller, "but I grew up at Laguna listening, and I hear the ancient stories, I hear them very clearly in the stories we are telling right now. Most important, I feel the power which the stories still have, to bring us together, especially when there is loss and grief."

Silko met the poet James Wright briefly in 1975 at a writers' conference. Three years later, after reading Ceremony, *Wright wrote a note of appreciation. A correspondence began between them, formal at first, until, in the words of Anne Wright, who edited their correspondence into the book* The Delicacy and Strength of Lace, *"Leslie began to relate stories about a tyrannical black rooster that lived on her ranch. Soon they were exchanging work, discussing the difficulties of writing when 'besieged by personal turmoil' and the rewards when it went well."*

Silko and Wright met only once more—in Mount Sinai Hospital, shortly before Wright succumbed to cancer. ". . . no matter if written words are seldom," Silko wrote in her last letter to her friend, "because we know, Jim, we know."

In these excerpts from her letters, Silko demonstrates the power
of stories and the power of love.

"Roosters and the Power of Love"

from *The Delicacy and Strength of Lace*

Tucson, Arizona
October 3, 1978

Dear Mr. Wright,
Dear Jim,

I just fed the rooster a blackened banana I found in the refrigerator. He has been losing his yellowish collar feathers lately, and I'm
afraid it might be that he isn't getting enough to eat. But I suppose
it could be his meanness too—he is the rooster out of all the rooster
stories my grandmother ever told me—the rooster who waited inside the barn on winter mornings when it was still dark and my
grandma was just married and going to milk her father-in-law's
cow. The rooster would wait and ambush her just when she thought
she had escaped him. It was a reflexive reaction the morning he
jumped to rake her with his spurs and she swung the milking bucket
at him. He collapsed and didn't move, and the whole time she was
milking the cow she wondered how she could ever tell her father-in-
law, my great-grandfather, that she had killed his rooster. She took
the milk inside and he was already drinking his coffee. (He was an
old man by then, the old white man who came from Ohio and
married my great-grandmother from Paguate village north of Laguna.) She told him she didn't mean to kill the rooster but that the
bucket hit him too hard. They tell me that my great-grandfather

was a gentle person. And Grandma said that morning he told her not to worry, that he had known for a while that rooster was too mean to keep. But as they went out to the barn together, to dispose of the dead rooster, there he was in the corral. Too mean to kill, Grandma said. But after that, he left her alone when she went to milk the cow.

There are all kinds of other rooster stories that one is apt to hear. I am glad I have this rooster because I never quite believed roosters so consistently *were* as the stories tell us they are. On these hot Tucson days, he scratches a little nest in the damp dirt under the Mexican lime tree by the front door. It is imperative for him that the kittens and the black cat show him respect, even deference, by detouring or half-circling the rooster as they approach the water dish which is also under the lime tree. If they fail to do this, then he jumps up and stamps his feet, moving sideways until they cringe. This done, he goes back to his mud nest.

He has all of us fooled, stepping around him softly, hesitant to turn our backs on him, all of us except for the old black hound dog. She won't let anyone, including the rooster, come between her and her food dish. The rooster pretends he does not notice her lack of concern; he pretends he was just finished eating when she approaches.

The lady at the feed store had to give him away. He was her pet and he let her pick him up and stroke him. But the men who came to buy hay got to teasing him and he started going after all the feed store customers. She was afraid he might hurt a child. So I took him and told her I didn't know how long he'd last here at the ranch because the coyotes are everywhere in the Tucson mountains. I didn't expect him to last even a week. But that was in June and now it is October. Maybe it is his meanness after all that keeps the coyotes away, that makes his feathers fall out.

I never know what will happen when I write a letter. Certain persons bring out certain things in me. I hadn't intended to go off with rooster stories when really I wanted to tell you how happy I was to hear from you again. . . .

Tucson, Arizona
October 17, 1978

Dear Jim,

. . . I am pushing to finish the first of the scripts which attempt to tell the Laguna stories on film using the storyteller's voice with the actual locations where these stories are supposed to have taken place. In a strange sort of way, the film project is an experiment in translation—bringing the land—the hills, the arroyos, the boulders, the cottonwoods in October—to people unfamiliar with it, because after all, the stories grow out of this land as much as we see ourselves as having emerged from the land there. Translations of Laguna stories seem terribly bleak on the printed page. A voice, a face, hands to point and gesture bring them alive, but if you do not know the places which the storyteller calls up in the telling, if you have not waded in the San Jose River below the village, if you have not hidden in the river willows and sand with your lover, then even as the teller relates a story, you will miss something which people from the Laguna community would not have missed. Laguna narratives are very lean because so much of the stories are shared knowledge—certainly descriptions of the river and the river willows are *not* included in the narratives because it is assumed the listeners already know the river and the willows. So with a wonderful cinematographer, I hope to bring the stories out in a manner most faithful to the heart of the Laguna storyteller. Film will be used to create a context, a place within which the narratives reside. It is all an experiment and film is such a complex and expensive medium. We will be lucky to ever see it on film. But the texts of the stories are beautiful and the visualization in the script is beautiful too, so I already feel that whatever the outcome, I will have written something interesting. I needed to wean myself from involved descriptions of the land, and the script has helped. I think I am learning something, too, about possibilities as well as the limits of visual imagery and verbal images. I am continually surprised at the things we writers think nothing of attempting with language—things which are impossible visually. On the other hand, film images can be strung together and the viewer's mind associates them in a way which dispenses with the "bridges" and "transitions" which writers must deal with.

Well, I hope this isn't too tedious—this discussion of visual and verbal, etc. I like to keep learning and this is one of my more ambitious undertakings.

The rooster is growing new feathers. The mares are fat but their hooves are dried-out from lack of rain and they shatter (This makes it sound worse than it really is. The old parts of the hoof break off and they lose their horseshoes.) when we ride over the rocks too fast. The coyotes haven't eaten the kittens yet, but one of the kittens tried to climb a cholla cactus yesterday and I spent the afternoon pulling cactus spines out of her belly, tail and paws. . . .

Tucson, Arizona
November 1, 1978

Dear Jim,

Writing to you is a special pleasure I save for myself, just as I look forward to your letters. If my letter has sent you back to your notebook, then your letters have sent me back to scribbles about played-out silver mines and the Grants, New Mexico, Train Robbery of 1918. . . .

You pointed out a very important dimension of the land and the Pueblo people's relation to the land when you said it was as if the land was telling the stories in the novel. That is it exactly, but it is so difficult to convey this interrelationship without sounding like Margaret Fuller or some other Transcendentalist. When I was writing *Ceremony* I was so terribly devastated by being away from the Laguna country that the writing was my way of re-making that place, the Laguna country, for myself. In sand paintings the little geometric forms are said to designate mountains, planets, rainbows—in one sand painting or another all things in Creation are traced out in sand. What I learned for myself was that words can function like the sand. I say "learned for myself" because I think most poets and writers understand this, but it is the kind of lesson that must be found on one's own. I wish I knew Plato better. But didn't he talk about the idea of the tree being more real or important than the actual physical tree itself? Well, I don't exactly agree with *that* either, but I think there is a materialistic impulse in Western thought which says that if you don't have "the real thing—untouched and unchanged" then you don't have anything of value/meaning. When the Army Corps of Engineers flooded the sacred shrines and land near Cochiti Pueblo, many non-Indian people (and Indians as well) said, "Well, it is all ruined. Why do they (the Cochitis) even go near those places?" But here it seems is an instance where this quasi-Platonic idea works well: the strong feelings, the love, the regard which the Cochiti people had for those places that were flooded, those feelings and the importance of those feelings, memories and beliefs are much more important than the physical locations. Which isn't to say that a great hurt and loss didn't occur when the shrines were flooded, but the idea or memory or feeling—whatever you want to call it—is more powerful and important than any damage or destruction humans may commit. How well you know this, express this in your writing—"Lament for the Shadows," "By the Ruins of Gun Emplacement," "One Last Look at the Adige." How much I love this!

It is the same with death. Death never ends feelings or relationships at Laguna. If a dear one passes on, the love continues and it continues in both directions—it is requited by the spirits of these dear ones who send blessings back to us, maybe with rain or maybe with the feeling of continuity and closeness as well as with past memories. And people still speak of old enemies as if the battle continues. For the family it means putting a pinch of food into a bowl for the spirits (family members/relatives) before eating the meal. I'm not sure what Plato would say to this, but here, it seems to me, we have an idea or memory or concept of a person enduring long after the actual, physical person is gone. And so, Jim, here is still another demonstration of the old saying "a little knowledge (of Plato) is dangerous."

Today is All Souls' Day and for both Mexican and Pueblo people it is the day when the dead are especially remembered, but not like Memorial Day exactly. Tonight at Laguna, there will be candles lighting the graves and there will be all kinds of food—favorite dishes like chili stew and roasted piñon nuts—for the souls of loved ones. People try to remember favorite foods of the dead person. At Laguna, when someone dies, you don't "get over it" by forgetting: you "get over it" by *remembering*, and by remembering you are aware that no person is ever truly lost or gone once they have been in our lives and loved us, as we have loved them. Which isn't to say that you conduct life exactly as if the person were alive. If Grandpa didn't like red paint, after he is gone you can feel free to paint the walls red because it is understood that those sorts of things are no longer concerns of the dead.

Navajos and some other tribes don't feel that way, of course—they fear the dead souls. And Eskimos actually name children for dead ancestors with the belief that the soul has returned in that child, though they also realize that this is *not* always the case. So it isn't a *strict* idea of reincarnation like some Asian cultures have.

Howard Rock was a wonderful man who began the first Alaska Native newspaper in Alaska, called the *Tundra Times*. He knew how much the Eskimo and Athabascan people wanted to hear about village news, so he recruited wonderful village correspondents whose use of the English language was unequaled for expressiveness, if a little ungrammatical. Anyway, I used to read his paper while I lived in Ketchikan, and each week he had a little story from childhood in a village near Nome. One week he recalled that when he was 5 years old, his aunt took him ice fishing for grayling. They traveled a distance from the village with their dogs and then she chopped a hole in the ice and they began fishing. This aunt called the boy "Grandmother" because he had been named, at birth, the same name his great-grandmother had had. This day, Howard Rock related, though he was just a little child, he caught many many grayling. And as they were going home that evening his aunt said to him, "Grandmother, you always were the best at ice fishing." . . .

The rooster has two little white hens now and he is *very proud.*

Love,
Leslie

Tucson, Arizona
January 24, 1979

Dear Jim,

Today it's gray and "cold" here, which means it's 45° and no sun, but for Tucson that's quite grim. I'm burning mesquite I chopped last evening—I like chopping wood. I like chopping wood better than most "household" chores. A sharp axe is so pleasurable to use, especially on this mesquite which is almost as tough as hardwood.

The rooster is very proud of his two little white hens and he'd lay down his life for them although they are not nearly his equals in beauty or spirit or intelligence. One of them especially loves to crawl *under* parked cars and motorcycles where she then sits for hours. Her feathers are grimy oily gray and she seems to be very comfortable with her slovenly appearance. The other hen is clean, but she is a throw-back to prehistoric days when reptiles were evolving into winged creatures which finally became birds. But he loves them both so much, and they make him very happy—his feathers are more beautiful than they've ever been. All of which goes to show us something, I guess. . . .

I always resented Shakespeare's use of the delayed messenger in *Romeo and Juliet,* maybe because such things are so ordinary and so possible, and so much can be lost for two people that way.

Love,
Leslie

Tucson, Arizona
March 2, 1979

Dear Jim,

The post card of Vermeer arrived yesterday. I have been carrying this ærogram around with me these past days waiting for a time when I could write to you with some semblance of peace. If I am frantic when I write, it sometimes affects the person receiving the letter; I don't want that.

The afternoon I wrote to you about the rooster and his hens we came back to the ranch to find them gone—the little white hens almost without a trace—and piles of rooster's green and bronze and black feathers scattered everywhere. By searching carefully I found four white feathers a short distance from the house. The coyotes had come—at least four of them I think because otherwise the dogs could have protected rooster and his hens. Coyotes waste nothing and so it is as if the white hens were never here; the rooster, on the other hand, was always a strange creature. A number of times I would be talking to Denny and would feel as if we were not alone; when I looked out the open window I'd find the rooster listening outside like a being out of some Haitian voodoo story. Now when the wind blows I find feathers, every time thinking that surely *now* I am seeing them for the last time, but finding them again and again. What is remarkable though are the colors of the feathers, which remain undimmed, and the texture of the feathers, which is as glossy as if they had only just fallen from him; and all this after weeks of the feathers blowing around the ground in dust and rain.

He was a mean and dirty bird but we loved him in a strange sort of way. Our friends who had been pursued or jumped by rooster find it difficult to appreciate our loss. I guess I am still surprised at the feeling we had for him—to realize that without wanting to, without any reason to, he had been dear to us. We are told we should love only the good and the beautiful, and these are defined for us so narrowly. Monday I will be 31. Maybe it has taken me this long to discover that we are liable to love anything—like characters in old Greek stories who set eyes on an oak tree or a bucket and fall in love hopelessly, there are no limits to our love. . . .

Love,
Leslie

Dorothy Allred Solomon

orothy Allred Solomon grew up as one of forty-eight children in a family of fundamentalist Mormons who practiced the Principle of Plural Marriage. Her father was Dr. Rulon Allred, a highly respected naturopathic doctor and spiritual leader who was eventually murdered by a violent sect; her mother was one of seven wives.

Because polygamy is illegal, within the eyes of both the state and the Church of Latter-Day Saints (the official Mormon Church), Solomon grew up in a world circumscribed by secrets. If the truth came out, Solomon and her siblings could be taken from their parents. Her early childhood was happy, cared for by so many "mothers." Later, a crackdown by authorities scattered her family over several Western states. "Although we were reared to treasure truth and 'cling to the light,'" she wrote in her autobiography, In My Father's House (1984), "our way of life was filled with secrets. . . . The secrecy that separated our family from the rest of the world pressed us back on each other. . . . As I grew older, . . . I learned that it wasn't always easy to tell the truth, even when it had nothing to do with the Principle of Plural Marriage."

Solomon eventually left the religion in which she was raised, and she has dedicated much of her writing to telling the truth about that closed world—its strengths of love and spirituality and mutual *commitment as well as its limitations. In this essay, she has changed names and identifying characteristics to protect the privacy of those dear to her.*

Sister-Wife

I WONDER IF I HAVE THE RIGHT TO TELL ALMA'S story, even though hers is a singular story and some good may come of it. Something in Alma's life testifies to her humanity although we grew up in a family that aspires to godlike perfection. My people pride themselves in serving only divine will, yet Alma's ordeal has opened a plot of common human ground. She broke that ground while tracking her own shadow, and in claiming her dark side, achieved a kind of perfection.

Alma and I are sisters—half-sisters, really, but because my father insisted that in the Principle of Plural Marriage we were all one family, we called each other sister and meant it. Alma has other sisters, like Karen with her imperious beauty, but none so like herself as I. Born less than a year apart, both without birth certificates, we mirrored each other's right to be here.

Alma began a lifelong obsession with horses the night our mothers wrapped us in blankets and stuffed us into the backseat of the big green Hudson. Another raid was brewing; we must escape the authorities that could take us from our mothers, or put the grown-ups in jail as had happened before Alma and I were born. When we returned from Mexico three months later, Alma was nearly dead of dysentery. That brush with death got her a tall sorrel horse she named "Babe." She wasn't strong enough to hoist a saddle, so she'd leap from the fence and hang over his bare back and kick one leg across. Then, clutching his long mane, she'd streak across the bare fields. Aunt Leah said it was a caution: ladies rode side-saddle for a reason, and Ellen should stop that girl before it was too late. But Aunt Ellen gave her daughter what she wanted. In fact, everyone gave Alma what she wanted, everyone except her older sister, Karen. A fierce love burned between the sisters, as if Karen knew Alma's frailty and intended to train it to strength. Karen reminded Alma that in the United Order she could not really own a horse, it would belong to everyone, and Alma should start her hope chest like other girls in the family.

In 1955, when another polygamous roundup scattered our big family to the four winds, Alma left Babe with the neighbors and headed north with Karen and her mother. My mother and Aunt Betty took us west to Nevada while our father closed the doors to his naturopathic office and went into hiding. But Alma and I wrote faithfully to each other, postcards in first-grade printing and later, neat penmanship on pale pink paper.

Several years later, when the political climate cooled so that we could return to Utah, Alma began dating a feisty young man from our religious group. Rowdy had grown up on a quartershare in Montana being settled by our people into a township of ten-acre parcels, each family with its own land the way Brigham Young had said it should be. Rowdy knew how to ride horses and drive a tractor and make hay. He was attracted to Alma, and she to him.

He was free-spirited, and the brethren worried about him. Karen—who was married by then—said Alma could never keep such a wild horse in hand. Aunt Leah predicted he would one day leave the group, and said Alma was too tender to survive out in the world where the natural man rules and hearts are godless.

The spring we graduated from high school, Karen gave a slumber party for all the girls in my father's family. Karen's husband, Anson, had refurbished a strong brick dwelling with apartments upstairs and down. His second wife lived in the basement with her new baby and took care of Karen's three little children while we giggled and told stories about the old days. Yet my stomach cramped all evening, not from food or excitement, but because I felt ill at ease with my own sisters. By then I was questioning everything, even dating outside the group, and the mothers worried that I was becoming worldly. Perhaps my jaded view stained the innocence of girl-talk, but our remarks seemed barbed with darker, sharper truths than those spoken. Alma left the room to take a phone call, and when she returned, Karen spoke pointedly.

"See how he can't go a whole evening without calling? It isn't right for a man who's going to live the Principle to be so gone on one girl."

Alma didn't take her eyes off her older sister. "You think he has a weak character?"

"You're meant for someone like Anson—someone who can take a firm hand with you." Karen's voice carried the authority of all older sisters.

"But," I started to say, "if she loves Rowdy, then. . . ." Both sisters turned to look at me. I had the awkward sense that I'd broken into a conversation that had been going on for years.

The next time I saw Alma—it was a year or more later—she showed me her hope chest full of linens edged with hand-crocheted lace and embroidered flowers made while I was writing papers for my classes at the university. I shook my head and wondered what happened to the horses. She told me that she and Rowdy had broken up for good and she had decided to become Anson's third wife. The wedding ceremony would be so secret I was not invited.

I had jumped the fence around our religious group by then, and people I had known all my life called me trouble. So after a glass of lemonade, we hurried off in opposite directions. I didn't see Alma and Karen again until the shower for my own baby—a shower thrown by big-hearted Aunt Ellen who must have known that my due date was a bare eight months beyond my wedding. Alma was happy for me, seemed happy for everyone. She occupied the back bedroom of Karen's house; she was a sister-wife. And that is where Alma's story really begins, a story that in many ways excludes me. I only know of it through other family members, through a few spare words Alma and I spoke when it was over, and through the knowing that defies time and space—the knowing of the heart.

As potential Mothers in Israel, we had inherited the legacy of Sarah, who laughed in God's face when told she would have a son in her old age, then gave birth to Isaac. In our little field, a woman's raison d'être was to raise a righteous seed unto the Lord. What good was a woman among many women if she could not bear children? The childless women in our group often became strange and witch-like, with their herbs and their sorrow. Some stood in meeting and made prophecies that were discounted before they were even heard. A barren woman was at best a child to be patronized, and at worst a thing to be pitied.

When Alma did not conceive, Aunt Leah blamed it on bareback riding and lifting heavy saddles. But the infertility was more likely due to the staph infection she caught while assisting in our father's office during the first year of her marriage. The infection rampaged through her body and none of my father's herbs contained it. Eventually he prescribed purging antibiotics that left her pale and bedridden. She lay in the back bedroom, waiting for the tides of her life to turn.

The tides did not turn. They continued as if each wave, once set in motion, must ripple around the world. Most of the ripples had met the shore by the time Alma and I met in a restaurant near our father's office—turned into an insurance agency after his murder by a violent religious cult. By the time we met, Alma had made her decision and there was no changing it.

On the basis of our shared history, I imagine Alma on that night when everything became clear. In my mind's eye, I see her arriving after work to help with the birth of Karen and Anson's ninth child. I imagine her lapsing into a moment of pretense that the eight children bathed and dressed and kneeling before the fireplace are hers.

"We say our prayers to the fire," Joseph, the youngest, says in his satisfied way.

"We don't pray to the fire, Joseph," Alma says, uneasy because she sees in him a familiar self-righteousness. "We pray facing north—and we pray to God."

"But how do you know God is north?" Rachel asks. "I thought he was straight up." She points past red curls at the ceiling.

"Rachel, five minutes don't pass without you asking impossible questions." Alma sighs and straightens her long, lean frame. "We kneel facing north because that's where the Ten Tribes will come from when they rescue the remnant of Israel in the Last Days. Your grandfather used to say that the City of Enoch was translated to the North Star near Kolob, where God lives."

As I imagine the scene, I wonder if Alma believes the litanies she recites for Karen and Anson's children. I think she must have clung to belief in something—otherwise, how could she get through that day?

"Anson!" she calls as though she is his mother. "Anson, we're waiting!" Then to Rachel, "Get your father for prayers."

Perhaps Joseph leans against her, asking, "Where's Mama?" and Alma strokes his red curls. "Your mama is having a baby." Then Anson enters, that distant gaze in his cobalt eyes. He kneels before the fireplace, his back to everyone, the family patriarch doing his duty.

"Hush, now," Alma whispers to the children. "Fold your arms."

Anson gives her a bemused smile, then speaks in a deep trombone: "Our dear Father in Heaven." And the other voices chime in: "Our dear Father in Heaven."

Anson prays for rain. He prays for peace. He prays that dear Karen will be delivered safely. He prays that the Lord will bless dear Alma with the desire of her heart.

And after each plea, the children echo, "Please bless dear Alma with the desire of her heart."

Alma clenches her arms and holds her body rigid. Perhaps she can feel the wind in her mind or sparks crackling behind her eyelids. At last the prayer is over and the children file up to kiss Anson and Alma good night. And Rachel whispers shyly, "Will you tuck us in, Aunt Alma?"

She nods, feeling Anson's sticky gaze on her. At last the children are folded in, neat and silent as eight white sheets on linen shelves. Alma descends to the kitchen and mixes bread in the blue porcelain pan. The cool batter salves her nerves. From the back bedroom float the voices of Karen and Anson. They have phoned the midwife, and now they are choosing a name for the baby. As always, Anson has left things for the last minute—something Alma complains about when the girls at the sewing shop where she works are chatting over lunch. She tells them that he bought her gold wedding band only an hour before he slipped it on her finger. She doesn't tell them that it is the third wedding band he has bought, or that she has sister-wives. She could lose her job over that. She smiles wryly, remembering the ceremony where Karen took Alma's hand and offered it to Anson and he covered both their hands with his and then pushed the gold band onto her ring finger. Back then the band had been too tight. Now her fingers are so thin the ring swivels; it could easily be lost in the batter.

Karen mews weakly from the bedroom. "Alma, what are you doing in there?" This morning Karen's voice had been strident as ever. "I want you to be here when this baby comes." The hint of something behind Karen's firm words, something Alma has prayed for and dreamed of for years, now hovers almost palpably.

"I'll be in as soon as I've set the bread to rise," Alma calls back.

She reaches into the flour bin. She is as at home here as anywhere, had once decorated and lived in the back room where she will stay tonight. Anson put those walls up when she agreed to marry him. Karen had chosen the wallpaper. Sometimes Karen came into the new room, broom and dustcloth in hand, rousing Alma still curved within Anson's crescent form to explain that she had saved this room for last, wasn't it time they got up?

After the infection, Alma had moved. Now she is a guest, "Aunt Alma" come to delight the children with molasses cookies she has too much time to make, and little trinkets she can afford because she has no little ones of her own.

Of course, she has every right to be here. Each month she turns her paycheck over to Anson who manages their United Order. Karen's needs are great. Alma's needs are small: a few clothes, the little she eats—although she is better about eating, now. Alma gets dry satisfaction from providing for her older sister, who has given her so much—sewed her wedding dress, handed down shoes and half-completed diaries, and shared her husband. I'm a hand-me-down kind of girl, she thinks, then stops to rephrase her thoughts.

She pushes the dough away, then pulls it toward her, tugging it apart with each movement of her arms, reshaping it into something palatable and nourishing, something to replace the dark red pain that nearly ate her alive.

At first, time at the apartment complex where she dwelt among divorced people and old couples had been luxurious: on her nights with Anson, they played chess, read poetry aloud, slept in till 7 A.M. Perhaps his face softened during those mornings alone, whispering over cantaloupe and hot biscuits, sharing stories of his boyhood and choosing names for babies to come. But the babies didn't come.

"Alma, I forgot to wash the bedroom with disinfectant." Knowing Karen, I suspect she would have roused her sister from her reverie by now.

Alma hears her, rinses the dough from her hands, and dries

them carefully. She draws a bucket of warm water and pours in a pine-smelling disinfectant that turns it milky; the fragrance of birth. In fundamentalist homes, this smell signaled the advent of a new brother or sister or cousin, and now nieces and nephews. The smell brings tears to Alma's eyes. She pauses at the door of the bedroom, puts down the bucket, and closes her eyes until the tears are gone. Then, with a deep breath, she enters.

Anson's rawboned frame roosts at the bottom of the bed as he softly reads scriptures. Karen sits against the pillows, her dark hair spread across white pillowslips embroidered with pink roses and edged with handmade lace. Alma had worked those sheets and cases for a month and gave them to Karen at Christmas. Karen had smiled tearfully and vowed to use them only for special occasions, a promise that left Alma imagining what those occasions might be.

It had been a memorable Christmas, the same Christmas she had ended up in the hospital. Alma was strong enough by then to work twelve-hour shifts, but she had been fasting for seventy-two hours and Christmas bore down like a vise—the children opening their stockings, Karen's announcement that a new one was on the way. A queasiness in Alma's stomach rose to her heart. Just as everyone was sitting down to Christmas dinner, Alma rushed from the house, leaving her coat draped on the hall-tree and Karen open-mouthed beside Anson at the head of the table. Alma had rushed to her little car, had driven through the cold empty streets until it started snowing and she could no longer see. She vaguely felt the bump of the other car, the door press against her hip, the cold windshield soothing her forehead like the cool cloth the mothers had used when she was so sick in Mexico.

In Karen's bedroom, Alma presses a cloth dipped in ice-water to her sister-wife's forehead. But Karen removes it and sits up. She fixes Alma with her bright eyes and interrupts Anson's reading to ask, "Are you all right, Alma dear?"

Alma laughs and shakes her head. "You're the one in labor!"

She turns away and takes a cloth from the bundle of oven-sterilized towels. Anson begins reading again, his voice like soft thunder. Alma washes the headboard and footboard and the dresser with disinfectant, drying the wood as she goes. She wipes the knickknacks and the frame of Grandmother's picture. She remembers how, when we were children, Grandmother was always complaining about our noise. Yet, once in a while she would pull us onto her lap to examine the baby-dolls we carried everywhere, then tell of the days when she had ridden her mare bareback through the Star Valley countryside.

"I was a happy girl," she'd say.

"What happened?" we'd ask.

Grandmother would dip her white head, then raise it. "Too much to do. I had eight of my own, and when Cordelia died, with hers I had sixteen. Don't make overmuch of babies, my girls. Babies don't always bring happiness—and they always bring work." Now Karen speaks into the deep silence. "Anson, Alma and I need to have a little talk."

"Alma . . ." Karen begins after Anson leaves, "each time I've given birth, I've wanted . . ." her face bleaching white as bone, ". . . wanted to have the strength to . . . do this. Before it was just too hard. And we hoped that you would still . . . be able to. . . ." Karen swallows. "But now . . . with no chance for you at all . . . I worry about you . . . and I've been so blessed—"

She stops as pain grips her face. Then she says matter-of-factly, "My water just broke. I hope the midwife hurries."

Alma starts up. "I'll send Anson for her. . . ."

Alma tells Anson, then brings fresh sheets and helps Karen into a fresh nightgown. She glances out the window, toward the drive. "I wish they would hurry," she says to no one in particular. Anxiousness for the midwife mixes with relief that Anson is out of the room. Just she and Karen, sisters, after all is said and done. Karen can't help the way she is; she was born to organize other people's lives. And neither can Alma help wanting to be free of other people's fences. Sweetness rises in her breast as she goes down the hall and puts the wet nightgown and pillowslips and sheets into the washer. The fluids of her sister's body and her sister's baby stain the white cotton. She pours in a little bleaching powder. When the washer begins its cycle, she retreats to the bread rising in her sister's kitchen. The yeasty smell opens her head; the bubbles popping as she kneads the dough effervesce in her heart; she is grateful to perform the tasks of love in her sister's home tonight.

The practice of marrying sisters is not considered peculiar among our people. My own mother and her twin sister were married to my father and the bonds of twinness were never severed; they became Siamese twins of the heart. Uncle Lawrence had married three sisters; even with the law watching him they had lived together in the same house and reared each other's children. Some men said it was easier to live the Principle if the women already knew how to live together, how to share.

Aunt Ilene had shared her sixth baby with Aunt Letha—let Letha name it and keep it in her bed at night. And Alma knows a family where the wives had not been sisters, not even relatives, but became the best of friends. The younger woman had given birth to seven children, while the older woman waited. Finally she was beyond child-bearing, and the younger woman gave her eighth baby to her sister-wife. The older woman had taken the child and raised it lovingly, a little boy who became his father's favorite. According to the story passed through our group, the younger woman had never interfered in the child's upbringing or tried to claim his gifts as her own. And the older woman had never reneged her motherhood. When the boy died in a motorcycle accident, the biological mother comforted her sister-wife as any sister would comfort a mother who lost her son. Although Alma had seen the two women at weddings and funerals, their legend preceded them, made people stand apart and stare at them, so often were they held up as the example of true sisterly love.

Sisterly love. It doesn't always look the way you think it should look. Alma watches the bread rise and listens. No sound from the bedroom. Perhaps the pains have stopped altogether. She gathers a slab of shortening and smooths it inside twelve blackened tins. Aunt Hilda had waited twelve years for her firstborn. Aunt Betty had waited eighteen years. But in Alma's case, time and faith have made no difference. She knows now it does no good to hold it against God, or Anson or Karen, either. She takes a deep breath, lifts the dough and throws it on the board. She can forgive Karen—even forgive Anson, too, if she can forgive herself. What will she forgive herself for? For riding horses? For getting sick? For being bare ground where seeds will not take root?

She works the dough into a smooth sphere. Once she had believed that if she were careful enough, had faith enough, all problems could be anticipated and solved. First she tried the herbal teas: althea, uvedalia, camphor, camomile. Then the powders, roots ground between mortar and pestle, sometimes moistened into salves: squaw root, birth bark, ergot. Then the exercises and the massages. Our father did everything he knew—used every chiropractic correction, every diathermal and ultraviolet machine. He referred her to people inside the group and gave her the names of colleagues in the medical community. The midwives of the religious group told her everything they knew about healing and fertility. There was a problem: her womb sat at an odd angle. But if she drank the teas diligently, if she put her faith in the Almighty, if she lay perfectly still on a slanted board afterward. . . .

Anson didn't like her going to doctors outside the group. Faith would be enough, he said. Their lives would prove that the Lord uses weak things of the flesh to accomplish his purposes. So she began fasting. Once a week for twenty-four hours, on her day off, she denied herself food and even water, spending most of the day on her knees. After two years she had increased the fasts to forty-eight hours, and six months later, to seventy-two. A three-day fast culminating at Christmas dinner preceded the accident.

She doesn't remember the crash. What she remembers is waking on the stretcher, Karen stroking her face like a mother with a sick child, saying, "Don't worry, darling, it will be all right." A siren shrilled so loud it seemed to be coming from inside her body.

They rushed her into the emergency room strapped down on a stretcher, Karen squeezing her left hand, and stroking her face, not minding the blood on her hands. By this time, Alma was certain that she was in labor, in the throes of an abnormal birth that had forced them to the hospital. She was oblivious to the huge lump lifting the hair on her brow, of the blood trickling across her left temple, was aware only of wrenching contractions. Soon there would be a child, the girl she had dreamed of named after her mother. That was all she could see, feel, believe, and so it must be true. All other semblances were only shadows.

Alma throws the perfect ball of dough down and punches it to shatter the silver image of herself on the hospital cart. But the image is not a glass to be broken, not an illusion. Like boiling soup it bubbles up, irreducible and real, its unforgettable traces seared in her mind.

As she shapes the dough in Karen's kitchen, bright fragments of memory fall like shards of a mirror. She hears herself calling out, "Hurry! It's time!" And Karen's martyred smile, and the emergency nurse running cold hands across Alma's arching stomach, then snapping on a milky glove to search beneath the sheet, then gazing into Karen's sad eyes while she, Alma, searched them for good news.

The emergency personnel took her into a room with doors that closed, strapped her to the bed, pried her fingers from Karen's, and left her wild-eyed and talking to the great white light which broke over her in waves like the white hot pain in her head. At last, the resident physician arrived, his white coat too big for him, his voice like warm milk.

"I'm Dr. Monroe. I'm getting you out of this," he said, unbuckling one strap, then the other. He lifted the sheet; his fingers gently probed. Then, sitting on the bed, brown eyes like soft earth drawing Alma down from her hot, white ride, he said, "Alma, you are not having a baby. Do you understand that? Tell me what's causing you so much pain."

And then the storm of weeping, while the young man rocked her like a baby. Then the blurting of secrets she had sworn to keep. About the Principle, about Anson, about Karen.

The young doctor sat still and silent for a long time. "Maybe if you and your husband could go away alone for a while—"

Alma shook her head and blew her nose, hard. "They think I'm jealous. And I am. And I have no right to be jealous." Tears ran like thin flames down her cheeks. "When we were married, my father asked, 'Why do you enter into this covenant?' and I knew it wasn't enough to say 'Because that's what I'm supposed to do.' That isn't reason enough. Our people serve God. And so I gave the right answer: 'To raise a righteous seed unto the Lord.'" Her voice thinned to hard wire. "It's the only good reason to live the Principle. And I can't fulfill it."

In the silence, the volcanic sphere was restored to clean, hard corners, right angles and solid lines.

The young doctor examined her again. "Let me talk to your husband. Things can be done. Amazing advances in fertility research."

Alma pressed a hand against her flat stomach. "He says we must have faith," she whispered.

"Medical intervention requires faith, too," the doctor said. "I'll talk to him." And then for no apparent reason, he laughed. And Alma thought of Sarah, mirthful in the face of the impossible.

Now she breaks the big ball of dough into twelve parts, then shapes the white loaves and sticks them in their black tins and covers them with cheesecloth. She stares out the window into the empty night, her reflection shimmering like a mirage.

Anson had visited her in the hospital. Her head was swathed in gauze, but her eyes were bright. She introduced him to the young doctor, gesticulating in a frantic dance of fingers, her heart rising in a joyous wave.

"Please, Anson," Alma pleaded when Dr. Monroe left.

Anson had shook his head and blushed. "The problem's not with me, Alma. I have children."

So began her lonely visits to the fertility clinic, the humiliation of tests that lit up her insides for the camera and then the medications and much later, the exploratory surgery, finding what blocked the way. And the bills, requiring longer hours at work. At the hospital she was always alone—even when her mother and Karen were there, she felt an aloneness so deep and long it seemed to have begun with her own birth.

Anson came to visit her when she was recovering from one surgery.

"Why did you come?" she asked.

"You are my other rib," he said gently.

"Then I'm a broken rib." She gritted her teeth to keep the tears back.

"Don't worry, Alma. You still have one ovary. God can do anything—even if there were no ovaries, He would bless you with a child if you had enough faith. Think of Sarah of Old. Think of Aunt Hilda."

And she pulled back from him and looked him straight in the face. "They've done everything they can for me, Anson. Now they need your help. There's a process that increases the chances fifty percent. They've done it with cows and mares for a long time. Artificial insemination."

Anson flushed. "Alma, we are not animals."

"But Anson—you have children. You don't know what it's like. . . ."

"We must have faith. We must fast and pray."

This made her shriek. If she had been stronger she'd have gone after him with her nails. "We! I have had faith! Enough to let them cut me open!" She pulled herself up, ignoring the stab of pain and grabbed his hand. "Please, Anson. Dr. Monroe says it's simple. They just take you into a little room, and give you a little jar and leave you alone. No one will see. No one will even know!"

A look of repulsion crossed his face and he backed away. "God would know."

And that was when her heart sank like a stone into a red sea of rage. When she spoke, her voice was authoritative. "It isn't me who has no faith. It's you." And her mouth closed like a dead-bolt.

That was when she truly began to live alone. She attended counseling sessions with a kind, strong woman who urged Alma to stand up for herself, to do everything possible to fulfill herself. She endured more surgeries. And when the surgeries didn't change anything, she applied to adopt as a single parent. But the adoption worker knew her maiden name as that of a polygamous family and terminated the process.

She visited Dr. Monroe one last time to say goodbye. There was no need to come back, with nothing left inside for him to fool with. Dr. Monroe promised that if he came across a baby through "channels," she would be the first to know.

"You'd do that for me?" Alma asked. "Why?"

He shrugged. "Because I want you to be happy."

Alma gathered her things in a whirl, banging her hip on the corner of the desk as she backed out the door. "Thank you," she whispered. "In the meantime, I'm going to . . . make myself happy."

And she had made herself happy. She found other seeds inside herself and saw them sprout and flourish. Her work took on new

dimension as she moved from tailoring to sewing wedding gowns.
She began to enjoy coffee breaks with the seamstresses, drinking
hot lemonade while they smoked and stirred sugar into their black
coffee. Wednesday afternoons, she took classes in dressmaking and
fashion design. At night, at a drafting table set up in the corner of
her apartment, she designed wedding gowns and trousseaus and
maternity dresses. Each had an old-fashioned flair. She bought a
stereo system and a tape library of Mozart, Beethoven, Chopin to
listen to as she worked. Anson's infrequent visits interrupted her
concentration. Even on the nights he slept at her apartment, she
stayed up late, the light of the drafting table throwing her magnified silhouette on the wall.

"Come to bed, Alma," Anson would say.

"I've work to do, Anson," she murmured.

"Don't lose sight of that which is truly important," he intoned,
as if reading from the scriptures.

She said nothing. Perhaps she had lost sight of what was truly
important. But children's clothing—long crinolines, calicos, pina-
fores—spun in her mind. Someday she would sew her creations.
Her name would be finely embroidered at the neck of every gar-
ment. Little children would go into the world dressed as apparitions
of light. A quiet glow would illuminate the halls of singular lives.

One year she held back her checks from the United Order to
buy a trailer and some land. Then she moved to a rural district outside the city. She adopted a wild filly through the Adopt-a-Horse
Program. It was absurdly easy. The officials didn't check for polygamous heritage; they only checked the size of the acreage, and made
her sign a paper promising not to sell the horse for three years. She
named the two-year filly Spirit. And gradually, the sky became
vivid, the wind stronger, water so very clear. Trees and flowers
seemed limned in rainbows of light. She came home from dressmaking to work with Spirit, gentling her to hackamore, then bit and
bridle, walking the horse with the weight of the saddle, then a bag

of feed, and then, finally, her own body. Astride the filly, Alma was whole.

But now, with Karen offering her ninth child, Alma's fine balance wavers. Karen wants to change the balance. Anson wants to change the balance. Perhaps even God wants to change the balance. Suddenly the dark window washes with headlights. The midwife hurries in with her little bag of instruments, Anson behind her. Alma ushers the birdlike woman to the bedroom and meets Anson at the bedroom door.

"I wish it was you, Alma," he says.

She steps back. "Don't, Anson. I'm fine. Really, I am. And so are you. Now get in there where you belong."

Always before, Alma had stayed in the room during Karen's birthings, standing at the foot of the bed as if trying to learn the miracle by heart. But tonight when Karen calls to her, Alma brings a cold towel for her forehead, ice for her cracked lips, then disappears to the kitchen to test the bread's golden crust, warm waves filling the house like good will. She doesn't want to watch Karen's face or the little head crowning. She wants to be strong enough to accept what is real, to serve others as she can, like these loaves of bread with honey and fresh milk. And when the midwife calls, "Come quickly, Alma, it's time!" and Anson's soft rumble, "Alma, quick—you'll miss it!" Alma calls back, "As soon as I get this bread out of the oven." And then the baby's burbling cry, and it is too late.

Later, when the loaves are turned out of their tins and the crusts swathed in butter, when Karen and the baby have been bathed, and when the midwife has bestowed a shadowy kiss and "I'm just sorry it wasn't you, Alma," just as the grandfather clock strikes the midnight hour, Karen's voice drifts down the hall. "Alma . . . Alma, darling. Please come here."

AND SO Alma gets up from the table where she has been staring out at the night, and she walks down the hall.

"Alma . . ." Karen reaches for her.

Alma kisses her sister's supple cheek. "Giving birth seems to make you younger," she smiles.

"Alma . . ." Karen takes a deep breath. Foreboding and excitement rise from Alma's stomach into her chest. Grimacing with an afterpain, Karen grips Alma's hand for a moment, then takes the small white bundle and holds it out. "Take this." Alma takes it, holds it close, peers at the little face.

And then Karen's voice, a strange mix of light and pain. "I want you to name her and keep her as if she were your own."

Alma looks at Karen, then back at the baby. Her heart thunders in her ears. She forces herself to breathe slow and deep. Her own? Her own sister's child. Her husband's child. Almost like her own.

Now, looking down at the tiny, wrinkled face, she is filled with a temptation strong as starvation. Something to fill her life. She looks past Karen's strangled smile.

"If ye be the son of God, turn these stones into bread." She could take it, keep it, let the world witness her worth.

Alma holds the baby close; the warmth fills her chest and spreads into the cavity of her womb. "As if she were your own." Perhaps a flicker of recognition flits through the baby's blank blue eyes. And in that instant she knows: something of this child belongs to her. Just as something of Joseph and Rachel, of Karen and Anson, and even of Dr. Monroe—in some way everyone belongs to her. There is no "as if." It is, or it isn't.

She looks at her sister. There's no use pretending that she can do things Karen's way. The Ten Tribes aren't coming to rescue her. On earth we must rescue ourselves, must reach with open arms to receive salvation. We must permit ourselves to be refined into something pure, something worth offering to God.

"Karen, thank you. But it wouldn't work." A surprising triumph lifts her voice and her heart as she speaks. She holds out the baby. "She's beautiful, Karen. But she's yours—yours and Anson's."

"But . . . but what will you do?"

"Live my life, Karen. It's precious—precious as that baby's."

Open-mouthed, staring, Karen takes the child, her tears suddenly gone.

Alma notices that her heart still beats strong, and that this bright fullness has not left her. Illusions take up a lot of space. When they are gone, life flows in naturally.

As she walks down the hall, Anson stops her. "Did Karen tell you? Isn't it a miracle—her giving so much?"

Alma smiles. "She told me. But I couldn't. Karen has already given so much to me. Besides . . . don't you know, Anson? The miracle had already happened."

She decides not to spend the night here—no matter how it looks. She floats on a draft out the door of the wonderful old house. There she stands, looking up. From habit, she searches out the Pole Star, then throws her arms skyward.

"Thank you, God," she says, surrendering to the countless bright holes in the blue blanket of the sky.

Kathleen Tyau

Kathleen Tyau was raised in a large Chinese-Hawaiian family on the island of Oahu. Until she left the island to attend college on the "mainland," at Lewis and Clark College in Portland, Oregon, she had always been in the majority. "I'm one-eighth Hawaiian, the rest Chinese, and maybe a pinch of Portuguese," she said in an interview in Glimmer Train. "I'm amazed at white Americans who don't think of themselves in terms of fractions. I can't imagine growing up without being aware of race. Race was present at every party, at every meal. For Thanksgiving we ate Chinese noodles and Japanese sushi with our roast turkey and stuffing. In Hawaii racial issues take on some strange forms. For example, my stepfather belonged to the Masonic Lodge. I remember asking him if he felt any discrimination. He said, 'No, but I told them we should start letting in more haoles [white people].' "

Tyau has written for as long as she can remember. She had her first piece published at the age of thirteen when the Honolulu Star Bulletin bought an essay titled "I Love Boys" for one dollar. More recently she has published essays and short fiction in a variety of periodicals including ZYZZYVA, Glimmer Train, and Left Bank. Her first collection of short stories, A Little Too Much Is

Enough, *was published by Farrar, Straus and Giroux in 1995.*
Here, she remembers the racial confusion that confronted her during
her first years of college.

The City I Colored White

THE PHOTOGRAPHER CIRCLED AROUND US, SNAP-
ping pictures. A stranger to us, he had strolled into the dining room
where my friend Alex and I sat at a table, talking. The other college
students had long since left. With every click of his camera, the photographer drew closer and closer until he crouched next to us,
pointing the camera straight at our faces. Intent on our conversation, we had ignored him until that moment.

"Do you mind?" said Alex, turning to the photographer.
"We're trying to have a conversation."

That's not entirely true, I wanted to add, but I was too embarrassed to lift my head. *It's more than that. We're breaking up.* But that
wasn't completely true either. How could we end what we'd never
had? The photographer took one last snapshot, then left.

I often wonder what happened to those pictures, taken years
ago when I was a college sophomore. How we must have looked to
this stranger, who saw us only as unusual subjects to photograph:
Alex, with his long, bony Nordic face, blond hair, cream-colored
fisherman's knit sweater and jeans; me, some kind of Asian with a
streak of dark blood and long, black hair, wearing a navy blue mo-
hair sweater and dark corduroy pants—a biracial couple, suitable
for shooting in black and white. Yet we never were a real couple,
never a match, and it seems ironic that a stranger memorialized our
inequality.

Alex (not his real name) was one of the first white men I came to know when I left my home in Hawaii to go to college in Oregon over twenty years ago. Although I never saw him again after graduation, our peculiar friendship has continued to puzzle me over the years.

I HAD LOOKED FORWARD TO going to the mainland for college. My mother was excited too, because she would be flying with me. We planned to visit relatives in California, go to Disneyland and Knotts Berry Farm, then head north to Oregon. There, my mother would help me set up a checking account, buy me some winter clothes, and make sure I was settled safely in the dorm.

A few weeks before we left the islands, my mother refused to let me go hiking with friends.

"You might break your leg," she said. "And then you won't be able to go away to school."

Later, as I packed my trunk, she said, "You don't have to go if you don't want to."

Neither of those statements may seem odd for a parent to say to a child leaving home, but for me, they reflect the ambivalence my mother had felt about leaving the islands herself. During the Second World War, after graduating from high school on the island of Oahu, my mother attended beauty school in San Francisco. When I was a child, I pored over photographs of my mother taken just before she left Hawaii.

In these photos she wears dresses tucked at the waist, orchids pinned above her left breast, her hair swept up in the style of the day. Even though the pictures are in black and white, her smiling lips gleam red. She was a beauty, the glamour girl I wanted to be. I scrutinized her photos, searching for my own features. I placed this vision of my mother in San Francisco and projected my likeness of her into my own dream city. I wanted to leave home and study on the mainland, just as my mother had.

San Francisco was a city I colored white, even though many of its inhabitants were not. I imagined life on the mainland through stories told by traveling relatives, photographs, television, and books. My scenes of a white America were never precise, blurred by all I did not know. Flying to the States, as we called the mainland U.S., was not common in the days before Hawaii became a state. The propeller-driven planes took eight hours or more to reach the West Coast, and natives of the islands did not leave except to go away to college or into the service.

Some years later—I don't remember exactly when—I asked my mother to tell me more about those years that were so magical in my mind. She confessed that she'd been unhappy and lonely in San Francisco. She had lived with a Chinese couple, paid them for room and board, but they didn't feed her enough.

"I was so hungry," she said. "I ate the burned rice that stuck to the bottom of the pot." She soaked the hard rice in hot water to make it soft.

AT MY MOTHER'S FUNERAL several years ago, one of her sisters pointed out a Japanese man sitting in the funeral parlor.

"He was your mother's boyfriend in high school," my aunt said.

It was then that I recalled something else my mother had told me about her stay in San Francisco, about how her father had sent her away so she wouldn't marry her high school boyfriend. As a child, I had seen pictures of him in the family photo albums at my grandmother's house. He was Japanese. When I asked my mother about him, she said he was just a friend, but now I realize that her father did not want her to marry this boy because of his race, because of the war with Japan. Besides, a respectable Chinese girl should marry Chinese, preferably of the same dialect.

What if my mother had been in my place, twenty-five years later? How would she have liked going to school with mostly whites and only a few Hawaiians, a sprinkling of Asian students from overseas, and a very small number of blacks? What would she think of my friend Alex? Even without the war, my grandfather still would have objected to her marrying outside her race. The fact that she fell in love with a Japanese boy against her parents' wishes suggested that she might have been like me. Curious, willing to challenge the expected.

While I was growing up in Hawaii, I was familiar with only a handful of white people, or *haoles,* as we called them. At school I played with service kids, most of them *haoles* from the mainland, but I never invited them to visit me at home. Not because my parents forbade me, but because it just wasn't done. Neither did I venture into their homes—the officers' quarters near Pearl Harbor or the enlisted men's housing across the way. The *haoles* who came to our house were mainly people who had grown up in the islands, tourists, or family friends. We welcomed them warmly and were close to some of them, but this didn't prepare me for living among whites in Oregon.

Sharing a dormitory with white women thrilled me. I thought of them as cameos, rosebuds, pale beauties I had admired from a distance. Now I would be close to them, and I hoped their attractiveness and style would rub off on me. Yet I felt awkward as a freshman. My clothes didn't look as fine as my dormmates'. Everything I wore seemed too flowery, too thin and bright, in contrast with the camel wool and creamy cashmere. Everything felt different—the clothes, the listless rice in the dining hall, the slang words, the way my roommates walked around in panties and bras, the tall, white men they dated.

I DON'T REMEMBER HOW I MET ALEX. He was an upperclassman. We had no mutual friends or classes. I believe he just saw me on campus, found out my name and called. We didn't "date" in the sense of going to football games, holding hands, partying with friends. Instead, we sat in the basement of my dormitory and talked about Nietzsche, Kierkegaard, the Soviet Union, John Cage.

On one of our rare evenings out, he took me to see a movie, *Lust for Life*, about the painter Vincent Van Gogh. I enjoyed the movie, my first "art" film; the night, how cool and misty it was; what I wore, a red-and-white knit top with a matching red wool skirt. I felt American in my Bobbie Brooks outfit bought in Oregon, not in the islands. Alex had borrowed his parents' car, and I was pleased to finally be out on a real date with him. But when we got back to the campus, he asked, "How did you feel about those people who stared at you?"

"What people?" I replied, trying to remember faces, but I could only recall his, upon which I had focused throughout most of the evening, even in the theater, where I had glanced at him to check his reactions to the film.

"The people on the street," he said. "When we were walking back to the car."

I remembered them then, the man and woman who had looked our way. I had stared at them too. The woman's dark hair fell below her waist, and I had coveted her boots, which rose way above her knees.

"I thought they were looking at you," I replied. That was why I hadn't remembered them right away, because I had presumed that Alex, with his blond hair and fair skin, was the one who looked strange, not me.

ALEX AND I TALKED A LOT ABOUT RACE. One day, he asked me, "How does it feel to be in the minority?"

"I don't know," I said. "I've always been in the majority. Where I come from, *haoles* are in the minority." I was adamant, matter-of-fact, but again, as on that night of the movie, I was surprised, and a blemish began to erupt in the image I held of myself.

I remember these words because my conversations with other college friends did not dwell so much on race. With them I discussed politics, but not race, at least not in a way that was personal to me. We talked about the Kennedys, Martin Luther King, the South, civil rights—but not Kathleen from the island of Oahu. My best friend (from Cody, Wyoming, the home of Wild Bill Cody) told about describing me to another student. She told him to look for a girl of medium height with long, black hair, rather than identifying me by race. She laughed as she told me this. She said she had forgotten to say I was Chinese-Hawaiian because, as she pointed out, my race didn't matter to her. I don't believe she ignored my race for lack of importance, but rather because she wanted me to know it made no difference to our friendship. It was this *indifference* that was absent in my relationship with Alex. I resented his interest, his careful tolerance. He forced me to acknowledge who I was, when what I really wanted was to forget.

A FRACTION OF HAWAIIAN BLOOD makes me taller, bigger than other Chinese-American women. Next to me my Chinese and Japanese girlfriends looked like dolls. The only advantage to being five foot seven was that I could wear clothes made for *haoles*. I didn't have to take up huge hems in dresses and pants. Yet, a part of me wanted to be small and look like the other Chinese girls. I was ashamed of my Hawaiian features, the dark skin and large bones that set me apart. I was not Chinese enough, yet not truly Hawaiian. I didn't feel like I belonged to either race.

So I longed to be *hapa haole*, part white, to merge with white skin and culture. I wanted to *think* like *haoles*, have what they had. Somehow I equated this with settling my own racial confusion. Even as a minority, *haoles* held positions of power. They owned the sugar and pineapple plantations, managed the lands held in trust for Hawaiians, controlled the politics of the islands. They wrote the books I studied in school; they wrote Hawaiian history, *my* history. Of course, I kept my feelings to myself. Although the Hawaiian sovereignty movement was not strong or widespread at that time, we "locals" still distrusted and ridiculed *haoles*. And envied, I should add. But to cross to the other side, to desire—this was something I could never admit.

ONE DAY AS I WALKED ON CAMPUS, a black woman joined me. She had come from a southern state on a special scholarship designed to bring black students to our college. As she told me about the problems she and the other blacks were having, she talked as if the whites were *them* and the blacks were *us*. I can remember thinking that this wasn't true. I didn't identify with her at all. I couldn't commiserate because I really didn't know what it was like to be outnumbered. My friends in the islands were Chinese, Japanese, Korean, Portuguese, Hawaiian, Filipino, *haole*—pure or mixed in some kind of combination. We lumped the mainland *haoles* into one group, and the rest of us constituted the other—the *kama'ainas*, the natives. We were clearly the majority. We traded racist jokes, poking fun at each other's race, often brutally, but always in jest. At the same time, we believed the advertisements we read about or saw on television, that Hawaii was a "melting pot," simmering contentedly, never boiling. We didn't fight or riot. I had no idea what this black woman from Alabama was talking about. My close friends in Oregon were white. I only attended Hawaiian parties on campus to which these friends could be invited. I wanted to be exotic, not political.

WITH ALEX I felt like Audrey Hepburn in *My Fair Lady*, learning to speak the King's English, except that what he taught me was commoner's Northwest. He taught me to say "ruff" instead of "roof" and "crik" instead of "creek." Yet, as we talked about philosophy, poetry, and art, the conversation always seemed to turn to race—usually mine. Pointing out my pidgin accent, my poor choice of words, and my lack of understanding of ordinary American sayings, Alex reminded me about how different I was. To me, Alex set the standard for the kind of white American I wanted to be. I felt hurt, embarrassed, but instead of defending myself, I asked him to teach me. I allowed him to scrutinize me, to help me become more American.

I like to believe he meant well, that he was genuinely interested and wanted to understand me. With Alex I couldn't pretend my race didn't matter. Yet as we discussed our differences, even in a gentle way, he seemed so sure and confident that I felt certain I could never be good enough.

Alex stood for something I didn't have. It was the *connection* I wanted. The feeling of not being different, of belonging. On the day the photographer fell upon us like a hawk, Alex and I had symbolically dressed the part. Maybe that's why I remember our contrasting hair and clothes so vividly. Our relationship failed in black and white, in what we wore and how we looked, and more.

I THOUGHT IT would be so simple for me to leave home and go away to school to Oregon. My mother had had a difficult time in California, but I thought this was because of the era in which she grew up—a prejudiced, unenlightened time—not at all like the sixties. I wasn't afraid my parents would send me away if I fell in love with someone outside of my race. I planned to leave home before they had the chance to stop me, so I could sample the forbidden on my own. Going away to school would be different for me, far better than my mother's exiled years in San Francisco. I chose Oregon because it was far away from Hawaii and not too close to my relatives in California. Oregon was my frontier.

I TRY TO PICTURE my mother meeting a man like Alex when she was my age. Would she have dated a white man? I remember her telling me how some people on the mainland mistook her for a "Jap." How she felt uncomfortable around those people even after they found out she was Chinese. At most, she could probably only observe white men from a distance.

I fantasize. What if she saw a white man on the trolley in San Francisco and followed him to a coffee shop on Fisherman's Wharf? Would she have caught his attention? Would they have found an opportunity to speak? But then I realized that she would not have been able to admire him discreetly. All eyes would have been focused on her. On what she was doing outside of Chinatown. On why she didn't go back to where she belonged. She would not like having people stare at her and would get up suddenly, jostling the waitress, spilling coffee in his lap. That's when he would finally look up, when her eyes would be searching for the door.

That's as far as I get. She does not parry playfully with him, articulate and bold, like the vivacious woman I see in her photographs. They don't date or become friends, and they certainly don't marry. But would she have felt awkward if the man had asked her about her race? How much did she grapple with what it meant to be Chinese living in America? Even though a problem of race had brought her to San Francisco, at least her boyfriend had been Asian. But a white man? I cannot imagine.

Perhaps my mother's years in San Francisco helped her to accept my first husband. I was the second in my family to marry a white man. I remember how upset my cousin's parents were when she became engaged to a *haole* from the mainland. They changed their minds when they saw their own prejudice reflected in *his* parents' doubts and *her*.

I CARRY THOSE PICTURES OF ALEX AND ME, the ones taken years ago by a stranger, not in my wallet, but in my memory of how it felt to be transplanted to foreign soil. We hang on a wall somewhere, nameless. "Who are they?" the photographer's friends ask, and he replies, "Don't they make a striking couple?" I wonder, does he ask himself, "What were they saying? How did they feel?" Has he made up a story for us, re-created what we meant to each other on that day and the days before? Has he figured out what happened to us in the end? He could not have known that Alex was telling me he planned to marry a white woman, someone he had known since grade school. While Alex spoke, all I could think of was that she was white. *She was white and I was not, I was not, I was not.* Perhaps the photographer thought of us only as a study in black and white. An abstraction, nothing more.

In those pictures, I don't have a voice. I was unable to say much at the time they were taken. I'd like to tell the photographer that I wasn't myself in those pictures. I wasn't yet comfortable with my own skin, with the intricacies of taking on a new culture without abandoning the old. Even now, living among white people in Oregon or visiting my family in Hawaii, there are times when I hover on the edges of conversations. I feel the boundaries of my body etched very precisely, separating me from people I care about and love. They know me only in the context of their lives in Hawaii *or* the mainland, not the collage of both that I have created over the years.

I'm not sure what Alex wanted from me or what I meant to him, and I am only now discovering what I wanted from him. Answers, clues, tools, anything to take me across the line. I thought that only on the other side could I be whole, because to me, being white meant to be complete. I did not yet know that insecurity and imperfection ignore the color of one's skin.

RECENTLY I DISCOVERED that I may have a small fraction of Portuguese blood from my mother's side of the family.

"One thirty-second," my uncle told me. Just a little, not enough to really matter.

But it does, of course. It does matter. Here I am, finally, possi-

bly part white, although the Portuguese in Hawaii are not traditionally thought of as *haoles.*

"It's funny," my uncle said, "because nobody in our family *acts
Pohtagee,* if you know what I mean."

Pohtagees, as we call them, have had to overcome another peculiar strain of racial prejudice, one that accuses them of being *not
white enough.* And they face the same problems of stereotype that all
of the racial groups in Hawaii have had to overcome.

"But why isn't it on my birth certificate?" I asked. "Why
haven't I known?"

"I don't know," he said. "We all knew. I guess we just didn't
talk about it."

Perhaps it's only fitting that now—after I have finally come to
appreciate and forgive the Hawaiian and Chinese in me, when I finally feel like my broken halves are put back together and make
sense and feel good—I face the irony of being part white—maybe.
Not really *haole,* not the "right" kind of white. I wonder why my
family didn't talk about this. Why, if it's true, our Portuguese blood
is not recorded. Maybe the confusion hasn't been mine alone. I long
to know about my Portuguese ancestors, if in fact they really exist. I
want to hear their stories, just as I have hungrily devoured my Hawaiian and Chinese family histories.

EVEN THOUGH I AM still a blurred image, I'm not the girl in
those black-and-white photographs. I welcome my new piece of
history. I'd like to replay those earlier years, give them an easier
beginning. Yet, that photographed scene plays again from time to
time, and I remember the flash of that moment, when a stranger
captured me as I was then, confused, suspended in time and place,
still struggling to understand and belong.

Evelyn C. White

E velyn C. White grew up as the eldest of five children in a working-class family in Gary, Indiana. She graduated with a bachelor's degree in drama from Wellesley and worked as a lighting designer in Denmark. She moved to Seattle, Washington, to enter the directing program at the University of Washington but eventually left the theater and became a legal advocate for battered women through the city attorney's Family Violence Project. Because of this work, she was asked to write a book about black women and abuse.

"I found that I liked to write," White says about the experience, "and that I had a knack for it. But the biggest shock was that someone would pay me for it. I remember the day I signed the book contract. Here I was, sitting in a fancy restaurant, being paid for signing my name. That idea was so far removed from my heritage as a black person whose ancestors had been forbidden to read or write. It made me aware of how far black people had traveled. I took it very seriously."

White earned a master's in journalism from Columbia University in 1985 and a master's in public administration from Harvard University in 1991. She has been on the reporting staff of the San Francisco Chronicle since 1986. Her books include Chain Chain Change: For Black Women Dealing with Physical and Emotional Abuse (1985) and The Black Women's Health Book:

Speaking for Ourselves *(1990; second edition 1994). She is co-author of the photography book* The African Americans *(1993). Always, she has tried to write clearly and compassionately about the concerns of black women, too often overlooked in the majority press.*

Black Women and the Wilderness

I wanted to sit outside and listen to the roar of the ocean, but I was afraid.
I wanted to walk through the redwoods, but I was afraid.
I wanted to glide in a kayak and feel the cool water splash in my face, but I was afraid.

FOR ME, THE FEAR IS LIKE A HEARTBEAT, ALWAYS present, while at the same time, intangible, elusive, and difficult to define. So pervasive, so much a part of me, that I hardly knew it was there.

In fact, I wasn't fully aware of my troubled feelings about nature until I was invited to teach at a women's writing workshop held each summer on the McKenzie River in the foothills of Oregon's Cascade Mountains. I was invited to Flight of the Mind by a Seattle writer and her friend, a poet who had moved from her native England to Oregon many years before. Both committed feminists, they asked me to teach because they believe, as I do, that language and literature transcend the manmade boundaries that are too often placed upon them. I welcomed and appreciated their interest in me and my work.

Once I got there, I did not welcome the steady stream of invitations to explore the great outdoors. It seemed like the minute I finished my teaching duties, I'd be faced with a student or fellow faculty member clamoring for me to trek to the lava beds, soak in the hot springs, or hike into the mountains that loomed over the site like white-capped security guards. I claimed fatigue, a backlog of classwork, concern about "proper" student/teacher relations; whatever the excuse, I always declined to join the expeditions into the woods. When I wasn't teaching, eating in the dining hall, or attending our evening readings, I stayed holed up in my riverfront cabin with all doors locked and windowshades drawn. While the river's roar gave me a certain comfort and my heart warmed when I gazed at the sun-dappled trees out of a classroom window, I didn't want to get closer. I was certain that if I ventured outside to admire a meadow or to feel the cool ripples in a stream, I'd be taunted, attacked, raped, maybe even murdered because of the color of my skin.

I believe the fear I experience in the outdoors is shared by many African-American women and that it limits the way we move through the world and colors the decisions we make about our lives. For instance, for several years now, I've been thinking about moving out of the city to a wooded, vineyard-laden area in Northern California. It is there, among the birds, creeks, and trees that I long to settle down and make a home.

Each house-hunting trip I've made to the countryside has been fraught with two emotions: elation at the prospect of living closer to nature and a sense of absolute doom about what might befall me in the backwoods. My genetic memory of ancestors hunted down and preyed upon in rural settings counters my fervent hopes of finding peace in the wilderness. Instead of the solace and comfort I seek, I imagine myself in the country as my forebears were—exposed, vulnerable, and unprotected—a target of cruelty and hate.

I'm certain that the terror I felt in my Oregon cabin is directly linked to my memories of September 15, 1963. On that day, Denise McNair, Addie Mae Collins, Cynthia Wesley, and Carol Robertson were sitting in their Sunday school class at the Sixteenth Street

Church in Birmingham, Alabama. Before the bright-eyed black girls could deliver the speeches they'd prepared for the church's annual Youth Day program, a bomb planted by racists flattened the building, killing them all. In black households throughout the nation, families grieved for the martyred children and expressed their outrage at whites who seemed to have no limits on the depths they would sink in their ultimately futile effort to curtail the civil rights movement.

To protest the Birmingham bombing and to show solidarity with the struggles in the South, my mother bought a spool of black cotton ribbon which she fashioned into armbands for me and my siblings to wear to school the next day. Nine years old at the time, I remember standing in my house in Gary, Indiana, and watching in horror as my mother ironed the black fabric that, in my mind, would align me with the bloody dresses, limbless bodies, and dust-covered patent leather shoes that had been entombed in the blast.

The next morning, I put on my favorite school dress—a V-necked cranberry jumper with a matching cranberry-and-white pin-striped shirt. Motionless, I stared stoically straight ahead, as my mother leaned down and pinned the black ribbon around my right sleeve shortly before I left the house.

As soon as I rounded the corner at the end of our street, I ripped the ribbon off my arm, looking nervously up into the sky for the "evil white people" I'd heard my parents talk about in the aftermath of the bombing. I feared that if I wore the armband, I'd be blown to bits like the black girls who were that moment rotting under the rubble. Thirty years later, I know that another part of my "defense strategy" that day was to wear the outfit that had always garnered me compliments from teachers and friends. "Don't drop a bomb on me," was the message I was desperately trying to convey through my cranberry jumper. "I'm a pretty black girl. Not like the ones at the church."

The sense of vulnerability and exposure that I felt in the wake of the Birmingham bombing was compounded by feelings that I already had about Emmett Till. Emmett was a rambunctious, four-teen-year-old black boy from Chicago, who in 1955 was sent to rural Mississippi to enjoy the pleasures of summer with relatives. Emmett was delivered home in a pine box long before season's end bloated and battered beyond recognition. He had been lynched and dumped in the Tallahatchie River with the rope still dangling around his neck for allegedly whistling at a white woman at a country store.

Those summers in Oregon when I walked past the country store where thick-necked loggers drank beer while leaning on their big rig trucks, it seemed like Emmett's fate had been a part of my identity from birth. Averting my eyes from those of the loggers, I'd remember the ghoulish photos of Emmett I'd seen in *JET* magazine with my childhood friends Tyrone and Lynette Henry. The Henrys subscribed to *JET*, an inexpensive magazine for blacks, and kept each issue neatly filed on the top shelf of a bookcase in their living room. Among black parents, the *JET* with Emmett's story was always carefully handled and treated like one of the most valuable treasures on earth. For within its pages rested an important lesson they felt duty-bound to teach their children: how little white society valued our lives.

Mesmerized by Emmett's monstrous face, Lynette, Tyrone, and I would drag a flower-patterned vinyl chair from the kitchen, take the Emmett *JET* from the bookcase, and spirit it to a back bedroom where we played. Heads together, bellies on the floor as if we were shooting marbles or scribbling in our coloring books, we'd silently gaze at Emmett's photo for what seemed like hours before returning it to its sacred place. As with thousands of black children from that era, Emmett's murder cast a nightmarish pall over my youth. In his pummeled and contorted face, I saw a reflection of myself and the blood-chilling violence that would greet me if I ever dared to venture into the wilderness.

I grew up. I went to college. I traveled abroad. Still, thoughts of Emmett Till could leave me speechless and paralyzed with the heart-stopping fear that swept over me as when I crossed paths with loggers near the McKenzie River or whenever I visited the outdoors. His death seemed to be summed up in the prophetic warning of writer Alice Walker, herself a native of rural Georgia: "Never be the only one, except, possibly, in your own house."

For several Oregon summers, I concealed my pained feelings about the outdoors until I could no longer reconcile my silence with my mandate to my students to face their fears. They found the courage to write openly about incest, poverty, and other ills that had constricted their lives: How could I turn away from my fears about being in nature?

But the one time I'd attempted to be as bold as my students, I'd been faced with an unsettling incident. Legend had it that the source of the McKenzie was a tiny trickle of water that bubbled up from a pocket in a nearby lake. Intrigued by the local lore, two other Flight teachers and a staff person, all white women, invited me to join them on an excursion to the lake. The plan was to rent rowboats and paddle around the lake Sacajawea-style, until we, brave and undaunted women, "discovered the source" of the mighty river. As we approached the lake, we could see dozens of rowboats tied to the dock. We had barely begun our inquiry about renting one when the boathouse man interrupted and tersely announced: "No boats."

We stood shocked and surprised on a sun-drenched dock with a vista of rowboats before us. No matter how much we insisted that our eyes belied his words, the man held fast to his two-note response: "No boats."

Distressed but determined to complete our mission, we set out on foot. As we trampled along the trail that circled the lake we tried to make sense of our "Twilight Zone" encounter. We laughed and joked about the incident and it ultimately drifted out of our thoughts in our jubilation at finding the gurgling bubble that gave

birth to the McKenzie. Yet I'd always felt that our triumph was un-
dermined by a searing question that went unvoiced that day: Had
we been denied the boat because our group included a black?

In an effort to contain my fears, I forced myself to revisit the
encounter and to reexamine my childhood wounds from the Birmingham bombing and the lynching of Emmett Till. I touched the
terror of my Ibo and Ashanti ancestors as they were dragged from
Africa and enslaved on southern plantations. I conjured blood-
hounds, burning crosses, and white-robed Klansmen hunting down
people who looked just like me. I imagined myself being captured in
a swampy backwater, my back ripped open and bloodied by the
whip's lash. I cradled an ancestral mother, broken and keening as
her baby was snatched from her arms and sold down the river.

EVERY YEAR, the Flight of the Mind workshop offers a rafting
trip on the McKenzie River. Each day we'd watch as flotillas of
rafters, shrieking excitedly and with their oars held aloft, rumbled
by the deck where students and teachers routinely gathered. While
I always cheered their adventuresome spirit, I never joined the
group of Flight women who took the trip. I was always mindful that
I had never seen one black person in any of those boats.

Determined to reconnect myself to the comfort my African
ancestors felt in the rift valleys of Kenya and on the shores of Sierra
Leone, I eventually decided to go on a rafting trip. Familiar with my
feelings about nature, Judith, a dear friend and workshop founder,
offered to be one of my raftmates.

With her sturdy, gentle and wise body as my anchor, I lowered
myself into a raft at the bank of the river. As we pushed off into the
current, I felt myself make an unsure but authentic shift from my
painful past.

At first the water was calm—nearly hypnotic in its pristine
tranquility. Then we met the rapids, sometimes swirling, other
times jolting us forward like a runaway roller coaster. The guide

roared out commands, "Highside! All forward! All back!" To my amazement, I responded. Periodically, my brown eyes would meet Judith's steady aquamarine gaze and we'd smile at each other as the cool water splashed in our faces and shimmered like diamonds in our hair.

Charging over the river, orange life vest firmly secured, my breathing relaxed and I allowed myself to drink in the stately rocks, soaring birds, towering trees, and affirming anglers who waved their rods as we rushed by in our raft. About an hour into the trip, in a magnificently still moment, I looked up into the heavens and heard the voice of black poet Langston Hughes:

"I've known rivers ancient as the world and older than the flow of human blood in human veins. I bathed in the Euphrates when dawns were young. I built my hut near the Congo and it lulled me to sleep. I looked upon the Nile and raised the pyramids above it. My soul has grown deep like the rivers."

Soaking wet and shivering with emotion, I felt tears welling in my eyes as I stepped out of the raft onto solid ground. Like my African forebears who survived the Middle Passage, I was stronger at journey's end.

Since that voyage, I've stayed at country farms, napped on secluded beaches, and taken wilderness treks all in an effort to find peace in the outdoors. No matter where I travel, I will always carry Emmett Till and the four black girls whose deaths affected me so. But comforted by our tribal ancestors—herders, gatherers, and fishers all—I am less fearful, ready to come home.

Terry Tempest Williams

T*erry Tempest Williams is naturalist-in-residence at the Utah Museum of Natural History in Salt Lake City. She is the author of seven books, two of them for children (*The Secret Language of Snow, *1984, and* Between Cattails, *1985). Two other books,* Pieces of White Shell *(1984) and* Coyote's Canyon *(1989), first earned her serious attention from critics, but it was* Refuge: An Unnatural History of Family and Place *(1991) that firmly established her national audience. Her major awards include a Conservation Award for Special Achievement from the National Wildlife Federation and a Lannan Fellowship for Nonfiction. Her most recent book is a collection of essays,* An Unspoken Hunger: Notes from the Field *(1994). She served four years (1990–94) on the Governing Council of the Wilderness Society. "The most radical act we can commit," she says, "is to stay home," and yet her work often underscores the point that home and homelessness are equally as endemic to the lives of Western Americans as rebellion and conformity. No group, of course, could be more in love with conformity and nonconformity, dislocation and placement, than Williams's own exiled people, the Mormons, who came West fleeing persecution and seeking religious freedom. In this essay she writes about her uncle Alan, whom she casts into the role of that characteristically Western American figure, the literal and symbolic orphan. She celebrates her* *uncle's uniqueness (he was a "sole-birth") by recognizing his sacred role as a Contrary and affirming the necessity of his place in the tribal family.*

"The Village Watchman"

from *An Unspoken Hunger*

STORIES CARVED IN CEDAR RISE FROM THE DEEP woods of Sitka. These totem poles are foreign to me, this vertical lineage of clans; Eagle, Raven, Wolf, and Salmon. The Tlingit craftsmen create a genealogy of the earth, a reminder of mentors, that we come into this world in need of proper instruction. I sit on the soft floor of this Alaskan forest and feel the presence of Other.

The totem before me is called "Wolf Pole" by locals. The Village Watchman sits on top of Wolf's head with his knees drawn to his chest, his hands holding them tight against his body. He wears a red-and-black-striped hat. His eyes are direct, deep-set, painted blue. The expression on his face reminds me of a man I loved, a man who was born into this world feet first.

"Breech—" my mother told me of her brother's birth. "Alan was born feet first. As a result, his brain was denied oxygen. He is special."

As a child, this information impressed me. I remember thinking fish live underwater. Maybe Alan had gills, maybe he didn't need a face-first gulp of air like the rest of us. His sweet breath of initiation came in time, slowly moving up through the soles of his tiny webbed feet. The amniotic sea he had floated in for nine months delivered him with a fluid memory. He knew something. Other.

Wolf, who resides in the center of this totem, holds the tail of Salmon with his feet. The tongue of Wolf hangs down, blood-red, as do his front paws, black. Salmon, a sockeye, is poised downriver—a swish of a tail and he could be gone, but the clasp of Wolf is strong.

There is a story of a boy who was kidnapped from his village by the Salmon People. He was taken from his family to learn the ways of water. When he returned many years later to his home, he was recognized by his own as a Holy Man privy to the mysteries of the unseen world. Twenty years after my uncle's death, I wonder if Alan could have been that boy.

But our culture tells a different story, more alien than those of Tlingit or Haida. My culture calls people of sole-births retarded, handicapped, mentally disabled or challenged. We see them for who they are not, rather than for who they are.

My grandmother, Lettie Romney Dixon, wrote in her journal, "It wasn't until Alan was sixteen months old that a busy doctor cruelly broke the news to us. Others may have suspected our son's limitations but to those of us who loved him so unquestionably, lightning struck without warning. I hugged my sorrow to myself. I felt abandoned and lost. I wouldn't accept the verdict. Then we started the trips to a multitude of doctors. Most of them were kind and explained that our child was like a car without brakes, like an electric wire without insulation. They gave us no hope for a normal life."

Normal. Latin: *normalis; norma*, a rule; conforming with or constituting an accepted standard, model, or pattern, especially corresponding to the median or average of a large group in type, appearance, achievement, function, or development.

Alan was not normal. He was unique; one and only; single; sole; unusual; extraordinary; rare. His emotions were not measured, his curiosity not bridled. In a sense, he was wild like a mustang in the desert and, like most wild horses, he was eventually rounded up.

He was unpredictable. He created his own rules and they changed from moment to moment. Alan was twelve years old, hy-

peractive, mischievous, easily frustrated, and unable to learn in traditional ways. The situation was intensified by his seizures. Suddenly, without warning, he would stiffen like a rake, fall forward
and crash to the ground, hitting his head. My grandparents could
not keep him home any longer. They needed professional guidance
and help. In 1957 they reluctantly placed their youngest child in an
institution for handicapped children called the American Fork
Training School. My grandmother's heart broke for the second
time.

Once again, from her journal: "Many a night my pillow is wet
from tears of sorrow and senseless dreamings of 'if things had only
been different,' or wondering if he is tucked in snug and warm, if he
is well and happy, if the wind still bothers him. . . ."

The wind may have continued to bother Alan, certainly the
conditions he was living under were less than ideal, but as a family
there was much about his private life we never knew. What we did
know was that Alan had an enormous capacity for adaptation. We
had no choice but to follow him.

I followed him for years.

Alan was ten years my senior. In my mind, growing up, he was
mythic. Everything I was taught not to do, Alan did. We were
taught to be polite, to not express displeasure or anger in public.
Alan was sheer, physical expression. Whatever was on his mind was
vocalized and usually punctuated with colorful speech. We would
go bowling as a family on Sundays. Each of us would take our turn,
hold the black ball to our chest, take a few steps, swing our arm
back, forward, glide, and release—the ball would roll down the
alley, hit a few pins, we would wait for the ball to return, and then
take our second run. Little emotion was shown. When it was Alan's
turn, it was an event. Nothing subtle. His style was Herculean. Big
man. Big ball. Big roll. Big bang. Whether it was a strike or a gut-
ter, he clapped his hands, spun around in the floor, slapped his
thighs and cried, "Goddamn! Did you see that one? Send me an-

other ball, sweet Jesus!" And the ball was always returned.

I could always count on my uncle for a straight answer. He was my mentor in understanding that one of the remarkable aspects of being human was to hold opposing views in our mind at once.

"How are you doing?" I would ask.

"Ask me how I am feeling?" he answered.

"Okay, how are you feeling?"

"Today? Right now?"

"Yes."

"I am very happy and very sad."

"How can you be both at the same time?" I asked in all seriousness, a girl of nine or ten.

"Because both require each other's company. They live in the same house. Didn't you know?"

We would laugh and then go on to another topic. Talking to my uncle was always like entering a maze of riddles. Ask a question. Answer with a question and see where it leads you.

My younger brother Steve and I spent a lot of time with Alan. He offered us shelter from the conventionality of a Mormon family. At our home during Christmas, he would direct us in his own nativity plays. "More—" he would say to us, making wide gestures with his hands. "Give me more of yourself." He was not like anyone we knew. In a culture where we were taught socially to be seen not heard, Alan was our mirror. We could be different too. His unquestioning belief in us as children, as human beings, was in startling contrast to the way we saw the public react to him. It hurt us. What we could never tell was if it hurt him.

Each week, Steve and I would accompany our grandparents south to visit Alan. It was an hour's drive to the training school from Salt Lake City, mostly through farmlands.

We would enter the grounds, pull into the parking lot of the institution where a playground filled with huge papier-mâché storybook figures stood (a twenty-foot pied piper, a pumpkin carriage with Cinderella inside, the old woman who lived in a shoe), and nine out of ten times, Alan would be standing outside his dormitory waiting for us. We would get out of the car and he would run toward us, throwing his powerful arms around us. His hugs cracked my back and at times I had to fight for my breath. My grandfather would calm him down by simply saying, "We're here, son. You can relax now."

Alan was a formidable man, now in his early twenties, stocky and strong. His head was large with a protruding forehead that bore many scars, a line-by-line history of seizures. He always had on someone else's clothes—a tweed jacket too small, brown pants too big, a striped golf shirt that didn't match. He showed us appearances didn't matter, personality did. If you didn't know him, he could look frightening. It was an unspoken rule in our family that the character of others was gauged in how they treated him. The only thing consistent about his attire was that he always wore a silver football helmet from Olympus High School where my grandfather was coach. It was a loving, practical solution to protect Alan when he fell. Quite simply, the helmet cradled his head and absorbed the shock of the seizures.

"Part of the team," my grandfather Sanky would say as he slapped him affectionately on the back. "You're a Titan, son, and I love you—you're a real player on our team."

The windows to the dormitory were dark, reflecting Mount Timpanogos to the east. It was hard to see inside, but I knew what the interior held. It looked like an abandoned gymnasium without bleachers, filled with hospital beds. The stained white walls and yellow-waxed floors offered no warmth to its residents. The stench was nauseating, sweat and urine trapped in the oppression of stale air. I recall the dirty sheets, the lack of privacy, and the almond-eyed children who never rose from their beds. And then I would turn around and face Alan's cheerfulness, the open and loving manner in which he would introduce me to his friends, the pride he exhibited as he showed me around his home. I kept thinking, Doesn't he see how bad this is, how poorly they are being treated? His words would return to me, "I am very happy and I am very sad."

For my brother and me, Alan was our guide, our elder. He was fearless. But neither one of us will ever be able to escape the image of Alan kissing his parents goodbye after an afternoon with family and slowly walking back to his dormitory. Before we drove away, he would turn toward us, take off his silver helmet, and wave. The look on his face haunts me still. Alan walked point for all of us.

Alan liked to talk about God. Perhaps it was in these private conversations that our real friendship was forged.

"I know Him," he would say when all the adults were gone.

"You do?" I asked.

"I talk to Him every day."

"How so?"

"I talk to Him in my prayers. I listen and then I hear His voice."

"What does He tell you?"

"He tells me to be patient. He tells me to be kind. He tells me that He loves me."

In Mormon culture, children are baptized a member of the Church of Jesus Christ of Latter-Day Saints when they turn eight years old. Alan had never been baptized because my grandparents believed it should be his choice, not something simply taken for granted. When he turned twenty-two, he expressed a sincere desire to join the Church. A date was set immediately.

The entire Dixon clan convened in the Lehi Chapel, a few miles north of the group home where Alan was now living. We were there to support and witness his conversion. As we walked toward the meetinghouse where this sacred rite was to be performed, Alan had a violent seizure. My grandfather and Uncle Don, Alan's elder brother, dropped down with him holding his head and body as every muscle thrashed on the pavement like a school of netted fish brought on deck. I didn't want to look, but to walk away would have been worse. We stayed with him, all of us.

"Talk to God," I heard myself saying under my breath "I love you, Alan."

"Can you hear me, darling?" It was my grandmother's voice, her hand holding her son's hand.

By now, many of us were gathered on our knees around him, our trembling hands on his rigid body.

And we, who have always thought
Of happiness as rising, would feel
The emotion that almost overwhelms us
Whenever a happy thing falls.
          —*Rainer Marie Rilke*

Alan opened his eyes. "I want to be baptized," he said. The men helped him to his feet. The gash on his left temple was deep. Blood dripped down the side of his face. He would forgo stitches once again. My mother had her arm around my grandmother's waist. Shaken, we all followed him inside.

Alan's father and brother ministered to him, stopped the bleeding and bandaged the pressure wound, then helped him change into the designated white garments for baptism. He entered the room with great dignity and sat on the front pew with a dozen or more eight-year-old children seated on either side. Row after row of family sat behind him.

"Alan Romney Dixon." His name was called by the presiding bishop. Alan rose from the pew and met his brother Don, also dressed in white, who took his hand and led him down the blue-tiled stairs into the baptismal font filled with water. They faced the congregation. Don raised his right arm to the square in the gesture of a holy oath as Alan placed his hands on his brother's left forearm. The sacred prayer was offered in the name of the Father, the Son, and the Holy Ghost, after which my uncle put his right hand behind Alan's shoulder and gently lowered him into the water for a complete baptism by immersion.

Alan emerged from the holy waters like an angel.

The breaking away of childhood
Left you intact. In a moment,
You stood there, as if completed
In a miracle, all at once.
—*Rainer Marie Rilke*

Six years later, I found myself sitting in a chair across from my uncle at the University Hospital, where he was being treated for a severe ear infection. I was eighteen. He was twenty-eight.

"Alan," I asked. "What is it really like to be inside your body?"

He crossed his leg and placed both hands on the arms of the chair. His brown eyes were piercing.

"I can't tell you what it's like except to say I feel pain for not being seen as the person I am."

A few days later, Alan died alone; unique; one and only; single; in American Fork, Utah.

THE VILLAGE WATCHMAN sits on top of his totem with Wolf and Salmon—it is beginning to rain in the forest. I find it curious that this spot in southeast Alaska has brought me back into relation with my uncle, this man of sole-birth who came into the world feet first. He reminds me of what it means to live and love with a broken heart; how nothing is sacred, how everything is sacred. He was a weather vane—a storm and a clearing at once.

Shortly after his death, Alan appeared to me in a dream. We were standing in my grandmother's kitchen. He was leaning against the white stove with his arms folded.